THE VERTICAL MOSAIC REVISITED
Edited by Rick Helmes-Hayes and James Curtis

When *The Vertical Mosaic* first appeared in 1965, it became an instant classic. Its key message was that Canada was not the classless democracy it fancied itself to be. In fact, Canada was a highly inegalitarian society comprising a 'vertical mosaic' of distinct classes and ethnic groups. This collection of papers by five of Canada's top sociologists subjects John Porter's landmark study to renewed scrutiny and traces the dramatic changes since Porter's time – both in Canadian society and in the agenda of Canadian sociology.

Based on papers written for a conference held in commemoration of the thirtieth anniversary of *The Vertical Mosaic*'s publication, the five essays revisit the central themes of the original work, including gender and race inequality; citizenship and social justice; and class, power, and ethnicity from the viewpoint of political economy. An introduction by the editors provides a historical biography of Porter and discusses his influence on Canadian sociology.

RICK HELMES-HAYES is Associate Professor of Sociology at the University of Waterloo.

JAMES CURTIS is Professor of Sociology at the University of Waterloo.

EDITED BY RICK HELMES-HAYES
AND JAMES CURTIS

The Vertical Mosaic Revisited

UNIVERSITY OF TORONTO PRESS
Toronto Buffalo London

HN
/03.5
.V47
/1998

© University of Toronto Press Incorporated 1998
Toronto Buffalo London
Printed in Canada

ISBN 0-8020-0917-4 (cloth)
ISBN 0-8020-7896-6 (paper)

Canadian Cataloguing in Publication Data

Main entry under title:

The vertical mosaic revisited

Based on a colloquium held at the University of Waterloo, Nov. 9–10, 1995.
Includes bibliographical references and index.
ISBN 0-8020-0917-4 (bound)   ISBN 0-8020-7896-6 (pbk.)

1. Canada – Social conditions – 1945– .   2. Porter, John, 1921–1979. The
vertical mosaic.   3. Social classes – Canada. ✓I. Helmes-Hayes, Richard C.
(Richard Charles), 1951– .   II. Curtis, James E., 1943– .

HN103.V47 1998   305 .0971   C97-932705-9

University of Toronto Press acknowledges the financial assistance to its publishing program of the Canada Council for the Arts and the Ontario Arts Council.

To the memory of John and Marion Porter

Contents

viii   Contents

Foreword

JAMES DOWNEY

Few books have been so important in the growth of social self-understanding in Canada as *The Vertical Mosaic*; few works of scholarship have had such a profound influence on academic and more general analyses of Canadian society. It is fitting and timely therefore that, a generation after its publication, we should revisit John Porter's great work. I was pleased to help sponsor the colloquium on *The Vertical Mosaic* that gave rise to this volume, and I am honoured to contribute this foreword.

I leave it to the able scholars who have contributed the essays that follow to assess Porter's work and build on it. My perspective is more personal and more partial. John Porter was for me a colleague at Carleton and, towards the end of his life, a friend. He was also a mentor. I learned as much from him during the summer of 1978 when we worked together on a new three-year plan for Carleton University as from any teacher I ever had – about how to define and evaluate issues, how to get and assess relevant data, how to reason through to usable conclusions, how to present analysis and results with economy and precision, and, perhaps most important of all, how to lead colleagues collegially.

He was above all a gifted scholar. But he was also a gifted academic leader, blessed with those qualities of mind and personality and character that inspire respect, confidence, and loyalty. When Carleton failed to appoint him president in 1978 it forfeited the opportunity to have its affairs directed by one of the strongest academic leaders and thinkers in Canada. By not appointing him, however, it allowed him the time to publish an outstanding collection of essays on Canadian society, which includes, in my opinion, the two best papers on higher education in Canada ever written: John's York lectures on 'Education, Equality, and the Just Society,' the last two essays in *The Measure of Canadian Society*.

Not included in that collection is a brilliant and charming essay on 'The Future of the University' which John gave to the Arts Faculty at Carleton in 1978. This paper has been nowhere published except in the annual report for 1978–9 of the dean of arts, which had only local distribution. I quote from it to evoke the voice, the style, the mind, and the values of the man himself. Here, he is describing what universities in England and elsewhere were like in the days when they were accessible only to a social elite.

What the scholarly communities wrote and said was largely for and to their members, and at the same time relatively inconsequential for their surrounding societies. Perhaps Harold Laski's remarks about American historians being like parasites living off one another's footnotes was made about Americans and not British, because the latter used smaller footnotes or none at all. These sheltered scholars provided little to the growth of the industrial epoch. Sometimes it was said that they had a civilizing influence, but they seemed remarkably blind to the brutality and human cost of the emerging industrial systems. Of course they defined what was civilized largely from their own inward-looking gaze or the narrow outward gaze afforded to them by the windows of their protective structures.

Before one wearied of the products of the Bloomsbury industry, one could be fascinated by its links with the Cambridge of G.E. Moore, Keynes, and Russell, and with the aristocracy. 'I hate democracy,' said Vita Sackville West. 'I hate la populace. I wish education had never been introduced. I don't like tyranny, but I like an intelligent oligarchy. I wish la populace had never been encouraged to emerge from its rightful place.'

John was not a shore hugger, either in his life or his scholarship. *The Vertical Mosaic* is, to be sure, his greatest deep-sea adventure, but in nearly everything he wrote the breadth and sweep and daring of his mind are observable: fresh literary allusions, a strong historical sense, a mordant wit, an egalitarian conscience, a moral framework, a fascination with education in all its multifarious dimensions, and a penetrating sociological perspective on class, power, ethnicity, and equality. Informing and infusing all is his powerful, disciplined, and focused intelligence.

John Porter's educational standards were as exacting as those of Vita Sackville West, but they were meritocratic not aristocratic. The university system he helped to design for Ontario was pluralistic, utilitarian, and democratic – accessible to all who demonstrated intellectual capability, regardless of means. But his commitment to quality was uncompromising. In the *Report of the Committee on Carleton University to 1982* (1978) he wrote, at a time when the Ontario system faced grim prospects of declining enrolments and revenues:

It is tempting to cast any discussion of living with the constraints to 1982 in quantitative terms only and to assume the task is largely one of budgeting and accounting where questions of educational quality must be left aside. The very urgency of the matter adds to the pressure to deal with quantities to the neglect of qualities. By qualities, in the briefest terms we mean the kind of university we are or might become, in spirit, in the sense of mission, and in the research and teaching we do. It might be thought that to entertain questions of quality in this time of urgency is a luxury we can scarcely afford. Yet to neglect questions of quality would be a great error. Not only must a university maintain a close watch on its academic priorities as a matter of course, but in the present competition for students, which has become more intense since every university is financed in the same way, questions of quality may well be paramount in the decisions that students make about where and what to study.

Carleton and some other universities paid a heavy price for not heeding this admonition. John, of course, may be (and was) criticized for his peremptory resignation as vice-president academic when he was not chosen president in 1978, and for thereby relinquishing his opportunity to ensure that a commitment to quality was sustained. One can only observe that he was a proud man who had expected and prepared himself to lead Carleton into the 1980s. He could not be persuaded to accept a subordinate role and lead from there. I know; I tried.

He did, however, with acute prescience, foresee what might lie ahead, and offered his sage advice and encouragement. I quote in conclusion from the end of his essay on 'The Future of the University':

That there are lean years ahead, or stormy weather, or whatever metaphor might be most apt, is inescapable. For that we must trim, but we must use our ingenuity, and what institution has more intellectual resources than the modern university to mobilize in the interests of its own future? We can all contribute. If, as I have suggested, the trends are not irreversible, it seems to call for a strategy of trimming and riding out the next decade with a collective determination to come through.

And come through we have, helped in our resolve as well as in our understanding, by the life and work of John Porter.

Preface

RICK HELMES-HAYES

For the past ten years, I have been working somewhat sporadically on an intellectual biography of John Porter. In the spring of 1994, at a University of Waterloo social function, I discussed the Porter biography with Dr James Downey, the president of the university. President Downey had a personal interest in the project as he had been a colleague and friend of Professor Porter at Carleton in the 1970s. Indeed, they had worked together on a volume dealing with the future of Carleton and the Ontario university system. Also, Dr Downey had replaced Porter as vice-president (academic) at Carleton in 1978 when Porter resigned from that position. During the course of the conversation, I remarked that 1995 was the thirtieth anniversary of the publication of John Porter's book, *The Vertical Mosaic*. Dr Downey immediately suggested that something be done to commemorate the event and honour Professor Porter. He even promised some money to get the project under way.

I went to work and, some months later, plans for a commemorative event were firmed up. I began by consulting with Professor Jim Curtis and involving him in the project. We decided that *The Vertical Mosaic* should serve as the analytic take-off point for a two-day colloquium. However, rather than simply reassessing *The Vertical Mosaic* thirty years after its publication, we decided to ask presenters to discuss in detail the nature and significance of major changes that had occurred in Canadian society and Canadian sociology over the past three decades, focusing in particular on issues that were central to Porter's work, especially in *The Vertical Mosaic*. More specifically, we commissioned five of Canada's best known sociologists in the broad area of social inequality studies to put together papers which would undertake three interrelated tasks that we thought would not only honour the memory of John Porter and *The*

Vertical Mosaic, but also be of substantial current interest to the Canadian sociological community. First, we asked the presenters to 'revisit' *The Vertical Mosaic* and briefly describe the formative and catalytic role that it played in the development of their respective areas of expertise in Canadian sociology thirty years ago. Second, we asked them to assess key developments in Canadian society in these areas between 1965 and 1995. Third, we asked them to outline significant research and theoretical developments in these substantive areas since 1965.

We constructed a 'wish list' of scholars in the discipline who would not only do a great job of the tasks we had in mind, but whose reputations as expert researchers would honour the memory of John Porter. Fortunately, each of the people we approached about the project – Pat Armstrong of Carleton University, Raymond Breton of the University of Toronto, Wallace Clement of Carleton University, Julia O'Connor of McMaster University, and Michael Ornstein of York University – immediately accepted our invitation.

The colloquium was held at the University of Waterloo on 9 and 10 November 1995. It was a great success; more than 100 faculty members and students (graduate and undergraduate alike) from thirteen universities and seven different disciplines attended. We were particularly pleased that Professor Porter's daughter, Ann Porter, a PhD candidate in Women's Studies at York University, was able to join us for the second day of the colloquium. Marion Porter, Professor Porter's wife and intellectual partner, had earlier accepted our invitation to attend, but was unable to come due to a serious health problem. The Porters' son, Professor Tony Porter of the department of political science of McMaster University, was likewise unable to attend; he was in Ottawa with his mother. We are sad to report that Marion Porter passed away on 3 September 1996.

Funding for the event came from a variety of sources at the University of Waterloo and Wilfrid Laurier University. In particular, we wish to thank Dr James Downey, president of the University of Waterloo, Dr Lorna Marsden, then-president of Wilfrid Laurier University, and Waterloo's dean of arts, Professor Brian Hendley, all of whom provided substantial resources for the project. We received contributions as well from the departments of sociology and political science and both the Women's Studies Program and the Canadian Studies Program at the University of Waterloo. Our colleagues at Wilfrid Laurier were likewise generous in their contributions to the success of the colloquium. In addition to President Marsden's contribution, financial support was provided by Laurier's departments of sociology and anthropology and political science. A grant from the Small Grants Selection Committee of the University of Waterloo (funds from the Social Sciences and Humanities Research Council of Canada) was also of considerable help.

For success, colloquia require more than good funding and excellent presentations. The advance planning and organizing of such events demands the skills of an experienced organizer. In this regard, we could not have been more fortunate. Professor Gary Waller, acting dean of research at the University of Waterloo, assigned Pamela Helmes-Hayes of his office to 'help us' organize the conference. Frankly, it is our view that it was really the other way around. Without Pam's experienced and meticulous attention to the thousand-and-one details that go into making such an event run smoothly, it would likely never have come to pass. A very special thank-you to her for her efforts.

Three students from the University of Waterloo – Jenna Hennebry, Geeta Kapur, and the late Shawn Mann – provided assistance during the colloquium itself. Since then, Alison Luke, a PhD candidate in the department, has helped to prepare the name and subject indexes, and Julie Dembski has skilfully and patiently typed and retyped countless versions of our Introduction, often on short notice. To each of them, too, we offer our thanks.

Above all, we thank the contributors. It is their collective wisdom and careful scholarship that make this volume a fitting tribute to John Porter.

THE VERTICAL MOSAIC REVISITED

Introduction[1]

RICK HELMES-HAYES AND JAMES CURTIS

The purpose of this volume is to commemorate the thirtieth anniversary of the publication of *The Vertical Mosaic* (1965), arguably the most important book in the history of English-language Canadian sociology. In this commemoration, we hope likewise to honour the memory of the book's author, John Porter, probably the best known and most influential sociologist this country has yet produced.

About John Porter (1921–1979)

Like many sociologists of the 1950s and 1960s, John Porter did not have the kind of straightforward career path we would now consider typical. Porter never finished high school, worked for several years at odd jobs, served a five-year stint in the army during the Second World War, and received his undergraduate degree only late in his twenties after returning to school following the war. His life and times were interesting ones – spanning the Depression, the Second World War, the baby boom, the Cold War, and the massive growth of the Canadian economy, educational system, and welfare state in the 1950s and 1960s. These and a few other details of his life story help us to understand him as a scholar.

John Porter was born in Vancouver on 12 November 1921, the eldest son of Arthur Porter, an accountant, and Ethel Cuffin, a schoolteacher. He was a bright student, especially accomplished at creative writing, who did extremely well in school until compelled to drop out in 1937, when his family was forced by a combination of circumstances to move to England. His father, never a great provider, had lost his job, and the Porters, like many other families during the Depression, had no choice but to go on welfare (or 'on relief' as they called it then). Sometime not long after, Porter's father abandoned the family, and the decision was made to return to England, from whence Porter's mother had originally come.

The Porters settled briefly in London, where John and his sister, Eileen, worked to support their mother and young brother, Alan. Two years later, the Second World War broke out and, in 1941, Porter joined the Canadian Army as a member of the Intelligence Section of the Seaforth Highlanders. He was stationed at Aldershot in England for a goodly portion of the war and did not see action until June of 1943, when his unit was shipped out to the Mediterranean, where it took part in the successful Allied invasion of Sicily and Italy.

Once the war ended and he was demobilized, now with the rank of Captain, Porter returned to London. There he worked during the day for Colonel C.P. Stacey as a writer-researcher, helping to put together the official history of Canada's involvement in the war. Evenings were spent at Regent Street Polytechnic, preparing for the entrance examinations for the University of London. It is a testament to Porter's intelligence and persistence that despite the fact he been out of school for seven years, and had not progressed beyond Grade 10, he successfully completed the entrance examinations on his first attempt and, in the fall of 1946, he entered the London School of Economics and Political Science (LSE).

Porter's time at LSE turned out to be a crucially important intellectual experience, because of the school itself and because of the times. The School, which was then among the very best places in the world to study the social sciences, was in its 'golden age.' Though originally founded by the socialist Fabian Society in 1895, LSE was by the 1940s an intellectually and politically diverse place where scholars as different in their points of view as the socialist Harold Laski and the ardent exponent of *laissez-faire* capitalism, Friedrich Hayek, could expound their ideas. Certainly, it was not a 'Fabian' institution. That said, it is also true that postwar England, and certainly LSE, was pervaded during this period by a spirit of liberal reformist optimism; a widely shared belief that the irrationality of war and suffering could be eliminated by the judicious application of humane rationality specifically manifested in the form of a generous and intelligent welfare state.

Porter sat in on courses offered by such social science luminaries as Karl Popper, Edward Shils, Donald MacRae, T.H. Marshall, R.H. Tawney, and most importantly, Harold Laski and Morris Ginsberg. Ginsberg in particular was important because he was a protégé and follower of L.T. Hobhouse, an influential sociologist, and theorist of the liberal welfare state whose ideas, via Ginsberg, left a deep and long-lasting impression on Porter. As he put it:

I was attracted to Hobhouse's principle of social development, that a community develops as it grows in scale, efficiency, freedom and mutuality: efficiency toward an end, freedom and scope for thought, mutuality in a service toward an end in which each participates. 'Social development corresponds in its concrete entirety to the requirements of rational ethics ... Good is the principle of organic harmony in things.' Hobhouse was a grand theorist of social evolution and he saw emerging in the process the principle of reason and progress. To him, the relationship between social values and social science was close. He was firmly convinced of the need for an empirical social science and believed one could be developed which was closely linked to ethical principles, or at least addressed itself to ethical problems ... In view of all the influences in those immediate post-war years, it is not surprising that ideas of social development, the global orientation, and a concern for ethical principles in social life became a dominant part of my outlook. (Porter 1987[1970]: 11–12)

Porter graduated from LSE in 1949 with a degree in economics and a specialization in sociology. Perhaps the most important thing he took away with him, though, was a multidisciplinary scholarly and political *Weltanschauung* – a world-view which accorded a central place to humanistic rationality combined with a 'left-liberal'/social democratic political outlook and a strong social reform orientation that stayed with him throughout his career.[2]

After graduating, Porter made a trip to Canada, though without any intention of remaining in the country. He wanted to return to Europe and become a writer or journalist. As fate would have it, however, on his way through Ottawa he looked up a friend from LSE days and, over lunch, was offered a job teaching political science at tiny Carleton College. He accepted, and two years later switched over to sociology, becoming the college's first full-time appointment in that discipline.

The first few years at Carleton College were difficult for Porter – he found Ottawa boring and provincial, his workload was heavy and his salary low – and, at one point, he came close to leaving the college and academia altogether. However, the exciting, multidisciplinary work environment created by his colleagues Paul Fox, Scott Gordon, Don Rowat, Kenneth MacRae, Pauline Jewett, and others helped him to persevere. Eventually, under pressure from the college principal either to get a graduate degree or publish a major work, he initiated the research project that culminated in the production of *The Vertical Mosaic*.

The process of writing *The Vertical Mosaic* was a slow one. Data for a comprehensive analysis of the structure of social inequality and power in Canada were either hard to come by (so Porter had to ferret them out of scattered library sources) or non-existent (so that Porter had to work them up himself). In addition, he was slowed by teaching and other research commitments. In fact, working solo, it took Porter eleven years to finish the first draft of the book. Revisions to the draft then took another year and a half. This does not mean, however, that Canadian social scientists had to wait a decade to benefit from the fruits of Porter's labour. Substantial sections of *The Vertical Mosaic* came out in 'instalment' form – ground-breaking and well-received articles in the *Canadian Journal of Economics and Political Science* (Porter, 1955, 1956, 1957, 1958) and two chapters in *Social Purpose for Canada*, a book edited by Michael Oliver (Porter 1961a, 1961b). These early publications not only made a name for Porter and secured his job at Carleton, but created a receptive audience for *The Vertical Mosaic* when it finally appeared in May 1965.

Professor Porter's work and influence did not stop with his writing in *The Vertical Mosaic* and the many publications which followed. During his career Porter's academic interest in education as a vehicle of social justice was mirrored by an interest in academic administration. Indeed, he was very active in academic administration beginning in 1963–6 when he was director of the Social Science Division at Carleton, through his long-term service as a member (and chair) of the Subcommittee on Research and Planning of the Committee of Presidents of the Universities of Ontario, to 1977–8 when he served as vice-president (academic) at Carleton. But after an unsuccessful attempt to become President of Carleton University in 1978, he withdrew from administration.

Porter died young on 15 June 1979 – he was just 57 years old – and three of his major projects – *The Measure of Canadian Society* (1979, 1987), *Stations and Callings* (1982), and *Ascription and Achievement* (1985) – were completed by his co-researchers and colleagues. As a 'final' tribute to Porter, in 1981, Wallace Clement edited a special issue of the *Canadian Review of Sociology and Anthropology* dedicated to a discussion of Porter's life's work and, in 1983, the Canadian Sociology and Anthropology Association established the John Porter Award, a prize given annually to the best book in Canadian sociology 'in the Porter tradition.'[3]

Introduction to *The Vertical Mosaic*

It is probably difficult for recent cohorts of students of sociology to understand the profound ground-breaking impact that *The Vertical Mosaic* had when it first appeared. The discipline of sociology is now well established, and each year the Canadian sociological community produces hundreds of articles and books about matters Canadian. Further, since the 1960s, the discipline has produced a staggering amount of scholarship dealing with a wide range of social issues – class, power, gender, race, ethnicity, education, work, the state, and so forth. As a consequence, we have considerable information on the structure of contemporary Canadian society, enlivened and enriched by a wide range of theoretical interpretations and constructions of these data.

None of this was true in 1965. Indeed, at this time, the Canadian sociological community was just embarking on its rapid-growth phase (the mid-1960s to the mid-1970s), so there were still only 115 university-based sociologists in Canada; and sociology departments were just being set up at a number of universities (Hiller 1982: 23; Table 3). There was not even a Canadian sociology textbook. The nearest thing was a collection of Canadian readings put together by Porter and three colleagues, Bernard Blishen, Frank Jones, and Kaspar Naegele (see Blishen et al. 1961, 1963, 1968, 1971).[4] Also, the first Canadian sociology journal, the *Canadian Review of Sociology and Anthropology*, was not founded until 1964. Certainly there was nothing even approximating the volume of published research on Canadian society that we now take for granted. Thus, Porter and his co-editors had to scour the literature in sociology and political science (including graduate theses) to find enough material to put together an edited book with reasonably broad coverage. In such an environment, the appearance of *The Vertical Mosaic* was of epoch-making significance. Not only did it help to establish the credibility of the discipline in the social science community at a key time in its development, but it provided a macrosociological baseline description and interpretation of Canadian society from which the entire Canadian sociological community could work. As Bruce McFarlane, then Porter's colleague at Carleton, put it, the publication of *The Vertical Mosaic* was the event that marked 'the coming of age' of Canadian sociology.[5]

The impact of *The Vertical Mosaic* was immediate and profound. It received almost universal acclaim when it appeared in 1965 (see Helmes-Hayes 1987) and the year after won the MacIver Award of the American Sociological Association[6], the only Canadian sociology book ever to receive that honour. It went on to become the most cited book in the history of Canadian sociology and has sold more copies than any other sociology work ever published by University of Toronto Press.[7] It remains in print to this day, three decades after it was originally released.

The book was influential not just because of its scope and depth, but because it was controversial. According to the scholarly and popular conventional wisdom of the time, Canada was a 'classless' or, at least, overwhelmingly 'middle-class' society. Most people had access to a middle-class lifestyle, it was believed. Porter's unflattering portrait of the country's class and power structure showed this to be a collective self-delusion. The phrase he felt captured the essence of Canadian society with respect to class and power was 'the vertical mosaic' – a term chosen to convey the idea that Canada was best understood not as an egalitarian melting pot but as a fixed hierarchy of distinct and unequal classes and ethnic groups.

Porter described how he arrived at the title, *The Vertical Mosaic*, as follows:

In a society which is made up of many cultural groups there is usually some relationship between a person's memberships in these groups and his class position and, consequently, his chances of reaching positions of power. Because the Canadian people are often referred to as a mosaic composed of different ethnic groups, the title, *The Vertical Mosaic*, was originally given to the chapter which examines the relationship between ethnicity and social class. As the study proceeded, however, the hierarchical relationship between Canada's many cultural groups became a recurring theme in class and power. For example, it became clear that the Canadians of British origin have retained, within the elite structure of the society, the charter group status with which they started out, and that in some institutional settings the French have been admitted as a co-charter group whereas in others they have not. The title, 'the Vertical Mosaic,' therefore seemed ... appropriate. (1965: xii–xiii)

The phrase and the image it conjured up were jarring ones that sent shock waves through the Canadian social science community.

Never before had anyone written such a detailed, comprehensive, theoretically informed analysis of Canada's dual systems of class and power (though see Marsh 1940). Such was the impact of *The Vertical Mosaic* that it helped to initiate a period of research interest in inequality-related themes that has not abated to this day. And, without wanting to attribute too much influence to *The Vertical Mosaic* – there were after all many forces that helped to push social inequality to centre-stage in Canadian sociology – we think it appropriate to say that, by successfully challenging the comfortable fiction that Canada was a classless society, Porter essentially set the agenda for English-language Canadian sociology for the next fifteen to twenty years (see Brym 1989: 92). Since the mid-1960s, many Canadian sociologists have continued to wrestle with precisely the issues that Porter asked us to try to understand in *The Vertical Mosaic*. In doing so, they have provided us with ever-richer portraits of inequality in all its forms – class, ethnic, race, gender, region, etc. – while at the same time giving us a better understanding of the role played by the state, education, corporate concentration, foreign ownership, and so on, in producing and reproducing the structure of inequality in this country.[8]

While this contribution – the provision of a compelling baseline analysis of class and power in Canada – earned Porter a place in the 'pantheon' of Canadian social scientists, there were still other contributions that further marked him as the key figure in the discipline during his career. Following the success of *The Vertical Mosaic*, he was involved in several other major studies. Some – such as 'Occupational Prestige in Canada' (1967) – examined further the structure of inequality in Canada, while others – such as *Towards 2000: The Future of Post-Secondary Education in Ontario* (1971), *Does Money Matter? Prospects for Higher Education* (1973, 1979), *Stations and Callings: Making It through the School System* (1982), and *Ascription and Achievement: Studies in Mobility and Status Attainment in Canada* (1985) – focused on the links between social inequality, education, and individual mobility (see also Porter 1977a, 1977b). In these latter studies, Marion Porter often assumed a major role. She had acted as a behind-the-scenes 'sounding board' and sometime 'research assistant' on some of his earlier projects. In the later works, especially *Does Money Matter?* and *Stations and Callings*, which focused on the potential of education to break down class barriers to individual achievement, she became more visible as his intellectual partner.

John Porter was richly rewarded for his labours by the scholarly community. We have mentioned that he is the only Canadian to have received the MacIver Award, in 1966. He also was elected a Fellow of the Royal Society of Canada in 1968 and honorary president of the Canadian Sociology and Anthropology Association in 1972. He was awarded honorary degrees by McMaster University (1973) and the University of Waterloo (1977). Further, *The Vertical Mosaic* came to be widely recognized as so definitive an interpretation of social inequality in Canadian society that it deserved to be placed alongside Harold Innis's *The Fur Trade in Canada* (1930), George Grant's *Lament for a Nation* (1965), and C.B. Macpherson's *Real World of Democracy* (1965) among the major classics of English-language Canadian social thought.

All this said, however, it *has* been three decades since Porter put the finishing touches on his *magnum opus*, and much has changed since. In this sense, the book is now to some degree a historical document; it gives us a window on the nation's past rather than a view of the current structure of Canadian society. In fact, we have seen over the past ten years or so a growing tendency among Canadian sociology students – even graduate students – to have little if any knowledge of *The Vertical Mosaic*. This would not have been possible even fifteen years ago. So pervasive was the effect of Porter's book in the 1960s and 1970s that it seemed that it was assigned reading in almost every course that dealt with Canadian society. Now, however, precious few courses make much use of it in this way.

This current failure to attend to *The Vertical Mosaic* strikes us as unfortunate and unwise. Students have much to gain by reading a classic study such as *The Vertical Mosaic*. Not only does this allow them to become familiar with a key work in the canon of Canadian social science, but they can begin to see contemporary debates in historical context and perspective. This alone makes a book like *The Vertical Mosaic* of much more than merely historical interest. As we have already noted, for about two decades after it was published *The Vertical Mosaic* acted as 'a point of inspiration and reference for literally scores of research projects in a wide variety of sub-fields within the discipline' (Helmes-Hayes 1987: 293). The volume became a central focus and 'take-off point' for later studies of economic, media, political, state, and other elites (e.g., Clement 1975, 1977; Olsen 1980) and for studies of occupational status attainment and occupational mobility (e.g., Blishen 1970; Blishen and Carroll 1978; Blishen and McRoberts 1976; Boyd et al. 1981; Cuneo and Curtis 1975; Goyder and Curtis 1977; McRoberts and Selbee 1981; Pineo, Porter, and McRoberts 1977). The book acted as a kind of 'lightning rod' for then-emergent Marxist and feminist theoretical and empirical approaches to the study of class, ethnicity, gender, and the state. As Wallace Clement's essay in this volume makes clear, a substantial portion of writings in Canadian Marxism and political economy was developed in the course of a theoretical and methodological debate with Porter and his work in *The Vertical Mosaic* (see also Clement 1988).

The Vertical Mosaic deserves continued careful study, too, because both its analyses – or what we will call its 'imagery' – and its overall approach have remained strongly influential in Canadian sociology. This has occurred because of the continued applicability of Porter's analysis and conclusions to contemporary patterns of social organization in Canada. We turn to these issues now.

The Vertical Mosaic as a Set of Images of Canadian Society

We have indicated that Porter's *The Vertical Mosaic* was important in establishing Canadian research benchmarks for work by his contemporaries and later generations in the Canadian social sciences. The book does this in two ways. First, it presents systematic data from Statistics Canada and other government documents and further library sources on various dimensions of Canadian society. Second, and probably more important, it summarizes the data in a set of *images of Canada*. By 'image' we mean a metaphor or concept that captures a central reality of Canadian history or contemporary social organization. These images are not theories so much as they are phrases that summarize concisely *sets of facts about central social patterns*. However, the images generally come complete with theories about how the social patterns came into being, and why they continue to exist. All national sociologies that are well developed have such images, and these provide inspiration and research guideposts for studies conducted in the society. What is remarkable about *The Vertical Mosaic* is how *widely* the book contributed to what are the prevailing sociological images of Canadian society. The *imagery heritage* includes 'the vertical mosaic' but goes well beyond it.

Curtis and Tepperman (1990) have identified nine central images of Canadian society in contemporary sociology. These images (slightly elaborated from the original) are as follows:

A vertical mosaic: In Canada, ethnicity and social class have been historically tied together, with the founding Anglophone group holding the positions of greatest attainment and power (Porter 1965).
A class society: Class is the primary fact of one's life; affecting everything from self-perception to education, life chances, and work experiences in Canada. The class structure and class relations have been and continue to be primary determinants of economic, political, and social change (Marsh 1940; Porter 1965; Marchak 1975).
Accommodating elites: Canada's economic, governmental, bureaucratic, ideological, and labour elites maintain contact and pursue their often competing interests by means of accommodation and compromise (Porter 1965).
Two solitudes / deux nations: Canada is a society of two quite different cultures, with different ways of thinking and living that have little contact with each other (Hughes 1943; Lower 1943; MacLennan 1945).
A British fragment: English-speaking Canada's institutional structure

and culture (values) reflect a British heritage, making Canadians more traditionalist, law-abiding, and so on than Americans (Lipset 1963; Hartz 1964).

A closed frontier: Canada's geography has allowed social control to remain firmly in the hands of powerful central interests exploiting the country's staple products (Innis 1930; Lower 1932, 1943; Clark 1959, 1968).

A metropolis and hinterland / Canada as a colony: Canadian regions, cities, and towns are tied one to another, and to the outside world, through a chain of dominance based on capital and, often, related to the exploitation of staples (Innis 1930; Creighton 1937; Lucas 1973).

A fragile federation: Canada's national culture and identity are not robust; its regions are weakly tied together in a confederation, but Canadians' sentiments, cultures, and allegiances are local, not national (Clark 1959, 1968; Marsden and Harvey 1979).

A double ghetto: Canadian society has a sexist institutional structure and culture so that women are disadvantaged in both domestic and paid labour. At home they do the bulk of domestic labour, and in the paid labour force they are concentrated in lower status, lower paying jobs (Armstrong and Armstrong 1978).

While only the first of these images is featured in the title of Porter's book, in point of fact the first *three* of the images – a vertical mosaic, a class society, and accommodating elites – are central to the book. Indeed, *The Vertical Mosaic* has been one of the major pieces of documentation for each of these images over the past thirty years. Furthermore, the next two images – two solitudes and a British fragment – were reinforced in the book – though they were neither devised by Porter nor as central to the volume as the other images. That is, while Porter characterized Canada as a 'vertical mosaic,' he also emphasized that Canada was replete with class inequality, had accommodating elites, had two solitudes, and was a British fragment. Even his analyses of these latter two dimensions of Canada were substantial and compelling. The book gave only minor attention to aspects of Canada's regionalism – the fragile federation, 'closed frontier,' and metropolis–hinterland patterns – and it more or less ignored the double ghetto.

Porter's three central characterizations of Canadian society were new to the Canadian scholarly literature. As we already have indicated, Canada was shown to be 'a class society' where people's social class backgrounds in large part determined how well they and their children lived. Class backgrounds affected people's chances of gaining better jobs, good income, higher educational credentials, and good quality of life, even good health. And, there was marked inequality in these opportunities and in class background among Canadians.

Further, Porter described a Canadian society where racial and ethnic minorities tended to occupy lower occupational positions for which they had been imported from other countries, sometimes generations earlier. There was limited occupational mobility out of these entrance statuses; ethnic minorities tended to continue holding down the worst positions, getting too little education, and having too little power in the society. The vertical structure of income and occupational inequality contained a mosaic of types of people. Different types of ethnic backgrounds were found more prominently at some levels in Canada's vertical structure than at others. People who were of British origin, English-speaking, and white were disproportionately at higher levels of income and occupational status, and their locations did not change much either within or across generations.

Porter went on to emphasize that 'the class society' and 'the vertical mosaic' were supported by the wishes of a more powerful middle- and upper-class Anglophone charter group, who wanted to remain advantaged in income, occupations, and so on. These patterns were supported by upper-class Anglophone control of Canada's elites and by the process of 'accommodating elites' in this country. According to Porter, Canada was ruled by five collaborating elite groups, all Anglo-dominated. These elite groups consisted of people in the top positions of each of five broad areas of Canadian society: the major economic corporations, political organizations, government bureaucracies, labour organizations, and ideological (church, educational, and media) organizations. Porter saw a plural set of elites with each elite having power by virtue of its organizational resources. Two of the elites – the economic or corporate elite and the bureaucratic elite – were found to be somewhat more powerful than the others because of the enormous economic resources each commanded and the fact that these two sections of the economy employed large percentages of the Canadian working population. They also provided better paying and more stable jobs than workers in the other sectors typically enjoyed.

In Porter's view, the general public and scholarly community seemed blind to each of the realities of vertical mosaic, class society, and control by accommodating elites. He saw this as a consequence of the middle-class backgrounds and class-determined interests and biases of most in the scholarly community. 'Even at times in what purports to be serious social analysis,' he wrote, 'middle class intellectuals project the image of their own class onto the social classes above and below them ... The idea of class differences has scarcely entered into the stream of Canadian academic writing' (1965: 6).

It is true that a few sociologists before Porter had described Canada's social class inequalities (see Helmes-Hayes 1985, 1988), but none was heard as well as Porter. Particularly notable among Porter's predecessors was Leonard Marsh.[9] His systematic, Fabian-inspired analysis, in *Canadians In and Out of Work* (1940), covered some of the same ground as Porter's, and in similar style, appeared twenty-five years earlier. Marsh's 500–page volume not only detailed the extent of inequalities of income and occupation in Canada, drawing heavily on 1931 census data, but came to conclusions very similar to those arrived at a quarter-century later by Porter:

Many Canadians are reluctant to admit that their country has a class structure. So far as social classes cannot be demarcated by a hard and fast line ... this reluctance is understandable. But this does not dismiss the other evidence of the class division of the population which exists in terms of inequalities of wealth, opportunity, and social recognition. The barriers are not the horizontal ones of geographic regions or distinctive ethnic cultures but the vertical ones of a large socio-economic hierarchy ... Communities and classes intersect; perhaps in few places more than in Canada, which has regional and ethnic variety ... of formidable magnitude. But these complications merely obscure, they do not eliminate the fundamental problems which class inequalities engender. (1940: 403–4)

Despite these noteworthy parallels between Porter's book and Marsh's, and despite the very important contribution *Canadians In and Out of Work* made to the literature of Canadian social science, Marsh's book garnered little attention from either Canadian academics or the Canadian public at large. The reasons for the different receptions accorded the two books are not entirely clear, but the outbreak of the Second World War must have had something to do with it. The war undoubtedly occupied the attention of the general public and academics, leaving little room for concern with class and ethnic inequality and elites in Canada. By contrast, Porter's book was published well after the war and just before the Canadian centennial celebration. Also, as we have indicated, prior to the 1960s few universities had sociology departments, and there were few sociological researchers in the universities or outside. Thus, Marsh's potential audience was relatively small. After 1960, in contrast, there was a major expansion of universities and colleges, and sociology departments, in all provinces. *The Vertical Mosaic* was, then, 'in the right spot to be acknowledged as the centrepiece of a newly-legitimated and rapidly-expanding academic discipline' (Helmes-Hayes and Wilcox-Magill 1993: 94).[10]

While Porter's book appeared at an opportune time, it would not have had the reception and impact it did without its strength and breadth of analysis. If Marsh painted a clear picture of the class structure of Canada in broad strokes, Porter's work did the same – and much else beside. For example, where *Canadians In and Out of Work* paid little attention to the ethnic and racial correlates of class position, *The Vertical Mosaic* emphasized these inequalities. Likewise, where *Canadians In and Out of Work* had almost nothing to say about the social origins and activities of Canada's elites and of the power structure they controlled, *The Vertical Mosaic* documented them in detail.

The Lasting Relevance of *The Vertical Mosaic*

The chapters of this volume give details on the important ways in which Canadian society has changed in the three decades since *The Vertical Mosaic* appeared. Relevant aspects of this change include: the sources of immigration (by country of origin) and the work qualifications required of immigrants have changed; multiculturalism has made the mosaic potentially even more unstable; Aboriginals have found a new voice and power; women have entered the workforce in much larger numbers; foreign ownership of the Canadian economy has increased; Canadian investment abroad has grown; industrial production has been internationalized; the computer and information revolutions have begun; regionalism has intensified; relations between Quebec and the rest of Canada (the latter particularly as represented in the federal government) have become more conflictual – witness the passage of Bill 101 and the results of the 1996 separation referendum; there has been some shift of powers from the federal government to the provinces and a decrease in federal and, more recently, provincial expenditures on social services and the like (see in particular the list in Clement's chapter).

Have the many changes in Canadian society meant that the basic images put forward in *The Vertical Mosaic* are no longer accurate characterizations of this society? Judging from the contents of the present volume, the images remain quite appropriate, but how appropriate depends on the image under consideration.

First, Porter's image of a society which locks certain ethnic and racial minorities into entrance statuses at the bottom of the occupational world applies to Canadian society today but less well than it did a generation or two ago (see, in particular, the chapters by Raymond Breton and Michael Ornstein). This is in part because changed immigration policies have altered the racial and ethnic composition of Canadian society. For example, in 1961, the population of European origin in Canada comprised 23 per cent of the total, and it is now just 15 per cent. Over the same period, the Asian proportion of Canada's population increased from less than 1 per cent to almost 6 per cent. Other ethnics of non-European origin increased from about 1 per cent to almost 5 per cent of the total. And, visible minorities (including Aboriginals) now make up 9 per cent rather than 3 per cent of the population (see Breton's chapter in this volume). So, Canada is now less British and less European in ethnic background, and it has a larger proportion of visible minorities, than was the case thirty years ago. Moreover, data on the occupational distribution of ethnic groups suggest that some non-charter ethnic groups have more successfully integrated into the occupational structure than was the case three decades ago. Also, they have done so while gaining sociopolitical acceptance. This has occurred because of changed requirements for better work credentials on the part of immigrants, policies of multiculturalism and affirmative action, and efforts by ethnic organizations. Income inequality across some ethnic groups has lessened, too, but income is still distributed unequally with northern and western Europeans and people of British origin remaining more advantaged, and blacks, Aboriginals, and those from Latin, South, and Central America towards the bottom in income. The 'visible' racial minorities generally remain lower in income. Native peoples in particular remain at or near the bottom of ethnic hierarchies of every kind – income, occupational status, labour force participation, and so forth (see the Breton chapter). In addition, there is still a problem of depressed entrance status for many immigrants, compounded by the structural barriers of labour markets and systematic discrimination. And, as elite studies over the past three decades show, access to the elites remains related to ethnic background. For example, people of British origin continue to do disproportionately well (see Ornstein's chapter in this volume).

In sum, the vertical mosaic imagery very successfully captured what was occurring in Canada during the first half of the century and before, but there have been some changes in a more egalitarian direction since.

This suggests that, sometime in the future, 'the vertical mosaic' may be only a memory – a historical image of ethnic relations in Canada. First, however, persistent inequalities for some minorities, particularly visible minorities, must disappear. Also, ethnic and racial barriers to elite entry must be eliminated. There is quite a way to go yet before 'the vertical mosaic' does not apply to Canadian society.

Second, the analyses in this volume show that 'the class society' image of Canada applies as well today as it did in Porter's time. Indeed, Armstrong's and O'Connor's analyses of public policy changes suggest that after a period during which class and gender inequalities were reduced in Canada, we may be entering a period of growing inequalities of each type (compare also Clement's and Ornstein's analyses). For example, data on the distribution of income suggest that Canada is just as unequal now as it was in 1965 – perhaps worse. Since 1961 the bottom quintile of earners (families) has received about 6 per cent of income, while the top quintile has received approximately 40 per cent. The bulk of investment income still goes to those at the very top of the class structure only, and RRSPs, which are a development since the period covered by *The Vertical Mosaic*, are for the most part a safe haven from taxes for those earners near the top of the income structure (Forcese 1997: 148). Further, something more than 20 per cent of Canadian children currently live below the poverty line (Forcese 1997: 47). In 1961 Canada had no food banks. In 1991 there were about 300 (Oderkirk 1995: 226; Figure 1). While more people have access to state-funded medical care, and more people have better education than thirty years ago, efforts at 'debt management' by federal and provincial governments have made even these gains precarious for the future.

Porter did not document gender differences in access to jobs and income. When these issues are explored, we find declining but persistent gender inequality, and the trends add moment to the 'class society' and 'vertical mosaic' images. There have been some gains for women over time in the world of paid work, but women still bear the burden of 'the double day' of paid and domestic labour. Thirty years ago less than 30 per cent of women were in the paid workforce; now 60 per cent are (Forcese 1997: 92). In 1965 women made less than 60 cents for every dollar a man made; that figure is now over 70 cents. Women now make up more than 50 per cent of the undergraduate population at Canadian universities, and they account for half those in master's programs and one-third of those in doctoral programs. There are more women in non-traditional occupations than ever before, and at higher levels of authority and pay. Women are still largely missing from the elites Porter described, but some gains have been made in elite access – particularly in the intellectual and labour elites (see Armstrong's chapter this volume). Legislation concerning pay equity, affirmative action, maternity leave, sexual harassment, and so on has been enacted. At the same time these gains have neither shattered nor homogenized the mosaic, for they are spread unevenly across the class and ethnic structure of Canadian society. Further, women suffer higher rates of unemployment and underemployment than men, and lower proportions of women than men are in paid employment full-time year-round (40 per cent today). Women, and particularly women among visible minorities, tend to be the first to suffer from government and private sector cutbacks because they remain overrepresented compared with men among the recently hired, and are concentrated in the clerical, service, teaching, and social service occupations that are currently under fire. Moreover, hard-won legislative gains such as affirmative action and pay equity are currently under attack.

Third, Ornstein's analyses of elite studies suggest that ethnic and racial inequalities in elite recruitment may have lessened somewhat, although a pattern of underrepresentation of minority groups persists. Further, he sees no reason from more recent analyses of who has power in Canadian society to reject or fundamentally alter the conclusions about elite control and elite accommodation presented by Porter. While various elites have received some research attention since Porter's analyses, only the economic elite has received much. For the economic elite, some data suggest that new, regionally based, ethnic capitalist class fragments have emerged (Jewish, Québécois) (Niosi 1981). Perhaps the clearest trend is the decline in the percentage of the economic elite that is Anglophone in background. Two recent studies (Hunter 1986; Ornstein and Stevenson, in press) suggest that while those of British origin are disproportionately high, they account for only about 55–65 per cent of elites; the French are underrepresented at 7–9 per cent, as are non-charter ethnics at approximately 26–38 per cent. Apparently, class origins of the economic elite also have changed; one major study (Ornstein and Stevenson, in press) shows that a smaller proportion (62 per cent) than in Porter's results come from middle-class or higher backgrounds. However, despite some shifts in class origin, there is evidence that the Canadian capitalist class is 'more robust, centralized, integrated and Canadian than previous studies suggested' and that Canadian, not foreign-controlled, industrial and financial firms are at the centre of this class (see Ornstein's chapter). The limited work on the political elite

(Olsen 1980; Ogmundson and McLaughlin 1992) suggests that some diversification of ethnic origins has taken place, with little change in class backgrounds. The situation in the bureaucratic elite at both the federal and provincial levels is different. There has been substantial 'downward' shifting of class backgrounds and a substantial decline in the percentage from British backgrounds with an increase in the percentage from French and other ethnic backgrounds (Campbell and Szablowski 1979).

None of the contributors to this volume, then, suggests that any of the three basic images from *The Vertical Mosaic* should be set aside in our attempts to analyse contemporary Canadian society. The images are still viable ones, given contemporary social patterns. At the same time, each contributor shows that today we should add some important caveats and qualifiers to Porter's analyses. Pat Armstrong's chapter provides a good case in point. While she does not dispute the continued relevance of the many social inequality-related images in *The Vertical Mosaic*, she takes up the topic of gender relations in Canada – one that Porter more or less ignored in *The Vertical Mosaic* – and discusses how the role of gender relations should be understood within the context of Canada as a class- and ethnically stratified society. Armstrong, who coined the phrase 'the double ghetto' for the title of one of her books, highlights the issue of gender relations and gender inequality and warns that the gains that have been made in breaking down this aspect of the vertical mosaic are now threatened – especially for women of colour and from visible minority ethnic backgrounds. Moreover, as a feminist political economist she sees a good portion of the push to limit or reverse these gains as coming from those with class-based power. She emphasizes that Canada is not 'just' a double ghetto for women; it is a class society. Thus, when we attempt to explain gender relations in Canada we have to explore class relations. Consideration of the most powerful class agents among 'accommodating elites' must come into play as well. Further, since classes, dominant or otherwise, are made up of 'agents' – real people with ethnic backgrounds, regional ties, and so forth – the facts of Canada as a colony (metropolis–hinterland relations), Canada as a 'British fragment,' and Canada as a 'fragile federation' of competing regions and two linguistic 'cultures' come into play as well.

We could do a similar analysis of each chapter in the volume. What such analyses would reveal is that the salience of Porter's three central images varies from one chapter to the next but that Porter's basic images constitute the foundation upon which their respective analyses of contemporary Canada are built.

Variations on a Macrosociological Theme: Porter and
Our Contributors Compared

A shared belief in the continued utility of the imagery of *The Vertical Mosaic* is not the only commonality among our contributors. They also share various other aspects of Porter's conceptual approach. It is useful to underscore these similarities because they constitute the defining characteristics of good macrosociology. This macrosociological approach has been one of the hallmarks of Canadian sociology since the 1960s.[11] Porter's work helped define for Canadian sociologists the proper approach to macrosociology and, because of the popularity of the approach, it is no surprise that the work of the contributors to this volume exemplifies good macrosociology. There are also some important differences between the approaches of Porter and the contributors, and among the contributors, that should be noted.

Perhaps the most obvious similarity among our contributors is that, like Porter, they use the *entire society* and its *history* as their focus of analysis. It is not that they are unmindful of individuals and smaller collectivities – groups, institutions, or regions – as fruitful take-off points for discussion. Indeed, all of them accord a good deal of weight to the agency of individual actors and the power of groups. Nor does this mean that their interests are insular; that their concerns and analyses stop at Canada's borders. In fact, there is a strong *comparative* element to their respective discussions of the class, gender, and ethnic inequalities that characterize contemporary Canadian society. For some, O'Connor and Clement in particular, the comparative element is front and centre; for others, it is less central. But each of our contributors views Canadian patterns of ethnic and class relations, structures of elite dominance, patterns of gender relations, and state power as not unique to this country. They believe that such patterns can and must be understood in terms of similar patterns and relations in other countries, particularly the United States and other capitalist societies. The same was true of Porter's *The Vertical Mosaic*, which was studded throughout with explicit and implicit comparisons with the United States, in particular. Canada's southern neighbour was an especially interesting point of comparison because it was allegedly an assimilationist 'melting pot' - a place where individual merit and universalistic characteristics rather than group loyalties and ethnic characteristics determined one's place in society.

The contributors have still more in common, beyond their holistic, historical, and comparative approaches. Each tends to see Canadian society as a *web of conflictual relations* between groups with different interests, resources, and agendas. This focus on relations and conflict is crucial for their descriptive and interpretive materials. In *The Vertical Mosaic*, John Porter documented the existence of widespread inequalities in the distribution of resources and rewards in Canadian society. But partly because of the kind of data he had available to him – information regarding the distribution of income, occupational status, power, etc. – he stressed *distributive* rather than the *relational* elements of class. Thus, while it is true that Porter understood class to be a relation – he certainly saw the struggles between the economic and labour elites as one aspect of class relations[12] – nonetheless, in *The Vertical Mosaic*, classes were presented as sets of positions or categories of people – large-scale statistical aggregations of individuals who shared various characteristics such as similar incomes, similar occupations and/or similar status rankings. By contrast, the contributers to this volume begin from the analytic premise that class (like gender, ethnicity, and race) is first and foremost a relation; more specifically, a set of conflictual relations between groups of people. The unequal distribution of resources across classes, genders, and ethnic and racial groups is, of course, important, but it is the relational element that is stressed by our contributors. This is a crucial difference of emphasis and analytic strategy. One of the problems with a simple distributive conception of class is that it tends to structure out the possibility of dealing with classes and ethnic groups as real groups; that is, as collections of agents with individual and collective histories, consciousnesses, and agendas, with in-group relations one to the other and out-group relations to those with whom they live and work. Seeing class, gender, ethnicity, and race as relations allows the analyst to use information about the distribution of resources but shifts the focus of analytical attention to the dynamics of intergroup struggle. Class, ethnicity, race, and gender become contested terrain. The disprivileged and the exploited become agents rather than victims. This shift of attention and emphasis from distributive to relational issues is one of the important changes in Canadian sociology since Porter's time, and our contributors are very representative of the changed approach.

Now, for some of our contributors – Armstrong, Clement, and O'Connor in particular – this relational focus comes from their explicit adoption of a 'materialist' (Marxian-inspired if not Marxian) *political economy* approach to the study of Canadian society. The political economy approach, broadly exemplified by Clement's piece in this volume, and originating in Canada with the work of Marx, Harold Innis's 'staples'

tradition, and C.B. Macpherson's writings on democratic theory, is suc-
cintly described in Patricia Marchak's masterful 1985 review of the
Canadian political economy tradition.

Political economy is the study of power derived from or contingent on a system
of property rights; the historical development of power relationships; and the
social and cultural embodiments of them ... Following Macpherson (1978), the
paradigm begins with property rights relative to things but not inherent in the
things themselves. The property rights of particular importance in an industrial
society relate to means of production ... Standard Marxist theory begins with
these rights and obligations, identified as the relations of production. Political
economy to the extent that it follows the Marxist paradigm likewise begins
there. But where political economy has challenged Marxism is the growing recognition of the existence of other property rights in capitalist systems as well, of
the importance of sources of inequality, subordination, and resistance either
unrelated to or not adequately explained within a standard class analysis ...
[e.g.] gender relations, ethnicity, nationalism, regionalism. How ... are these to
be understood? In addition, there is impatience with the reduction of cultural
and political phenomena to the history of class relations, yet insistence on the
centrality of class in a capitalist world economy. Much of contemporary political
economy is a debate about the relationships between culture, politics, and class.
(Marchak 1985: 673)

But not all the contributors are political economists, and the relational
approach is not dependent upon this. Certainly, neither Ornstein nor
Breton would see themselves as political economists. Nonetheless, Breton's approach clearly focuses on the struggles between ethnic and
racial groups and conceives of them in relational rather than just distributive terms. Ornstein's analysis likewise shares some of the sensibilities
of Marxian political economy – a focus on class structure and relations,
the importance of the ownership of the means of production, and so
forth – but he characterizes elite studies and their approach to class and
class relations as simply 'good *sociology*' which wisely pays more attention to 'the social backgrounds, careers, and interpersonal networks of
elites and the organizations they control' than does political economy
(Ornstein, this volume).

The macrosociological focus on class and group struggles among the
contributors extends to a common interest in the state as well. The contributors see the state as a key 'player' in modern industrial society.
They do not see the state as either a neutral referee among competing

interest groups (say, a liberal view) or as a more or less manipulable instrument of powerful class interests (a Marxist view). They see the state as a set of relations between citizens – a terrain where disadvantaged individuals and groups with rights and resources, however meagre, can empower themselves through resistance and activism. Women, for example, can win legislation supporting pay equity. Ethnic and racial groups can lobby successfully for affirmative action programs. But such gains are always hard won, for the state is a site where Anglophone dominance, wealth, and patriarchy often win out. With regard to the role of the state, too, the contributors very much echo Porter's concern with the nature and role of the state as a site where class and other groups contest for control of social resources and rewards.

One final point of comparison deserves brief mention. In the 1960s and early 1970s, in the heyday of the expanding Canadian welfare state, many people placed a great deal of faith in education as the solution to the problems of class, ethnic, and, to the extent they focused on it, gender inequality in Canada. Until late in his career, John Porter was among them (cf. Porter 1961b, 1965, 1987: 241–2). By contrast, while none of our contributors would see a less extensive and less open educational system as a good thing, each suggests in one way or another that in a class society such as ours the educational system does little to alter either the logic or structure of the system. Education allows for upward mobility for some individuals, but it does not do away with classes or the property relations on which they are based. This is the perspective that Porter came more and more to adopt in his later work (1977a, 1977b). However, in *The Vertical Mosaic*, he gave greater credence to greater educational opportunities as a panacea for ethnic and class inequalities.

Insofar as our contributors would presume to offer comprehensive solutions to the problems of social inequality in Canada, their prescriptions would vary. The chapters by Clement and O'Connor address the issue most pointedly. They would urge us to examine carefully the adequacy of a liberal conception of citizenship. The civil, political, and social rights that form the basis of citizenship in modern liberal capitalist democracies like Canada are seen to be necessary to breaking down the barriers to inequality and full participation among those that constitute Canada's 'mosaic.' At the same time, Canadian history seems to demonstrate that *while necessary*, civil, political, and social rights are *insufficient preconditions* to the development of a maximally inclusive and participatory democracy.

Organization of the Volume

The five essays appear here in the order in which they were presented at the colloquium. Each addresses three issues: (a) the character of Porter's original analyses on the topic, including both his findings and theoretical interpretations; (b) changes in Canadian society, from 1965 to 1995, which are especially relevant for the topic being considered; and (c) recent developments in research and theory.

The book begins, fittingly, with a paper by Wallace Clement. This author is probably Porter's best known student. He did both his master's and doctoral theses under Porter's supervision, and, in the course of his career, Clement has continued to work in substantive areas that were central to Porter's interests. Clement's early work in *The Canadian Corporate Elite* (1975) and *Continental Corporate Power* (1977) was clearly influenced by the elite studies tradition within which Porter worked. Since then, however, much of Clement's research has been rooted in the alternative Marxist political economy approach. This is clearly apparent in Clement's chapter – the plenary address at the colloquium – which not only provides an insightful and wide-ranging introduction to the interrelated themes of class, power, and ethnicity that constituted the analytic focus of *The Vertical Mosaic*, but also offers an account and justification of his shift into political economy. It also is much more than this. First, it is a description of some of the changed economic, social, and political circumstances of the past three decades in Canada that social analysts are trying to understand. Second, and more centrally, it is a concise overview of the theoretical underpinnings of a 'new,' holistic approach to the study of the myriad forms of social inequality in Canada. As Clement's review of selected empirical studies in the political economy tradition points out, such analyses have moved a long way from the approach to sociological analysis employed by John Porter. The political economy approach differs in that it is based on a view of class and power, gender and ethnicity as dynamic, relational, and interrelated phenomena. Moreover, while retaining a Canadian empirical focus, many studies in the political economy mode are comparative. This is a consequence of two facts: first, capitalism has come to assume many forms or 'faces,' and a comparative theoretical and methodological approach is required to understand them; second, the dynamics of Canada's internal economic development and class and power relations can be understood only in terms of the operation of capitalism as a global system.

Next, Raymond Breton's chapter considers, in fine-grained detail, trends around ethnicity and race in Canadian society. Like Clement, Breton takes a sweeping, macrosociological and historical approach that emphasizes group conflict and organizational bases for power. He emphasizes that Porter, for the most part, focused on the *distributive aspect of ethnicity and race*, on how people with different ethnic and racial backgrounds tended to receive different levels of scarce resources of occupations, income, education, and power; *relations among ethnic and racial groups*, get short attention in *The Vertical Mosaic*. Breton demonstrates that much of what is significant in the area of ethnicity and race in the past thirty years falls under this latter topic. He also emphasizes that, to the extent that there has been change in ethnic/race relations in this period, it has come at the insistence of the non-dominant group, not at the initiation of the dominant English-speaking white group. The role of language use in ethnic stratification received little attention from Porter either but, as we are all well aware, language has become an important issue since the 1960s, particularly as it became a primary consideration on the public policy agenda in Quebec. Breton reports on the significant developments in ethnic/race relations and language policy since the 1960s. Also, he updates the analysis of differences in socioeconomic circumstances according to ethnic and racial backgrounds. In the process, he shows that some of Porter's expectations about ethnic relations and ethnic inequalities for the future have come to pass, while others have not. Breton's analyses, then, present assessments of both 'the vertical mosaic' and 'two solitudes' images found in Porter's book. For the former, he shows that social and ethnic inequalities are still very much with us, particularly for visible minorities, and that differential power and conflictual relations have become much more prominent issues. Concerning the latter – 'the two solitudes' – Breton's analyses must lead us to question the applicability of the image to contemporary Canadian society. There are two linguistic cultures and societies – *deux nations* – but the extent to which they are isolated 'solitudes' has changed markedly in the past thirty years; the relations between them are now much more combative.

In the next chapter, Pat Armstrong reminds us that the analysis of gender inequalities and gender relations were obvious areas of inattention in *The Vertical Mosaic*. She points out that this is partially because women are essentially absent from many of the situations studied by Porter – particularly the elites. This was an important issue of social inequality in Canadian society that Porter simply observed without making any attempt to explain through sustained theoretical or empirical analysis. Armstrong emphasizes, too, that Porter's central theoretical concepts and overall approach do not lend themselves well to the explanation of the subordination of women. For these reasons, among others, Armstrong concludes that it is inappropriate to revise and extend the theoretical approach Porter employed in *The Vertical Mosaic* as a way of incorporating women into the analysis. One must instead look at where women *are* as well as where they *are not*, and an improved theoretical approach is required. Armstrong goes on to analyse the situations of women over the past thirty years, guided by a feminist theoretical approach. In short, she looks at Porter's concerns but this time from the point of view of the phenomenon of 'the double ghetto.' She documents important gains in jobs, income, education, and power that women have made over recent decades, and she indicates why these gains have occurred – generally through the collective actions of women, with some assistance from the activities of labour unions and the state. She also identifies recent public policy threats to women's gains which put them in danger of participation in 'an unequal race to the bottom.' Armstrong believes that Porter writing *The Vertical Mosaic* today, and considering gender inequality, would have arrived at the same analysis and conclusions that she reaches, because of the value he placed on equality of opportunity and his critical approach to public policy.

Michael Ornstein's chapter looks at Porter's analysis of elites in Canada and the three decades of elite research since Porter's work. In part, Ornstein's analyses harken back to and expand upon issues of class and ethnic inequalities raised in the chapters by Clement and Breton. He reviews and assesses Porter's study of class and ethnic inequalities in attainment of elite positions in this country and the research on these topics that followed Porter's work. Porter's and others' work on (a) the structure of corporate capital and the economic elite, (b) relations between corporations, and (c) corporate ideology come in for careful assessment as well, as do studies of the labour elite, political elite, bureaucratic elite, and relationships between the elites. Ornstein also critically assesses the concepts of elites and power in Porter's study and related work and the theoretical underpinnings of such elite studies. Ornstein speaks, too, of an 'unfulfilled legacy' of Porter's work in this area. By this he means that no equivalent holistic, detailed study has been done to replicate Porter's work on elites. What we have instead, he says, is several scattered smaller studies of some specific elements of Porter's analysis. Ornstein speculates on the reasons for this lack of follow-up, suggesting that (a) the large investment in time and effort required to replicate Porter's work in a systematic, holistic way is daunting for researchers, (b) sociological research has become more specialized and piecemeal over recent decades, and (c) the theoretical tradition that is best suited to follow up on Porter's elite analysis, that is, political economy, has become more concerned with other issues central to studies in economics and politics.

The chapter by Julia O'Connor concludes the book by examining Canada in relationship to other welfare state societies, answering the question: 'To what degree has the welfare state lessened the inequalities of condition and opportunity in Canada that Porter documented in *The Vertical Mosaic*?' More specifically, O'Connor asks: 'How does Canada fare relative to other countries that are members of the Organization for Economic Cooperation and Development (OECD), not only in terms of social expenditure, but in terms of the scope and quality of social citizenship rights, and has its position changed over the 1960–1995 period?' O'Connor assesses Porter's conceptual approach to equality, justice, and citizenship and its theoretical underpinnings. Rooting herself in a 'gender-sensitive critique' of theories of citizenship, she identifies four defensible and measurable dimensions on which societies' records on citizenship rights and justice may be compared. The comparisons are then performed for Canada and other OECD societies. Porter's *The Vertical Mosaic* was often implicitly comparative – he drew many implicit comparisons with the United States and Britain. For example, he saw Canadian society as often standing between the United States and Britain in egalitarianism and conservatism, with Canada less egalitarian and more conservative than the United States, but more egalitarian and less conservative than Britain – thus providing support for 'the British fragment' imagery. However, this side of *The Vertical Mosaic* was more conjecture than empirical and explicitly comparative. O'Connor shows that the explicit comparisons can quite readily be made for certain concrete measures of inequality and citizenship. Among other things her analysis identifies a period of growth of citizenship rights and social equality in the Canadian welfare state (1960–73) and a later period (1974–present) of retrenchment and maintenance.

Taken together, the five chapters provide clear and abundant testimony as to why the Canadian sociological community should celebrate the thirtieth anniversary of *The Vertical Mosaic*. Not only do they show the magnitude of Porter's contribution to the mapping and interpretation of Canadian society, but they also demonstrate that in many instances we will continue to start out with Porter's maps and his analytical images for some time to come, as we cover this territory. That this is the case testifies to both the thoroughness and appropriateness of Porter's analyses in *The Vertical Mosaic* and the persistence and centrality to society of the phenomena he chose to research in the book. The chapters also illustrate how maps and images change with time. We must ask how the maps we have before us are incomplete or outdated and must be redrawn. Likewise, we must ask if the images and symbols we use to capture and communicate the salient features of the social landscape remain vital and useful. Our contributors undertake this activity, and researchers who follow them will do the same. Always though, the benchmark contributions of *The Vertical Mosaic* will provide reference points. Like us, those who update Porter's book in the future will by so doing continue to celebrate the book and honour its author.

These two goals will be served, too, when the five chapters that follow prompt readers who are not particularly familiar with John Porter's book to have a closer look at it. We are sure you will find rewarding these chapters, and *The Vertical Mosaic*.

Notes

1 Parts of this Introduction were presented by Rick Helmes-Hayes as the 17th Annual University of Waterloo Arts Lecture on 24 February 1997.
2 For a detailed discussion of the influence of Porter's LSE years, see Helmes-Hayes (1990).
3 Further details on the John Porter Award, and on the Porter Memorial Lectures, which are given by the recipient of the award at the annual meeting of the Canadian Sociology and Anthropology Association, may be found in *The Porter Memorial Lectures* (Curtis and Richardson 1988). This short volume contains the first few lectures, presented between 1984 and 1987.
4 Indeed, as late as 1972–3, only 25 per cent of required texts in 17 sociology departments across Canada were written by Canadians (Redekop 1976: 113; cited in Brym 1989: 20).
5 Interview of Bruce McFarlane by Rick Helmes-Hayes, 2 November 1986.
6 The citation reads: 'For his comprehensive analysis of stratification in Canadian society, and his contribution to macrosociology' (contained in John Porter, *Curriculum Vitae*, privately held copy, Rick Helmes-Hayes).
7 The observation that *The Vertical Mosaic* has sold more copies (over 100,000 copies) than any other sociology book (indeed, any other book) published by University of Toronto Press is based on correspondence from Virgil Duff, at the Press, to Rick Helmes-Hayes, 13 May 1997.

8 Stocktakings of studies on patterns of social inequality in Canada over the 1970s to 1990s are contained in Curtis and Scott (1973, 1979), Curtis, Grabb, and Guppy (1988, 1993), Forcese (1975, 1980, 1997), and Hunter (1981, 1986).

9 The paragraphs below draw on the detailed discussion of Leonard Marsh's *Canadians In and Out of Work* in Helmes-Hayes and Wilcox-Magill (1993).

10 Porter expressed his own guesses about why the book was so well received as follows: 'Canada was approaching a centennial and occasionally, in the range of celebration, questions were being asked about the kind of society that had been established. More importantly, perhaps, Canada was being torn by ethnic conflict which no amount of celebration could conceal' (1975: ix).

11 The macrosociological approach has been described as more prominent in English-language Canadian sociology than in American sociology (see Harp and Curtis 1971; cf. Lambert and Curtis 1973). American sociology has been much more 'individualistic' and social psychology oriented; Canadian sociology has been more 'society realist' – society and social change are more often the central referents. Some have argued that because of the greater isolation of French-language Canadian sociology from American sociology and the greater influence of the historical tradition of sociology in France, French-language Canadian sociology is even less social psychology oriented and more macrosociological than English-language Canadian sociology (see, e.g., Vallee and Whyte 1968; Harp and Curtis 1971).

12 Quite correctly, Ornstein argues, in his chapter in this volume, that Porter's analysis was based at least in part on an understanding of class as involving *relations*, and on the proposition that the economic elite was a representative of the capitalist class. Likewise, Ornstein contends, Porter's discussions of elites clearly emphasized relational aspects of elite arrangement. However, these relations were seen to lead more to 'accommodations' than to conflict.

References

Armstrong, Pat, and Hugh Armstrong. (1978). *The Double Ghetto: Canadian Women and Their Segregated Work*. Toronto: McClelland and Stewart.

Blishen, Bernard. (1970). 'Social Class and Opportunity in Canada.' *Canadian Review of Sociology and Anthropology* 7(2): 110–27.

Blishen, Bernard, and William K. Carroll. (1978). 'Sex Differences in a Socio-Economic Index for Occupations in Canada.' *Canadian Review of Sociology and Anthropology* 15 (3): 352–71.

Blishen, Bernard, and Hugh McRoberts. (1976). 'A Revised Socioeconomic Index for Occupations in Canada.' *Canadian Review of Sociology and Anthropology* 13(1): 71–9.

Blishen, Bernard, Frank Jones, Kaspar Naegele, and John Porter (eds.). (Four editions, in 1961, 1963, 1968, 1971). *Canadian Society: Sociological Perspectives*. Toronto: Macmillan.

Boyd, Monica, John Goyder, Frank E. Jones, Hugh A. McRoberts, Peter C. Pineo, and John Porter (1981). 'Status Attainment in Canada: Findings of the Canadian Mobility Study.' *Canadian Review of Sociology and Anthropology* 18(5): 657–73.

Brym, Robert, with Bonnie Fox. (1989). *From Culture to Power: The Sociology of English Canada*. Toronto: Oxford University Press.

Campbell, Colin, and George J. Szablowski. (1979). *The Superbureaucrats: Structures and Behaviour in Central Agencies*. Toronto: Macmillan.

Clark, S.D. (1959). *Movements of Political Protest, 1640–1940*. Toronto: University of Toronto Press.

– (1968). *The Developing Canadian Community*. Toronto: University of Toronto Press.

Clement, Wallace. (1975). *The Canadian Corporate Elite: An Analysis of Economic Power*. Toronto: McClelland and Stewart.

– (1977). *Continental Corporate Power: Economic Linkages Between Canada and the United States*. Toronto: McClelland and Stewart.

– (1988). 'Class Cleavages and Canadian Political Economy." Pp. 165–203 in Wallace Clement, *The Challenge of Class Analysis*. Ottawa: Carleton University Press.

Connor, Desmond M., and James Curtis. (1970). *Sociology and Anthropology in Canada*. Montreal: Canadian Sociology and Anthropology Association.

Creighton, Donald. (1937). *The Commercial Empire of the St Lawrence, 1760–1850*. Toronto: Ryerson.

Cuneo, Carl, and James Curtis. (1975). 'Social Ascription in the Educational and Occupational Status Attainment of Urban Canadians.' *Canadian Review of Sociology and Anthropology* 12(1): 6–24.

Curtis, James, and James Richardson (eds.). (1988). *The Porter Memorial Lectures*. Montreal: Canadian Sociology and Anthropology Association.

Curtis, James, and William G. Scott (eds.). (1973; 2nd ed. 1979). *Social Stratification in Canada*. Scarborough: Prentice-Hall.

Curtis, James, and Lorne Tepperman (eds.). (1990). *Images of Canada*. Scarborough: Prentice-Hall.

Curtis, James, Edward Grabb, and Neil Guppy (eds.). (1988; 2nd ed. 1993). *Social Inequality in Canada*. Scarborough: Prentice-Hall.

Forcese, Dennis P. (1975; 2nd ed. 1980; 3rd ed. 1997). *The Canadian Class Structure*. Toronto: McGraw-Hill Ryerson.

Goyder, John, and James Curtis. (1977). 'Occupational Mobility in Canada over Four Generations.' *Canadian Review of Sociology and Anthropology* 14(3): 303–19.

Grant, George. (1965). *Lament for a Nation: The Defeat of Canadian Nationalism.* Toronto: McClelland and Stewart.

Harp, John, and James Curtis. (1971). 'Linguistic Communities and Sociology.' Pp. 57–70 in James E. Gallagher and Ronald D. Lambert (eds.), *Social Process and Identities: The Canadian Case.* Toronto: Holt, Rinehart, and Winston.

Hartz, Louis (ed.). (1964). *The Founding of New Societies.* New York: Harcourt, Brace, and World.

Helmes-Hayes, Rick. (1985). 'Images of Inequality in Early Canadian Sociology, 1922–1965.' Unpublished PhD dissertation, University of Toronto.

– (1987). 'Writings about John Porter and His Work: An Annotated Bibliography.' Pp. 283–92 in John Porter, *The Measure of Canadian Society* (2nd ed.) (Wallace Clement, ed.). Ottawa: Carleton University Press.

– (1988). 'The Image of Inequality in S.D. Clark's Writings on Pioneer Canadian Society.' *Canadian Journal of Sociology* 13(3): 211–33.

– (1990). '"Hobhouse Twice Removed": John Porter and the LSE Years.' *Canadian Review of Sociology and Anthropology* 27 (3): 357–88.

Helmes-Hayes, Rick, and Dennis W. Wilcox-Magill. (1993). 'A Neglected Classic: Leonard Marsh's *Canadians In and Out of Work.*" *Canadian Review of Sociology and Anthropology* 30 (1): 83–109.

Hiller, Harry H. (1982). *Society and Change: S.D. Clark and the Development of Canadian Sociology.* Toronto: University of Toronto Press.

Hughes, Everett C. (1943). *French Canada in Transition.* Chicago: University of Chicago Press.

Hunter, Alfred A. (1981; 2nd ed. 1986). *Class Tells: On Social Inequality in Canada.* Toronto: Butterworths.

Innis, Harold. (1930). *The Fur Trade in Canada: An Introduction to Canadian Economic History.* Toronto: University of Toronto Press.

Lambert, Ronald D., and James Curtis. (1973). "Nationality and Professional Activity Correlates among Social Scientists.' *Canadian Review of Sociology and Anthropology* 10(1): 62–80.

Lipset, Seymour M. (1963). *The First New Nation: The United States in Historical and Comparative Perspective.* New York: Basic.

Lower, A.R.M. (1932). *The Trade in Square Timber.* MA thesis, University of Toronto.

– (1943). 'Two Ways of Life – the Primary Antithesis in Canadian History.' *Canadian Historical Association Report*: 5–18.

Lucas, Rex. (1973). *Minetown, Milltown, Railtown.* Toronto: University of Toronto Press.

MacLennan, Hugh. (1945). *Two Solitudes.* Toronto: Popular Library.

Macpherson, C.B. (1965). *The Real World of Democracy.* Toronto: Canadian Broadcasting Corporation.

McFarlane, Bruce. (1986). Interviewed by R. Helmes-Hayes, 2 November.

McRoberts, Hugh A., and K. Selbee. (1981). 'Trends in Occupational Mobility in Canada and the United States: A Comparison.' *American Sociological Review* 46: 406–21.

Marchak, Patricia. (1975). *Ideological Perspectives on Canada*. Toronto: McGraw-Hill Ryerson.

– (1985). 'Canadian Political Economy.' *Canadian Review of Sociology and Anthropology* 22(5): 673–709.

Marsden, Lorna, and Edward Harvey. (1979). *Fragile Federation: Social Change in Canada*. Toronto: McGraw-Hill Ryerson.

Marsh, Leonard C. (1940). *Canadians In and Out of Work: A Survey of Economic Classes and Their Relations to the Labour Market*. Toronto and Montreal: Oxford University Press and McGill University.

Niosi, Jorge. (1981). *Canadian Capitalism: A Study of Power in the Canadian Business Establishment*. Toronto: Lorimer.

Oderkirk, Jillian. (1995). 'Food Banks.' Pp. 225–40 in E.D. Nelson and Augie Fleras (eds.), *Social Problems in Canada Reader*. Scarborough: Prentice-Hall.

Ogmundson, Rick, and J. McLauglin (1992). 'Trends in the Ethnic Origins of Canadian Elites: The Decline of the BRITS.' *Canadian Review of Sociology and Anthropology* 29(2): 227–42.

Olsen, Dennis. (1980). *The State Elite*. Toronto: McClelland and Stewart.

Ornstein, Michael, and H. Michael Stevenson. (in press). *In the Bosom of the State: Ideology and Politics in Canada*. McGill-Queen's University Press.

Pineo, Peter, John Porter, and Hugh McRoberts. (1977). 'The 1971 Census and the Socio-Economic Classification of Occupations.' *Canadian Review of Sociology and Anthropology* 14(1): 91–102.

Porter, John. (1955). 'Elite Groups: A Scheme for the Study of Power in Canada.' *Canadian Journal of Economics and Political Science* 21(4): 498–512.

– (1956). 'Concentration of Economic Power and the Economic Elite in Canada.' *Canadian Journal of Economics and Political Science* 22(2): 199–220.

– (1957). 'The Economic Elite and the Social Structure in Canada.' *Canadian Journal of Economics and Political Science* 23(3): 376–94.

– (1958). 'Higher Public Servants and the Bureaucratic Elite in Canada.' *Canadian Journal of Economics and Political Science* 24(4): 483–501.

– (1961a). 'Power and Freedom in Canadian Democracy.' Pp. 27–56 in Michael Oliver (ed.), *Social Purpose for Canada*. Toronto: University of Toronto Press.

– (1961b). 'Social Class and Education.' Pp. 103–29 in Michael Oliver (ed.), *Social Purpose for Canada*. Toronto: University of Toronto Press.

– (1965). *The Vertical Mosaic: An Analysis of Social Class and Power in Canada*. Toronto: University of Toronto Press.

- (1967). 'Canadian Character in the Twentieth Century.' *Annals of the American Academy of Political and Social Science* 370 (March): 49–56.
- (1970). 'Research Biography of a Macrosociological Study: *The Vertical Mosaic.*' Pp. 7–39 in J. Porter, *The Measure of Canadian Society* (2nd ed. 1987) (Wallace Clement, ed.). Ottawa: Carleton University Press.
- (1975). 'Foreword,' in Wallace Clement, *The Canadian Corporate Elite: An Analysis of Economic Power.* Toronto: McClelland and Stewart.
- (1977a). 'Education and Equality: The Failure of a Mission.' Pp. 242–62 in J. Porter, *The Measure of Canadian Society* (2nd ed. 1987) (Wallace Clement, ed.). Ottawa: Carleton University Press.
- (1977b). 'Education and the Just Society.' Pp. 263–80 in J. Porter, *The Measure of Canadian Society* (2nd ed. 1987) (Wallace Clement, ed.). Ottawa: Carleton University Press.
- (1979). *The Measure of Canadian Society* (1st ed.). Toronto: Gage.
- (1987). *The Measure of Canadian Society* (2nd ed.) (Wallace Clement, ed.). Ottawa: Carleton University Press.

Porter, John, Bernard Blishen, et al. (1971). *Towards 2000: The Future of Post-Secondary Education in Ontario.* Toronto: McClelland and Stewart.

Porter, John, et al. (1985). *Ascription and Achievement: Studies in Mobility and Status Attainment in Canada.* Ottawa: Carleton University Press.

Porter, John, and Peter Pineo. (1967). 'Occupational Prestige in Canada.' *Canadian Review of Sociology and Anthropology* 4(1): 24–40.

Porter, John, Marion Porter, Bernard Blishen, et al. (1982). *Stations and Callings: Making It through the School System.* Toronto: Methuen.

Porter, Marion, John Porter, and Bernard Blishen. (1973). *Does Money Matter?* Toronto: York University Institute for Behavioural Research.

Vallee, Frank G., and Donald R. Whyte. (1968). Pp. 833–52 in Bernard Blishen et al (eds.), *Canadian Society: Sociological Perspectives* (3rd ed.). Toronto: Macmillan.

Power, Ethnicity, and Class: Reflections Thirty Years after *The Vertical Mosaic*[1]

WALLACE CLEMENT

Thirty years have passed since publication of *The Vertical Mosaic*, the defining book in Canadian sociology and a benchmark for Canadian social science. John Porter was then forty-three years of age. He was only fifty-seven years old when he died prematurely in 1979. Porter's entire teaching career spanned thirty years. He graduated from the London School of Economics in 1949 and returned to the Canada he had left at the age of fifteen. That year he began teaching at Carleton College, which had been established to train war veterans like himself.

John Porter began research for *The Vertical Mosaic* (1965) in the summer of 1952, having negotiated a thesis topic with his supervisor, Morris Ginsberg, back in London the previous summer. Like many doctoral theses, this one took on proportions larger than its author originally intended. It was, however, scaled down from his grandiose desire to 'write an interpretation of Canada as a modern democracy' much as de Tocqueville, Laski, and Lord Bryce had done for the United States (Porter 1987a: 12).

The public beginning for his remarkable project was the publication of his 'Elite Groups: A Scheme for the Study of Power in Canada' in the *Canadian Journal of Economics and Political Science* published in November 1955. It was revised to become Chapter 7 in *The Vertical Mosaic*. Porter's classic work consumed his talents for the next decade. From today's perspective, it is hard to appreciate just how radical a departure this book was for Canadian academics. Not only did the book take up a theme – class inequality – that had been all but ignored by academics, but it took a critical stance towards the position of 'value neutrality' that mainstream social scientists adopted during that era. John Meisel acknowledged its importance in the book's Foreword but felt bound to say that 'it departs from a long-standing tradition in Canadian academic circles concerning the degree to which a scholarly work can be simultaneously respectable and polemical.' As Meisel went on to inform the reader, 'A sense of commitment, of *engagement*, has, in short, been a sign of scholarly impurity' (Meisel 1965: x).

Immediately upon its publication, *The Vertical Mosaic* received scholarly and popular acclaim, setting the Canadian sociological agenda for the next two decades, including fifteen scholarly productive years for John Porter. However, this past decade has seen Canadian sociology's agenda range far beyond that pursued in *The Vertical Mosaic*. There has been an entrenchment of feminism and the women's movement, the intellectual autonomy of Quebec, the rise of Native people's claims, a new international political economy including North American free trade, the economic unification of Europe, the rise of the Pacific Rim as an economic power, and the development of a strong tradition of comparative analysis in political economy. This is not to say that the issues of education, ethnicity and migration, class and power, are *passé*. Far from it. They remain as relevant today as when Porter was writing, but they are now being expressed and understood in Canadian scholarship in a very different way than they were in 1965.

The Vertical Mosaic was so significant because of the silences it addressed. When published in 1965, Canadian social sciences, and sociology in particular, were underdeveloped; this was especially the case *vis-à-vis* the link between academic and public discourse. *The Vertical Mosaic* did not fill this void, but it was a key first volley, a foray into an uncharted domain – the development of a macrosociology of Canada accessible to the reading public. This remarkable book was a synthetic piece, but one where the parts often needed to be custom crafted. John Porter had to pioneer at the level of 'the homework'; that is, the basic research. He was able to cover as much ground as he did because of his exceptional journalistic and analytical skills. He knew there were gaps and softness to the data. Every area covered demanded more in-depth research than he was able to undertake, yet he managed to weave a tapestry which captured in vivid and colourful terms the whole of a society. His was an extraordinary accomplishment.

My intent here is to revisit the major themes that informed *The Vertical Mosaic* and reflect upon some of the research and ways of thinking in these areas today. I will do so by describing the logic of my own shift into political economy and comparative research. It is not possible here to review the discipline of sociology – even only those parts most directly influenced by Porter. There are four other essays in this collection covering the specific areas of race and ethnicity, gender inequalities, elites, and comparative welfare states. There is also an intellectual biography provided by the editors. Instead, I will critically locate my research in the context of the research agenda established by John Porter in his seminal work and use my own work to exemplify trends within the political economy tradition as they have developed since the 1970s in particular. As those essays demonstrate, there are important continuities between the research tradition established by John Porter and the research that continues to engage contemporary scholars, myself included. The differences between Porter's work and the work I do are partially those of time and changed circumstances, but mainly they are differences of theory and assumptions. After all these years, I continue to be motivated by the thinking of John Porter and have enormous respect for the contribution he made to Canadian scholarship and, in particular, to my own intellectual development. But times change.

In all the key areas of Canadian society there have been major developments since the publication of *The Vertical Mosaic*. Notable has been the rise of foreign ownership in the Canadian economy, its continentalization, and the internationalization of production. Canada and its capital are now intertwined with U.S. capitalists, the dominant fraction of which has gained hegemony over a continental trade bloc which now also includes Mexico. Regionalism, always an element of Canadian society, has taken on expanded importance. Fostered in no small part by demands for nationhood emanating from Quebec, and the concessions to all provinces by federal politicians seeking to placate the demands for decentralization, regionalism has intensified. Porter actively supported increased federal powers as a way to promote more universalistic, national goals rather than the more particularistic goals of the provinces, although he did support the distinctiveness of Quebec.

Part of the diminished role for the federal state has been motivated by its desire to reduce state expenditures, an initiative Porter would have fought. This not only undercuts the idea of national standards and provision of fundamental social entitlements, but it also reduces the number of good jobs in the state sector where women have made some inroads in recent times. The structure of power under the promotion of the so-called market enhances private and particularistic interests over public and universalistic ones. Such actions promote further opening of Canada to the agenda of U.S. neo-liberal interests which have captured the hearts and minds of many Canadian politicians and the pocketbooks of many business interests.

Also notable has been the shift of Canadian immigration from Europe to Asia and the Caribbean, magnifying the place of racism within discussions of difference. The immigrant society Porter characterized as a 'vertical mosaic' is in many ways even more colourful and volatile today. 'Multiculturalism,' which Porter did so much to problematize, continues to be a contested notion both in public policy and in scholarly terms.

Finally, class struggles have far from dissolved away with postindustrialism. Class formation has changed, but it has not disappeared as a real factor in the dynamics of contemporary Canadian society. In many ways, the restructuring, reducing, and diminishing of the state have caused a resurgence of class struggle with new challenges for the labour movement. This movement remains nearly as fragmented as Porter's prescient analysis of the labour elite revealed it to be over thirty years ago, but it is considerably more resilient than its counterpart in the United States.

Power, Elites, and Mobility

Two-thirds of the space in *The Vertical Mosaic* addresses the theme of power and elites. This was also Porter's point of departure in 1955 as he began to construct his sociological map of Canada.

Porter began with a map of power based on the assumption of plural functional institutional systems headed by decision makers he called elites. Consciously he opposed this view to one he labelled as 'materialist.' In that original 1955 blueprint article, Porter wrote: 'This materialist view holds that the economic function has a primacy over the others. The view here taken is that not only must all five functions be undertaken, but also that in any given case economic, political, bureaucratic, defensive, or ideological considerations might dominate' (Porter 1955: 502). On this formulation John Porter and I disagreed (see Porter 1975). We differed in 1975 when, *The Canadian Corporate Elite* (Clement 1975; see Porter 1975a) was published, and we differ even more two decades later. Now I even more thoroughly support the materialism of political economy, a tradition where all these features of society are holistically integrated.

John Porter's portrayal of power was strongly influenced by Raymond Aron, the French journalist and sociologist, well known for his hyperindividualism. According to the Aron/Porter view, there is a dichotomy between the 'Soviet' and 'Western' types of elites, with the former bound by 'the party' and the latter 'clearly separated – by a floating equilibrium of compromise' (Porter 1965: 210). For Porter, these were two 'models' rather than actual societies. He deemed the 'Western' type to be 'more desirable,' but granted that a society's actual place on the 'continuum' was a matter for empirical investigation (ibid.: 215).

Porter's elites corresponded to the power roles in each of the 'five functional systems.' The task was 'to isolate these power roles and to examine the way in which persons are selected to fill them' (Porter 1955: 503). Not only did this perspective assume the existence of five functional 'systems' which, in modern times, each demand greater 'specialization,' but also it assumed that the major social problem is to create conditions that allow mobility into the elites by society's most talented members. Such a problematic of 'elite circulation' stems back to the classic works of Gaetano Mosca in *The Ruling Class* (1939), Vilfredo Pareto in *The Mind and Society* (1935), and Robert Michels in *Political Parties* (1962).

Porter's views differed significantly from those of C. Wright Mills, who published *The Power Elite* (1956), a year after Porter's initial article and the year both men met. Porter held views more liberal-democratic than those of radical populist Mills whose 'monolithic' portrayal of power Porter rejected.[2] Porter supported the notion of equality of opportunity on both ethical and practical grounds. He saw the liberating quality this had for 'talent' and that 'talent' had for the quality of governance. Porter clearly believed in the creative role of politics and in political institutions as the means of reform. Mills, by contrast, saw politics in the United States as subordinate to the 'military-industrial complex' and regarded dissent as the best means of opposition. Mills's goals were more populist and radical than were Porter's, founded in a tradition Mills characterized as 'plain marxism' (see Mills 1962).[3]

My agenda for the 'updating' of Porter's study of Canada's economic elite (Clement 1975) introduced the importance of time (social change) and space (relations between nations). It included a sense that power was to be understood in relational class terms, especially in terms of the effects of power. This work was more akin to the analysis of C. Wright Mills than that of the plural elitists followed by Porter.

Current discussion has moved beyond the power elite versus plural elite versus ruling class debates of the late 1950s (C. Wright Mills), 1960s (John Porter), and 1970s (myself). Each tended, by definition or neglect, to pose a 'mass' population or an ill-specified 'working class,' as the counterpoint to a ruling elite or ruling class, and none focused much on class *relations*. In contrast to the crude materialism which Porter rejected, and which I would reject, I take the position that all large-scale societies need to attend to the economic alongside the state (political, bureaucratic, and military powers) and the legitimacy of the social order (cultural and ideological understandings).

Porter was not naïve about the power of corporations and the hegemony of capitalism. As he stated in *The Vertical Mosaic*: 'Corporations ... are governed by human beings who behave in accordance with a set of institutional norms – those of corporate capitalism. To argue that national sentiments and the "national interest" would supplant the historical and inexorable norms of capitalist enterprise is to reveal an ignorance of the capitalist economy' (1965: 269). Although John Porter was influenced by and familiar with the work of Antonio Gramsci (see Clement 1987), much of his agenda reflected a liberal view that equated issues of 'equality' to those of 'mobility' and rejected a Marxist materialist analysis.

Porter's sociological concerns about equality of opportunity were expressed in the language of 'ascription' versus 'achievement' so popular in American sociology during the 1950s. Sociologists focused, that is, on the interrelated issues of (a) role allocations to elite positions and (b) barriers to social mobility experienced by the talented. Education was regarded as the master institution which could overcome both inequities. Late in life Porter questioned his earlier concern with issues of occupational mobility and educational achievement. Neither was necessarily progressive, and neither facilitated equality, justice, or fairness (ibid. 1987: xiv).

As I argued in my Foreword to the second edition of *The Measure of Canadian Society* (1987), one of the main differences between Porter's power and stratification analysis and my own more class-oriented approach is that he focused on *inequality*, while I sought to address *exploitation*. Somewhat crudely put, this may be seen as the difference between inequality of opportunity and inequality of condition, although that language itself is mired in an earlier problematic. Inequality of opportunity has a 'mobility problematic,' whereby the fluidity of movement between positions and access to the 'best' jobs for the 'most' talented is seen as central. An inequality of condition concern is with the hierarchy of power and the structure of the labour market (the way good and bad jobs are created). Inequalities in 'opportunity' paradigms are specified in terms of recruitment, while those in the 'condition' paradigm are located in terms of the structure of positions in a hierarchy. Underlying these paradigms are different assumptions and values. As expressed by Frank Parkin (1971), the 'meritocratic critique' focuses on recruitment and opportunity, while the 'egalitarian critique' has the structure of positions and disparity of power as its concern (see Clement 1975: 6–8). To put it otherwise, my analysis of class has been based on relations between classes (Clement 1990; Clement and Myles 1994) rather than on barriers to individual mobility opportunities. Even in the elite studies, I took access to elite positions as indicators of other relational differences rather than as ends in themselves. While Porter was more motivated to show that mobility to the 'inevitable' structures was based upon ascriptive characteristics rather than achievement by the most meritorious, I was concerned to reveal the *structures* of power. Consequently, my work paid more attention to property ownership, corporate structures, and economic development than did Porter's, which focused more on 'fairness' and the 'wastage' of society's talent.

Other Canadian sociologists have continued to work broadly within the 'elite' tradition, most notably William Carroll (1986), Michael Ornstein (1984, 1989), and Jorge Niosi (1981).[4] They have produced rich and sophisticated research that goes well beyond the elite analysis of Porter or myself in terms of its statistical detail and depth of empirical coverage. What remains unique about Porter, however, is his range of coverage for all elites. The elite theories and methodologies he pioneered in his early work, especially *The Vertical Mosaic*, have never been duplicated in terms of their insight, clarity, and vitality.

Ethnicity and Nation

In his Foreword to *The Vertical Mosaic*, John Meisel referred to what was then the 'present crisis' – by which he meant matters before the Royal Commission on Bilingualism and Biculturalism. His comment on the 'current problems in maintaining national unity' has a contemporary ring (Meisel 1965: ix, x). Next to power and elites, the most frequently noted feature of Porter's book was its focus on ethnicity and, to a lesser extent, the national question in Quebec. Despite the current familiarity of statements such as, 'The French struggle to retain their identity, while the non-French are looking for one,' much has changed since 1965. Note, for example, Porter's observation: 'The dominance of the two charter groups has never been seriously challenged because of French natural increase and high levels of British immigration' (Porter 1965: 49, 61). Neither practice reflects our contemporary reality: in fact, just the opposite.

Much of what Porter had to say about Quebec followed publication of *The Vertical Mosaic*. The French in Quebec Porter regarded as a 'nation' rather than an 'ethnic group.' While he campaigned against ethnicity as an appropriate basis for organizing a society, he made an exception in the case of Quebec. Indeed, in 'Mr Trudeau and Canadian Federalism,' written in 1968, Porter argued for a 'new federalism which would give special status to Quebec and at the same time seek to draw the rest of Canada together in a strong centralist frame' (Porter 1987b: 183).

The distinction between nation and ethnicity mattered for Porter, although there were certainly some tensions in his argument. As he explained in his 1972 inaugural address to the Royal Society of Canada, there are 'problems which are likely to emerge when we deal with inequality on the basis of group rather than individual claims.' Which groups and which identities clearly matter, even in Porter's own terms. He cited Frank Vallee's study of how minority group claims can limit individuals' opportunities for upward mobility 'unless, of course, it is characteristic of the ethnic group to put a special stress on educational and vocational achievement.' While some ethnic groups may in fact promote mobility and educational attainment, this seems not to have been Porter's fundamental concern. Rather, it was because 'racism and culturalism stem from the fact that both are linked to the maintenance of descent group solidarity and endogamy' that Porter feared promotion of ethnicity. He was clear about his reasons: 'In seeking to choose between the ethnic stratification that results from ethnic diversity and the greater possibilities for equality that result from the reduction of ethnicity as a salient feature of modern society I have quite obviously chosen an assimilationist position, and in seeking to choose between the atavistic responses that can arise from descent group identification and the more liberal view that descent group membership is irrelevant to human interaction I have chosen the latter' (Porter 1972: 205).

Multiculturalism continues to be a controversial idea in Canada (as an official policy, as a value, and as an analytical tool). Porter may have accepted aspects of liberal multiculturalism (folklore) which encourage festive aspects of ancestral cultures, but he clearly saw more danger than advantage. There are now those who would promote radical multiculturalism that emphasizes the politics of difference to maintain authentic alternatives rather than transcend them in favour of common goals like 'equality.' To some extent this may be portrayed by some groups as the politics of 'emancipation.' But such formulations do not do justice to the quality of research that has been produced in the field of ethnicity in recent times. An exemplar is Kay J. Anderson's book, *Vancouver's Chinatown: Racial Discourse in Canada, 1875–1980* (1991), an empirically rich and theoretically sophisticated study which, in 1992, was an appropriate winner of the Porter Book Award given annually by the Canadian Sociology and Anthropology Association.

Most of John Porter's work focused on the nation state and thus ana-

lysed national-level data dealing with ethnicity and opportunity/mobil-
ity structures. He paid little attention to the practices of immigration
and/or the formation and dynamics of ethnic communities. What
Anderson demonstrated so elegantly in *Vancouver's Chinatown* was the
specific construction of ethnicity around the Chinese community in
Vancouver and what this revealed about how 'Anglo-dominance'
operated against Asian populations. Anderson struggled against distinctions (analytical or otherwise) based on biological conceptions of
'race.' She revealed race to be a social construct created and maintained
as part of the cultural hegemony of the British settler society. She offered
an intriguing analysis based upon territory and 'otherness,' including
differences supported by multiculturalism, whereby the 'Chinese'(who
were and are far from homogeneous) offered resistance and challenge to
their subordination. Obviously much more could be said about this
work, but one aspect I wish to mention is its authorship. Kay Anderson,
who I would consider to be a political economist who employs a materialist analysis of culture and ideology, is an Australian geographer. She
produced this book from her doctoral thesis which was done in the
Department of Geography at the University of British Columbia. This
helps support a contention I will make below that political economy not
only gives us permission to transcend disciplinary boundaries, it actually 'forces' us to do so – and provides novel insights in the process.

There has been a revival of sociological work in the area of ethnicity,
much of which has a continuity with Porter's work. There are direct
links, for example, with Monica Boyd and Raymond Breton (see, e.g.,
Breton 1991; Boyd 1992). At the same time, however, the field has
changed dramatically in terms of the approach and issues addressed by
the researchers. For example, issues of racism in major metropolitan
centres, refugees, and the migration of domestic labourers within the
context of international developments have each received detailed
attention (see, e.g., Stasiulis 1997). Equally noteworthy has been the
revival of research on Native peoples within Canada and the special
place they have within the complex relations of race and ethnicity (see,
e.g., Satzewich and Wotherspoon 1993; Abele 1997).

Classes

As with power, elites, and ethnicity, Porter's critique of class was motivated by a desire to maximize individual opportunity and the rational
societal utilization of talent. Early in *The Vertical Mosaic* he wrote: 'Class

barriers act to prevent the full use of Canada's human resources in an age when high levels of skill are essential to future development' (Porter 1965: 6). This statement includes his view on class but also assumptions about 'postindustrial society' to which I return below.

Porter addressed the methodological problem of defining classes by specifying two approaches: the objective and subjective. Subjective classes, based on prestige social rankings, are 'no more than artificially constructed social groups.' Objective classes are groups that share economic characteristics: 'income, the ownership of property, level of education, degree of occupational skill, or position of responsibility and power' (ibid.: 9, 10). Thus, the 'reality' of the classes described in Porter's work has been contentious. Were classes to be understood as relational or as distributive? Did classes have interests, and engage in collective actions and struggles as actors, or were they to be statistical compilations meant to communicate inequalities of valued resources such as income, education, or occupational attainment?

There is little doubt for me that classes used in Porter's 'objective' sense are real in both experiential and explanatory ways. As one of his stated goals, Porter had challenged the 'middle class image' of Canada. He used the example of low-income family heads 'moonlighting' to maintain consumption at 'a middle class style of life in the middle 1950s, the high tide of post-war affluence' (ibid.: 5). We know the times are now different. In Porter's work, unemployment goes virtually unmentioned, except for historical references to the Depression. Unemployment stood at less than a quarter million in 1955, mostly young people and immigrants who were in transition within the labour force (ibid.: 110). Today the number of unemployed is over six times as great, hovering around one and a half million, a chronic problem demanding resolution.

Class analysis has changed since Porter's time. Let me illustrate using *Relations of Ruling: Class and Gender in Postindustrial Societies* (Clement and Myles 1994). There John Myles and I argued that class and class relations are real and mediated by gender, race, ethnicity, and nation, among other things. Often the effects of class are contingent (that is, dependent) upon other relations.

We began by reconceptualizing how capitalist relations are to be understood, arguing that key features of these relations concern decision making regarding the forces of production (strategic decisions) and authority over labour (tactical decisions). We offered a key distinction about directing the forces and relations of production. Following Poulantzas (1975) and Carchedi (1977), we distinguished control and surveillance from coordination and unity (see Clement and Myles 1994: Chapter 1). Coordination and unity are requirements of any large-scale organization of production and distribution (thus adding value), whereas control and surveillance are based on disciplining labour and extracting surplus (thus recovering value for capital). Bearing these relationships in mind, we then offered an innovation to class analysis using a 'minimalist,' domination-based relational approach. This 'minimalist approach' focuses on two dimensions: commanding the means of production and directing the labour power of others, adding complexities such as skill, education, and management and supervision as refinements.

Relations of Ruling is based on an original conception of class in which we 'took apart,' explored and put back together the four major classes of advanced capitalism. This was done in relationship to gender located in the context of transformations in national economies. We examined class structures and relations of ruling, including how people reproduce their material and ideological existence. Located in the macrocomparative context, we asked about the fate of the old middle class, the rise and activism of the new middle class, and issues of labour regulation and surveillance.

We contended that the new middle class is the most volatile (and variable) class actor in the postindustrial world. The new middle class has emerged as an important force within both the state and corporate worlds. Its 'loyalty' or identification with either the capitalist/executive class on the one side or working class on the other has become a key variable in class analysis, analogous to the important role in the past held by the old middle class (or petty bourgeoisie) in class politics. Our studies indicated that the alliances of the new middle class are conditional, varying by nation, economic sector, and degree of feminization.

Alongside this development has been the feminization of the 'new working class' as salesclerks, office workers, and personal service workers. The feminization of the labour market, for example, transforms the material interests of the working class and produces demands for pay equity, child care, paid leaves, sexual harassment policies, different forms of training, flexible working hours, and an overall feminization of class struggles.[5]

We argued that there is more to production relations than class relations. Also embodied are relations of ruling governing men and women, inside and outside the household. Included here are cultural practices and ideologies fundamental to maintaining structures of control. We moved well beyond simply identifying 'gender differences' in the class structure to explore how gender is embodied in relations of ruling at home and in the paid labour force. For example we explored authority and decision making within the home as influenced by the amount of income individuals earn and gendered differences in how supervision occurs for men and women in employment.

By using understandings of class embodied in conservative, populist, left-labour, and corporatist class orientations as a typology of the 'class cultural repertoire' used in North America and Nordic settings, we also took a novel look at class culture/consciousness. Our findings suggested that populism is a remarkably important mind-set in North America and confirmed a strong left-labour orientation in Sweden. Beyond that, however, we showed that class cleavages between the working class and both the capitalist/executive and old middle class remain wide in Sweden. Questions were raised about both intraclass solidarity and class cleavages.

Sensitive to the limitations of using countries as units of analysis, we examined some basic social cleavages inside North America: regionalism, the national question in Quebec, and ethnicity in Canada, and regionalism and race in the United States. That specific analysis involved the culture of gender and the influence of trade unions on these cleavages.

The progressive features of 'postindustrial society' seemed less convincing to us than they were to John Porter in *The Vertical Mosaic* and his writings up to the mid-1970s. Like many sociologists of his era, Porter accepted the argument that there was a direct link between the development of postindustrial society and the overall upgrading of the labour force. Evidence changed his mind. Revealing about John Porter is that the methodological appendix critiquing census data entitled 'A Final Note on Skill' was what convinced him about many points in Harry Braverman's *Labor and Monopoly Capital* (1974; see Porter 1978: 25), a scathing critique of assumptions Porter once had shared.

The context of postindustrialism conveys the changes in the character of goods production in favour of service employment which has strong class and gender effects as well as differences by nation. For example, we found that in North America women were concentrated in the private sector consumer and business services, Nordic women were still in public sector health, education, and welfare, while men everywhere were concentrated in goods production characteristic of the 'old working class.' Considering this evidence, we concluded that the postindustrial experience is gendered and differs nationally, and therefore it is contingent in its effects and subject to human agency.

In conducting our analysis in *Relations of Ruling*, Myles and I challenged traditional assumptions, such as those held by Porter, that even with the increasing number of women in the paid labour force 'it is unlikely that their occupations have replaced those of men as the main factor determining the class position of the family' (Porter 1965: 154). Over three chapters (6, 7, and 8) we dealt in detail with such head-of-household assumptions in *Relations of Ruling*.

Has postindustrialism produced different or new ways of organizing gender relations, or has it simply reinforced traditional ways? There is some evidence of changes in what we called unconventional households where women earn at least half the total household income and succeed in changing traditional patterns of organizing housework. The effects were evident in both the behaviours and attitudes accompanying economic powers. Most households remained 'traditional' in our terms, but there was evidence of transitional patterns, especially in Sweden. There were even some 'modern' households where the housework barrier has been broken. We were interested in finding under what conditions these changes occur. To conduct such analysis requires using households instead of individuals as the appropriate units of analysis. Not using 'heads of households' but relations within the household was the key. Furthermore, we explored classes within households. Empowerment was specified in relational terms. We found some definite effects of class on gender attitudes.

Much, much more work needs to be done on class and gender in Canada and comparatively. Analyses such as ours only begin to touch upon the enormous complexity of this real world. Class and gender are very real in their experiences and effects. Both matter.

Political Economy and Comparative Analysis

John Porter was not a political economist. Though he had some background in economics, he was more of a European sociologist and political scientist with journalistic experience. He had a 'faith,' not well grounded empirically, in the meritocratic, democratic, and 'melting pot' character of the United States.[6] As an aside, in his 'Introduction' to 'Research Biography of a Macrosociological Study: *The Vertical Mosaic*,' written in 1979, he wrote: 'Although I always admired American sociologists for their methodological skills, I was never particularly attracted to the kinds of problems to which they were bringing their skills' (Porter 1987d: 8). There is an implicit comparative analysis throughout *The Vertical Mosaic* between the United States (the meritocratic melting pot) and the United Kingdom (where class was real and transparent).[7]

An important development within Canadian sociology has been the development of comparative political economy.[8] An excellent example is the special issue of the *Canadian Review of Sociology and Anthropology*,[9] edited by John Myles,[10] called 'Comparative Political Economy Perspectives.' Much of this literature engages with Gøsta Esping-Andersen's *The Three Worlds of Welfare Capitalism* (1990) which establishes a typology of welfare-state regimes: the conservative, liberal, and social democratic.[11] Each type is exemplified by a social security regime: continental European conservatism combines labour market attachments and financial contributions; Anglo-Saxon liberalism establishes entitlements around means-tested benefits; Scandinavian social democracy provides universal rights of citizenship.

As John Myles pointed out in his 'Introduction' to the special issue, Canadian sociology, including Porter's, has always been comparative, at least implicitly, but the comparators have been the United Kingdom and the United States because of their similarities and common roots. What the new political economy approach to comparative analysis has done is to shift the focus of methodological attention from similarities to differences, arguing that variation among industrial societies requires explanation. Myles remarked that the main conclusion of this approach has been that 'politics matters' and that 'class politics matter the most' (1989a: 2–3). At stake in current discussions of comparative political economy methodologies are the issues of which comparators are appropriate under what conditions and how comparisons should be conducted, that is, using countries as exemplars of particular types or examining countries transforming from one type to another. In this era of global forces and restructuring, how can our explanations draw upon both national distinctiveness and common international pressures?[12]

'Regime analysis,' which includes comparative research based upon 'types' of nations presented as exemplars, designates a system of rule and periodization when particular policy regimes are 'in place' or ruling groups are 'in power.' This approach recognizes the national integrity and distinctiveness of nations, but acknowledges as well that there are important parallels in social formations, such as those that characterize all liberal democracies. The scheme is not only one of 'classification' but of movement between types of nations, such as Sweden's movement from a social-democratic formation to a liberal regime and Canada's shift from a liberal to neo-conservative regime (see Ahrne and Clement 1994a). My work on Sweden has explored the issue of regime change and raised questions about the limits of social democracy (see Ahrne and Clement 1994b; Clement 1994a).

Pat Marchak's *The Integrated Circus: The New Right and the Restructuring of Global Markets* (1991) leads a strong corpus of work within Canadian sociology in the political economy tradition. Marchak is noteworthy because of her enormous contribution to political economy within sociology, including her leadership in the 'Fish and Ships' project, her work on British Columbia and international forestry, and her chapter 'Canadian Political Economy' in the special issue of the *Canadian Review of Sociology and Anthropology* dedicated to 'approaches' (see Marchak 1983, 1985, 1991, 1995; also Marchak, Guppy, and McMullan (eds.) 1987).

Also exemplary of contemporary political economy is the collection *Production, Space, Identity: Political Economy Faces the 21st Century* (1993), edited by Jane Jenson, Rianne Mahon, and Manfred Bienefeld. Its title is revealing. *Production* signifies transformations in economic relations; *space* marks boundaries and spatial relations; *identity* includes gender, class, race/ethnicity, age, nation, and region. Political economy studies the marginal *as part of* the powerful, not isolated on their own where only some *internal logic* ('blaming the victim') can offer an explanation or account.

A new collection of original essays called *Understanding Canada: Building on The New Canadian Political Economy* (Clement, ed. 1997), which includes sociologists in seven of its seventeen chapters, develops a materialist perspective. Its 'Introduction' argues that political economy, at its best, connects the economic, political, and cultural/ideological moments of social life. Materialist analysis in this sense recognizes that the organization of consumption, distribution, and production of goods and services is inherently cultural, social, and political. Moreover, all require both immediate and long-term reproduction. Such organization requires justification and the appearance of legitimacy. Political economy is also historic and dynamic, seeking to understand change and transformation through identification of tensions and contradictions. Equally important is the spatial dimension of political economy understood as relational in both domestic (regional) and international contexts. Politics in political economy involves human agency and encompasses all power relations from the household to the international economy. This perspective is particularly important to counter images of the 'market' as simply economic forces; markets are also social and political in how they are directed and with what implications. Political economy resists the surrendering of markets to strictly economic paradigms.

In the new political economy the material base is much more than the economic. To say, for example, that race relations have changed enormously in Canada over the past three decades because of the new material conditions in which immigrants find themselves means that we look at not only the numbers, location, and density of immigrant populations (formerly from Europe, now increasingly from the Caribbean and Asia) but also the particular skills and wealth they bring with them. Likewise, to say material conditions have been part of the increasing demands for day care means greater women's labour force participation produces the circumstances for such demands. The material is embedded in the ecosystem and environment (part of 'space'), thus changing the material conditions of, for example, fish stocks. Political economy embedded in a comparative and international context is, in my view, the richest and most fruitful perspective available for contemporary social scholars.

Envisioning Alternatives

Late in his career John Porter began to adopt a new vantage point based upon John Rawls's book, *A Theory of Justice* (1971), extending the writings of T.H. Marshall with which he had been familiar.[13] My own line of influence differs, leading from T.H. Marshall to the writings of the eminent Canadian political theorist, C.B. Macpherson.

As I suggested, Porter's liberalism initially drew him to undertake studies of social mobility and education, while his fundamentally meritocratic critique led him to fight against ascriptive barriers to individual upward mobility, whether based on race, ethnicity, or gender. His judgment about postindustrialism led him to make optimistic projections: 'What distinguishes a modern industrial society from earlier times,' Porter wrote, 'is that, because of greater productive capacity, it can implement all the rights of citizenship according to the principles of justice.' Porter (1975b: 3) then identified John Rawls's study, *A Theory of Justice* as 'perhaps the best contemporary attempt to develop a socialist ethic,' and took it as his guide. The principles of liberty and justice as articulated by Rawls became the key theme of Porter's final years (Porter 1977).

In T.H. Marshall's scheme of rights there are three types: *civil rights* are necessary for individual freedom – liberty of the person, freedom of speech, rights to own property, justice through the law courts; *political rights* are for the exercise of political office, to elect or be elected to Parliament; *social rights* provide a modicum of welfare and security, allowing citizens to share in standards of a society's education, health, and social services (Marshall 1964). To these rights C.B. Macpherson added *economic rights* as claims to a say in the distribution of work, income, and wealth plus, *industrial rights* as claims to a say in control over production, including the conditions of work, methods of production, and the goals and allocation of production. Economic and industrial democratic demands are claims for an extension of justice beyond distribution (the entitlements of social rights) to involvement in power arrangements. For Macpherson, economic democracy was 'an arrangement of the economic system that will give a just distribution of work, income and wealth in a country.' For this to come about will require substantial political control over the economy, not only control over production as implied in industrial democracy. These twin demands merge since demands for industrial democracy are likely to be the stimulus for pressures towards economic democracy in Macpherson's thinking (Macpherson 1985: 35–7).

The formulation required for economic justice by Macpherson contrasts with the limited demand for distributive justice advocated by Rawls (and by extension Porter). Macpherson's reading of Rawls's model is that it 'is essentially a liberal-democratic capitalist welfare state' that accepts class-based inequalities and is primarily about issues of distribution (Macpherson 1973: 88). It is essentially a modern-day meritocracy with a dash of 'chance.' Macpherson's critique was that Rawls has 'a general principle of distribution which will justify the class differences in life prospects which any market society ... is bound to produce' (Macpherson 1985: 12). Absent is an alternative arrangement of power relations.

The liberal democracy with the most advanced struggle for industrial and economic rights has been Sweden. Those struggles have pushed social democracy to its current limits, both in work life and in attempts to develop worker-controlled investment funds (Clement 1988). In 'Exploring the Limits of Social Democracy: Regime Change in Sweden' (Clement 1994a) I examined some of the dilemmas and contradictions of this exemplary social-democratic regime. Unlike the classificatory regime analysis of Esping-Andersen, which seeks to describe exemplars for various regime types, I attempt to understand a regime *under transformation* and identify what forces are contingent, that is, the logic of the conditions that are responsible for such changes and their effects.

Regime change reveals a 'field of power' that includes capital, labour, the state, and popular forces (none of which is in itself homogeneous) configured in relation to one another. Regimes are always contested so they must seek to maintain their own hegemony against other groups with alternative agendas, hence the key 'cementing' role of ideology as a construction of what is 'normal, right, just, and proper' for effective rule. In Sweden this ideological struggle has become open since the early 1980s, led by the remarkably powerful Swedish Employers' Confederation's declared 'Farewell to Corporatism' and responded to by the increasingly divided labour movement embodied in the social democratic party and Swedish Trade Union Confederation (see Ahrne and Clement 1994b). The particular configuration of power includes considerable human agency, but always within the context of the limitations of capitalism and the international system expressed as interests for continentalization (entry into the European Union). Such forces pre-empt pressures for industrial democracy, bowing instead to 'market forces' and exposing the limits to social democracy in one country. Progressive forces in Sweden now face the formidable task of mobilizing across Europe.

My current research includes comparisons of six countries: Sweden, Germany, Canada, the United States, Australia, and Japan. Using regime analysis, the investigation analyses changing labour market practices in these countries, including how their labour markets are created, entitlements for employees, and issues of education and training, all in the context of international restructuring. For example, I have recently completed a comparison of Canada and Japan in terms of their immigration and citizenship regimes as they influence the way each has built its labour markets (see Clement 1996). Canada, like Australia and the United States, exemplifies the 'law of soil' regime, while Japan, like Germany and Sweden, exemplifies the 'law of blood' regime in terms of how they create their citizenry. These were issues of great interest to John Porter and his insights about 'two streams' of migration continue to shed light on these issues.

Like Porter, I, too, am interested in the release of society's 'talent,' but less in the individual 'upward social mobility' sense used by Porter than in the 'being fully human' sense of Macpherson. Therein lies my interest in labour markets and how they work. Labour markets are not simply matters of the number of people who work (or seek work but are unemployed). Also important are the quality of work available, including its remuneration and benefits (in the largest sense). At stake is not simply a matter of the 'distribution' of jobs but democratic control over the creation and allocation of work, as well as control over decisions regarding what kind of work is valued (such as social services and work in the household). Work is an essential ingredient of the ability to become fully human so the absence of work or the predominance of degrading or undervalued work are all key barriers to the good society.

Conclusion

John Porter was optimistic about the potential for postindustrial society to liberate people and to mobilize talent to take advantage of that potential. He assumed that a more equitable distribution of these new-found resources would follow postindustrialism. Many social democrats put forth Sweden as an exemplar of a society where the possibility existed not only to improve the distribution of society's advantages but to give a greater say in its organization to the 'common people.' Both have been disappointments. In the current era we are seeing not only greater inequities throughout liberal democracies, but also diminishing social rights as welfare states retrench in the fundamentals of health, education, and welfare. Rogue liberalism, with its blind faith in the market, seems to have taken over.

The Measure of Canadian Society (1987c), John Porter's final book, was meant not as a 'count' but as an 'accounting,' that is, an assessment of standards and directions against which social progress in Canada could be measured. If we were to take account of present-day Canada we should be concerned about the quality of our social rights. It would be difficult to be optimistic about the development of economic rights, especially with the North America Free Trade Agreement. It is frightening to imagine a 'level playing field' with the anemic American labour movement and squalid Mexican employment conditions used as 'baselines' for comparison and a 'levelling down' of standards. Democratic interests are clearly on the back burner, but need to be pressed ahead if we are to recover from the present malaise.

From a scholarly point of view there is much more reason to be encouraged about the current state of affairs (although the universities are part of the attack on social institutions). The quality of graduate students pursuing novel research has never been better. The classic issues at the heart of The Vertical Mosaic – class, power, ethnicity, immigration, and education – remain central. Obviously, nation, gender, region, race (especially Native people), and employment are now added to the mix. It has become even more apparent that the international context and its imposed restructuring are also pertinent. There continues to be struggle over the state, its policies, and practices. It is no longer clear that social democratic governments are or can be progressive in this respect, especially at provincial levels or even in small states.

For John Porter the analysis was the intellectual goal: theory, method, and data were means. Moreover, analysis had an agenda – it was always motivated by value concerns though never blinded by ideological strictures. It was important for Porter that the university maintained an autonomous, critical place within public policy discussions, but that it did have relevance for such issues. John Porter would continue to ask today: What is an appropriate research agenda and how can Canadian sociology contribute? As a rough guide, today there are at least five related areas demanding scholarly attention:

1 We need to continue refining our theoretical and methodological tools *as a means to analysis*; how to think about problems and how to do research are crucial to scholarship.
2 Labour market practices demand study: who is included, how are demands for work created, and what are the appropriate links between school and work?
3 Households remain key sites for investigation: the division of labour, power relations (including abuse, partner and parent/child relations), and links to paid labour must be better understood.
4 The state, too, must be better understood. State services demand reform, justification, and renewed support for education, health, housing, pensions, and welfare – those social rights that help to make us fully human.
5 We must continue to study immigration; it remains a key site of ideological struggle. New immigrants have new needs; they continue to struggle against racism and require compassionate treatment from the rest of society.

Besides these specific points, there is the broader agenda of undertaking a full-scale macrosociology of Canada – a project that had been John Porter's original goal and one to which he returned late in his short life. Such an undertaking would of necessity continue to focus on power, ethnicity, and class (in ways modified by contemporary scholarship), but it would also have a strong social justice focus and a comparative context. A macrosociology of that order today would have to challenge the fundamentals of what it means to be a modern democracy, while locating Canada in its international setting. Such an approach would demand the injection of the social into the political/ideological debates now dominated by business and narrow economic motives. To this end the political economy tradition provides a means I think Porter would have found attractive.

John Porter could relate to such concerns and would make a valuable contribution to today's discussion. I am confident we would continue to be impressed by his insights and compassion as English Canada's premier sociologist. His work continues to demand our attention and his person to command our respect.

Notes

1 I thank Bruce McFarlane, Janet Siltanen, and Frank Vallee for insightful comments on an earlier draft. Rick Helmes-Hayes, Jim Curtis, and two University of Toronto Press reviewers provided useful editorial advice for the published version.
2 C. Wright Mills had a contingent argument, clearly saying, 'What I am asserting is that in this particular epoch a conjunction of historical circumstances has led to the rise of an elite of power' in the United States characterized as a 'triangle of power.' His empirical point was that 'there is no longer, on the one hand, a political order containing a military establishment unimportant to politics and money-making. There is a political economy linked, in thousands of ways, with military institutions and decisions' (Mills 1956: 7–8, 28).
3 For an insightful account of this see Miliband (1964). Miliband had been a classmate of Porter's at the London School of Economics.
4 Both the Carroll and Niosi books received the Porter Book Award. Robert J. Brym (1985) and the chapter by Michael Ornstein included in this collection are important reviews of this field.
5 See the seminal work by Pat and Hugh Armstrong, *The Double Ghetto: Canadian Women and Their Segregated Work*, now in its third edition (1994), and the article by Pat Armstrong in this collection.
6 See many of his essays in *The Measure of Canadian Society*, especially 'The Human Community" (1987e) and "The Future of Upward Mobility' (1987f) and, also, the assumptions underlying many of his critiques of Canada in *The Vertical Mosaic*.
7 Another Porter Award winner is Gordon Laxer (1989). Laxer calls for comparisons based on 'late-follower' countries like Sweden and Australia rather than the traditional North Atlantic triangle.

8 Canadian sociology departments tend to be quite eclectic, and sociologists often find themselves outside formal departments of sociology, for example, a half dozen of the best-known sociologists at Carleton University make their academic homes outside the department and as many 'inside' are cross-appointed within the university to other academic units.

9 A second example, from the same journal, is the 'Globalization,' special issue, edited by Gordon Laxer, *Canadian Review of Sociology and Anthropology* 32(3), 1995.

10 See the 'Comparative Political Economy Perspectives,' special issue, edited by John Myles, *Canadian Review of Sociology and Anthropology* 26(1), 1989.

11 See Gøsta Esping-Andersen (1990); important critiques may be found in Orloff (1993), O'Connor (1993), and Olsen (1994).

12 The chapter by Julia S. O'Connor in this collection is a thorough review of contemporary comparative research.

13 T.H. Marshall had been John Porter's tutor for his final two years of study at the London School of Economics. Thanks to Bruce McFarlane for this point.

References

Abele, Frances. (1997). 'Understanding What Happpened Here: The Political Economy of Indigenous Peoples.' Pp. 118–40 in W. Clement (ed.), *Understanding Canada: Building on the New Canadian Political Economy*. Montreal: McGill-Queen's University Press.

Ahrne, Göran, and Wallace Clement. (1994a). 'Making Labour Forces in Canada and Sweden: Neo-Conservative Directions?' Sweden–Canada Academic Foundation Annual Conference, 'Labour and Social Policy: The Experience of the 1980s and 1990s,' Arbetslivscentrum, Stockholm, Sweden, May.

– (1994b). 'A New Regime? Class Representation Within the Swedish State.' Pp. 223–44 in Wallace Clement and Rianne Mahon (eds.), *Swedish Social Democracy: A Model in Transition*. Toronto: Canadian Scholars' Press.

Anderson, Kay J. (1991). *Vancouver's Chinatown: Racial Discourse in Canada, 1875–1980*. Kingston and Montreal: McGill-Queen's University Press.

Armstrong, Pat, and Hugh Armstrong. (1994). *The Double Ghetto: Canadian Women and Their Segregated Work* (3rd ed.). Toronto: McClelland and Stewart.

Boyd, Monica. (1992). 'Gender, Visible Minority and Immigrant Earnings Inequality: Reassessing an Employment Equity Premise.' Pp. 279–321 in Vic Satzewich (ed.), *Deconstructing a Nation: Immigration, Multiculturalism and Racism in the 1990s in Canada*. Toronto: Fernwood.

56   Wallace Clement

Braverman, Harry. (1974). *Labor and Monopoly Capital: The Degradation of Work in the Twentieth Century.* New York and London: Monthly Review Press.

Breton, Raymond. (1991). *The Governance of Ethnic Communities: Political Structures and Process in Canada.* Toronto: Oxford University Press.

Brym, Robert (ed.). (1985). *The Structure of the Canadian Capitalist Class.* Toronto: Garamond.

Carchedi, Guglielmo. (1977). *On the Economic Identification of Social Classes.* London: Routledge and Kegan Paul.

Carroll, William. (1986). *Corporate Power and Canadian Capitalism.* Vancouver: University of British Columbia Press.

Clement, Wallace. (1975). *The Canadian Corporate Elite: An Analysis of Economic Power.* Ottawa: Carleton University Press.

– (1977). *Continental Corporate Power: Economic Elite Linkages between Canada and the United States.* Toronto: McClelland and Stewart.

– (1987). 'Foreword.' Pp. xi–xxxv in John Porter, *The Measure of Canadian Society* (2nd ed.). (Wallace Clement, ed.). Ottawa: Carleton University Press.

– (1988). 'Technological Change and Its Effects on Employees: Some Canadian Experiences (with Swedish Subtitles).' Pp. 33–45 in W. Clement, *The Challenge of Class Analysis.* Ottawa: Carleton University Press.

– (1990). 'Comparative Class Analysis: Locating Canada in a North American and Nordic Context.' *Canadian Review of Sociology and Anthropology* 27(4): 462–86.

– (1994a). 'Exploring the Limits of Social Democracy: Regime Change in Sweden.' Pp. 373–94 in Wallace Clement and Rianne Mahon (eds.), *Swedish Social Democracy: A Model in Transition.* Toronto: Canadian Scholars' Press.

– (1996). 'Blood versus Soil: Immigration and Labour Markets in Japan and Canada,' Keynote Address for 7th Canadian Studies Seminar, 'People on the Move: Canada and Japan in a Smaller World,' Kwansei Gakuin University, November.

– (1997). *Understanding Canada: Building on the New Canadian Political Economy.* Montreal: McGill-Queen's University Press.

Clement, Wallace, and John Myles. (1994). *Relations of Ruling: Class and Gender in Postindustrial Societies.* Montreal: McGill-Queen's University Press.

Esping-Andersen, Gøsta. (1990). *The Three Worlds of Welfare Capitalism.* Princeton, NJ: Princeton University Press.

Jenson, Jane, Rianne Mahon, and Manfred Bienefeld (eds.). (1993). *Production, Space, Identity: Political Economy Faces the 21st Century.* Toronto: Canadian Scholars' Press, 1993.

Laxer, Gordon. (1989). *Open for Business: The Roots of Foreign Ownership in Canada*. Toronto: Oxford University Press.

Macpherson, C.B. (1973). 'Rawl's Distributive Justice.' Pp. 87–94 in C.B. Macpherson, *Democratic Theory: Essays in Retrieval*. London: Clarendon Press.

– (1985). *The Rise and Fall of Economic Justice*. Oxford: Oxford University Press.

Marchak, M. Patricia. (1983). *Green Gold: The Forest Industry in British Columbia*. Vancouver: University of British Columbia Press.

– (1985). 'Canadian Political Economy.' *Canadian Review of Sociology and Anthropology* 22(5): 673–709.

– (1991). *The Integrated Circus: The New Right and the Restructuring of Global Markets*. Montreal: McGill-Queen's University Press.

_–(1995). *Logging the Globe*. Montreal: McGill-Queen's University Press.

Marchak, M. Patricia, Neil Guppy, and John McMullan (eds.). (1987). *Uncommon Property: The Fishing and Fish-Processing Industries in British Columbia*. Toronto: Methuen.

Marshall, T.H. (1964). *Class, Citizenship and Social Development*. Westport: Greenwood Press.

Meisel, John. (1965). Foreword. Pp. ix–x in John Porter, *The Vertical Mosaic: An Analysis of Social Class and Power in Canada*. Toronto: University of Toronto Press.

Michels, Robert. (1962). *Political Parties: A Sociological Study of the Oligarchical Tendencies of Modern Democracy*. New York: Free Press.

Miliband, Ralph. (1964). 'Mills and Politics.' Pp. 76–87 in Irving Louis Horowitz (ed.), *The New Sociology*. New York: Oxford University Press.

Mills, C. Wright. (1956). *The Power Elite*. New York: Oxford University Press.

– (1962). *The Marxists*. New York: Dell.

Mosca, Gaetano. (1939). *The Ruling Class*. New York: McGraw-Hill.

Myles, John. (1989a). 'Introduction: Understanding Canada: Comparative Political Economy Perspectives.' *Canadian Review of Sociology and Anthropology* 26(1): 1–9.

Myles, John (ed.). (1989b). 'Comparative Political Economy Perspectives.' Special Issue, *Canadian Review of Sociology and Anthropology* 26(1).

Niosi, Jorge. (1981). *Canadian Capitalism: A Study of Power in the Canadian Business Establishment*. Toronto: Lorimer.

O'Connor, Julia. (1993). 'Gender, Class and Citizenship in the Comparative Analysis of Welfare State Regimes.' *British Journal of Sociology* 44(3): 501–18.

Olsen, Gregg. (1994). 'Locating the Canadian Welfare State: Family Policy and Health Care in Canada, Sweden and the United States.' *Canadian Journal of Sociology* 19(1): 1–20.

Orloff, Anne Schola. (1993). 'Gender and the Social Rights of Citizenship.' *American Sociological Review* 58(3): 303–28.

Ornstein, Michael. (1984). 'Interlocking Directorates in Canada: Intercorporate or Class Alliance?' *Administrative Science Quarterly* 29: 210–31.

– (1989). 'The Social Organization of the Canadian Capitalist Class in Comparative Perspective.' *Canadian Review of Sociology and Anthropology* 26(1): 151–77.

Pareto, Vilfredo. (1935). *The Mind and Society.* New York: Harcourt Brace.

Parkin, Frank. (1971). *Class Inequality and Political Order.* London: Paladin.

Porter, John. (1955). 'Elite Groups: A Scheme for the Study of Power in Canada.' *Canadian Journal of Economics and Political Science* 21(4): 498–512.

– (1972). 'Canada: Dilemmas and Contradictions of a Multi-Ethnic Society.' Royal Society of Canada. *Transactions* Series 4, vol. 10: 193–205.

– (1975a). 'Foreword.' Pp. ix–xv in Wallace Clement, *The Canadian Corporate Elite: An Analysis of Economic Power.* Ottawa: Carleton University Press.

– (1975b). 'Notes as a Commentator for the Macrosociological Issues,' at the Annual Meetings of the Canadian Sociology and Anthropology Association, Edmonton, May.

– (1977). 'Address,' in *Options for Canada,* A Report on the First Options for Canada Conference, St Patrick's College, Carleton University, Ottawa, 6–8 May.

– (1978). 'Comments by John Porter.' *Alternate Routes: A Critical Review* 2: 23–5.

– (1987a). 'Research Biography of a Macrosociological Study.' Pp. 7–39 in John Porter, *The Measure of Canadian Society* (2nd ed.). (W. Clement, ed.). Ottawa: Carleton University Press.

– (1987b). 'Mr Trudeau and Canadian Federalism.' Pp. 163–84 in John Porter, *The Measure of Canadian Society* (2nd ed.). (Wallace Clement, ed.). Ottawa: Carleton University Press.

– (1987c). 'Prologue.' Pp. 1–5 in John Porter, *The Measure of Canadian Society* (2nd ed.) (Wallace Clement, ed.). Ottawa: Carleton University Press.

– (1987d). 'Introduction' to 'Research Biography of a Macrosociological Study: *The Vertical Mosaic.*' Pp. 7–9 in John Porter, *The Measure of Canadian Society* (2nd ed.). (Wallace Clement, ed.). Ottawa: Carleton University Press.

– (1987e). 'The Human Community.' Pp. 41–63 in John Porter, *The Measure of Canadian Society* (2nd ed.). (Wallace Clement, ed.). Ottawa: Carleton University Press.

– (1987f). 'The Future of Upward Mobility.' Pp. 65–87 in John Porter, *The Measure of Canadian Society* (2nd ed.). (Wallace Clement, ed.). Ottawa: Carleton University Press.

Poulantzos, Nicos. (1975). *Classes in Contemporary Capitalism*. London: New Left Books.

Rawls, John. (1971). *A Theory of Justice*. Cambridge: Harvard University Press.

Satzewich, Vic, and Terry Wotherspoon. (1993). *First Nations: Race, Class, and Gender Relations*. Scarborough: Nelson.

Stasiulis, Daiva. (1997). 'The Political Economy of Race, Ethnicity, and Migration.' Pp. 141–71 in Wallace Clement (ed.), *Understanding Canada: Building on the New Canadian Political Economy*. Montreal: McGill-Queen's University Press.

Ethnicity and Race in Social Organization: Recent Developments in Canadian Society[1]

RAYMOND BRETON

Considerable change has taken place in the relations between ethnic groups in Canada and between them and the institutions of the society since the publication of *The Vertical Mosaic* three decades ago. The transformations, as will be seen, are partly a matter of degree, but they also are in some ways changes in the nature of the relationships. In this essay the evolution of groups and of their societal relationships will be examined for these three major axes of ethnic differentiation in Canada: Native peoples in relation to the larger society; English and French relations; and immigrants, their descendants, and the 'mainstream' society. This latter section includes the relationship between whites and visible minorities.

In most instances, the process of change was set in motion by the non-dominant groups in the relationship. These groups changed in their demographic composition, in the level of education and socioeconomic achievement of their members, and in their self-conceptions, aspirations, and expectations. The economic and political context also changed, not only in Canada but in the rest of the world. As a result, the feeling grew among members of ethnic minorities that changes in their relations with other groups and with societal institutions were not only desirable, but possible.

Some of the changes under way in the 1960s are extensively dealt with in *The Vertical Mosaic*. In his monumental study, John Porter devoted considerable attention to the participation of immigrants and ethnic minorities in the socioeconomic structure and to the question of ethnic stratification. In fact, this is largely what the title of the book refers to; it is a condensed symbolic expression of his argument. Porter saw the economic and political power structure as dominated primarily by the British charter group, the prevailing theories of race of the time being used to justify this dominance (Porter 1965: 61–8). Other groups were located in lower strata. When economic expansion began after the Second World War, Canada's skilled labour force was inadequate: 'the necessity in the 1950's of importing skills from abroad to meet the labour force increment in skilled occupations suggests that Canadian institutions – particularly educational and industrial – were not geared to provide mobility opportunities.' While in the United States the low skill levels of most immigrants 'pushed up the existing population to higher educational levels,' in Canada this process was less prevalent because immigration was designed to obtain 'skilled and professional workers as an alternative to educational reforms' (ibid.: 49). Highly skilled immigrants came primarily from Great Britain and the United States. Others came primarily from Southern and Eastern Europe. The entrance status of these two categories of immigrants was an important factor in the formation and maintenance of a vertical mosaic.

With time, however, those who had entered at the lower echelons of the occupational hierarchy progressively improved their situation and especially that of their children, leaving the lower positions to new waves of immigrants. This mobility, however, was predicated on 'Anglo-conformity,' that is, to conformity to the rules of the game established by the charter group and to its values and way of life. This required relinquishing one's ethnic identity at least in the public domain. Porter saw ethnicity as a problem because it was an obstacle to mobility.[2] He would no doubt have argued that this is even more so when groups are racially different from the charter group.

The other lines of ethnic differentiation were barely touched upon or were dealt with much less extensively by Porter. For instance, his book does not deal with the changes that were beginning to be felt in the relationship of Native peoples with the rest of Canadian society. This may have been because, at the time, the momentum for change was just beginning. But it may also have been because sociologists, as other Canadians, saw Native peoples as marginal to the mainstream social and political structure. Studies of social inequality, for instance, did not at the time pay much attention to the place of Native peoples in the class structure. This was deemed to be the domain of anthropologists.

The relationship between English- and French-speaking Canadians was also beginning to change. One of the manifestations of this change was the resurgence of nationalistic sentiments in Quebec, especially the emergence of a separatist movement at the end of the 1950s. Others were the establishment of the Royal Commission on Bilingualism and Biculturalism in 1963 and the various expressions of grievances and expectations that were part of the Quiet Revolution in Quebec.

These transformations, however, were a secondary component of Porter's analysis of ethnicity and interethnic relations in Canada. While *The Vertical Mosaic* did not address the question of ethnic separatism and its underpinnings, Porter did think that there was some validity to the notion of cultural particularism in the case of Quebec, and he felt that 'as Quebec becomes more industrialized it will become culturally more like other industrialized societies,' an evolution that would seem to have suggested to him that there was no need for a special accommodation within Canadian federalism because, with time, Quebec's similarities with the other provinces would be far more important than the differences (Porter 1965: 383). This has, in fact, been the nature of socioeconomic change in Quebec. However, the evolution of nationalism and of the independentist movement strongly support those who criticize social scientists for giving too much importance to economic factors in the shaping of intergroup attitudes and relationships (Connor 1972).

Porter did not deal either with the question of language and its impact on ethnic stratification and mobility and on the control of economic institutions in Quebec. This, however, is somewhat understandable as language was not yet an issue of public policy. It became so in the late 1960s with the recommendations of the royal commission and with the legislation introduced by the Quebec government in 1968 (Bill-85 concerning the language of education). Porter did, however, address the unfavourable socioeconomic situation of French Canadians (to be considered in a subsequent section).

In concluding this overview of Porter's approach,[3] it is worth mentioning that, generally, his 'analyses had little to offer on *relations* among ethnic groups. For the most part he concentrated on the *distributive* aspect of ethnicity, on the question of how people in different ethnic categories were distributed in the system of power and stratification' (Vallee 1981: 640).

Native Peoples and the Larger Society

A little before the publication of *The Vertical Mosaic*, a major reversal had begun in the sociopolitical organization of Native peoples and in their relationship with the larger society and governments. There had been, of course, developments before the 1960s. Political confrontations between whites and Métis occurred in the late 1800s, ending with the rebellion of 1885. Aboriginal political movements sparked by land issues began in British Columbia at the beginning of the twentieth century. Indians in other regions eventually joined the movement. The League of Indians of Canada was formed in the interwar years. In the 1930s and 1940s, other organizations were established in British Columbia, Alberta, and Saskatchewan (Miller 1989: 214–19). This organizational expansion was triggered in part by the emergence of new issues – agriculture and schooling were added to land claims – and in part by the Native participation in the First World War and 'their understandable tendency afterwards to claim a right to be heard' (Miller 1989: 217).

But, in spite of these efforts, the structure and culture of dominance was not seriously challenged. Native communities remained dependencies administered by external agencies under the restrictive Indian Act. The idea that this could be modified in any significant way entered the public agenda only after the Second World War and gained ground at a very slow pace.

The war itself had an impact in launching this process. Indeed, the attitudes of white Canadians were shaken by the systematic racism and atrocities of the war. These events forced Canadians to begin to face the racism embedded in their own institutions, legal practices, and social mores. The Hawthorn Report published in the mid-1960s was one manifestation of this new concern with the conditions of the country's Aboriginal population (Hawthorn 1966–7). By documenting these conditions in a systematic way, the report had the effect of increasing the willingness to accept significant changes. Also, it introduced the notion of 'citizens plus' for Native peoples whereby, because of their Aboriginal title and treaty rights, Indians possess certain rights as charter members of the Canadian community in addition to their normal rights and duties as citizens (Hawthorn 1966–7: 13). This constituted a call for a drastically new relationship between them and the larger society.

The war also had an impact on Native peoples themselves. Having contributed to the first war effort, their aspirations were further increased by their participation in the second. Re-establishing control over their own community life and institutions became a significant component of their political agenda (Miller 1989; Ponting and Gibbins 1980). The economic growth and the related exploration for raw materials and energy that followed the war gave a new significance and urgency to the question of land claims. The civil rights movement in the United States also had an impact: Red Power was the slogan that corresponded to Black Power in that country. Another significant element 'was the fact that in the later 1960s Indian groups up to and including the National Indian Council were beginning to receive better funding, and, with their better organization and funding ... found themselves able to present their views in a series of cogent, effective arguments' (Miller 1989: 225).

Finally, the 1969 White Paper (Canada, Department of Indian Affairs and Northern Development 1969) generated a sort of crisis because it put on the public agenda the very fundamental question of the social and political philosophy that was to guide public policies of social and institutional change. One of the basic ideas of the White Paper was that the appalling conditions in which Native peoples found themselves were the result of the legal status that kept them apart from the larger society. Thus, it was necessary to dismantle the legal and bureaucratic arrangements that had decimated their traditional social and political organization, kept them in a situation of dependency, and prevented their social, economic, and political development. The remedy envisioned by the White Paper was the elimination of the separate status and the integration of Native peoples in the larger social and economic structure. It was *not* to replace the distant, white-controlled bureaucracy by self-administered Native organizations and agencies.

The reaction to the White Paper was such as to force the government to withdraw it and to begin, very reluctantly, to explore other avenues of change. As a result, a new process was set in motion, one in which Native peoples were very much in the driver's seat, at least in terms of defining the political agenda, if not in terms of actual changes.

Dimensions of Sociopolitical Change

Change is sought and is taking place along six major dimensions. These involve issues pertaining to collective identity, to the social and normative infrastructure of community organization and its territorial and economic basis, and to the social and political participation of women. Such changes require a redistribution of institutional control which, in turn, implies that Aboriginal peoples be recognized as legitimate political actors by the larger society and its institutions, and, in the case of women, within the Aboriginal power structure as well. Finally, they require transformations of the institutions of the larger society.

The ultimate objective of these changes is the improvement of the economic and social condition of Native peoples – a condition that is among the worst of any groups in Canada. This is so with regard to income, occupational status, labour force participation, educational attainment, and the various manifestations of a poor economic situation, including shorter life expectancies (Siggner 1986; Frideres 1993).

Social Identity

The construction of a new social identity was essential if Native communities were to be internally transformed and the traditional relationship with the larger society reversed. Indeed, the Indian social identity had definite connotations of inferiority, backwardness, dependency, and irrelevance. 'Native peoples' and especially 'First Nations' affirm a positive status in relation to the larger polity. The discourse surrounding this identity includes concepts of 'citizen plus' mentioned earlier and of inherent rights of self-government within Canada.

Another evolution is the progressive formation of a pan-Aboriginal collective identity, that is, an overarching identity that de-emphasized internal differences and emphasized commonalities.

Institutional Control and the Rebuilding of Community Structures

Being in a situation of externally administered dependency has weakened considerably the traditional social, economic, and political organization of Aboriginal communities (Frideres 1993). Rebuilding social and organizational structures to cope with the needs and aspirations of their members has been an important component of change.

The drive to rebuild community infrastructures required the control of an increasing range of their institutions. Thus, pressure has built up to end administrative dependency and replace it with administrative autonomy and self-government. In the 1970s the transfer of the administration from the federal government to Native organizations began. Core funding was provided to Native organizations. Self-government became a serious issue in the relationship between Native peoples and governments.

In recent decades there have also been a number of developments in building organizations based on insights and the social logic specific to Aboriginal cultures. These have taken place in the fields of political decision making, education, economic development, the administration of justice, and the rehabilitation of delinquents and criminals, alcoholics, and sexual abusers.

Some prominent illustrations are provided by the three Aboriginal communities that have recently won awards for 'demonstrating an outstanding collective approach to environmental issues and the social development of their inhabitants' (Valpy 1995). Their success was not due to external support but rather to the organizational resources and activities of the communities themselves.[4]

Establishing a Territorial and Economic Basis
Land claims have been one of the main fronts of action in this regard. Control over territory and access to part of the rents from the exploitation of resources are critical to community formation and maintenance. Control of land and of the capital that can be generated from it are essential for the economic development of any community or society. The alternative is integration into the enterprises and the social structure of the community that controls the land and the rents drawn from it.

The question of land control is the fundamental issue raised by the White Paper, and it continues to be part of the public debate, regarding whether Native peoples should acquire the means necessary for the building of enterprises and other institutions or integrate as individuals into the white-controlled institutional system. That is, there are two types of integration involved: corporate and individual. In the first case, the idea is that the Aboriginal communities and organizations are integrated in the larger interorganizational system (in a way analogous to the way in which municipalities, provinces, and national institutions are part of an integrated whole). In the second, it is individuals and their families that are integrated into the socioeconomic and political structure.

Land has been an issue ever since Europeans came to settle on this continent. At first, because of their skills and environmental knowledge, the Aboriginal population was progressively incorporated into a commercial system shaped by the interests of European trading companies. Defence and culture (i.e., 'civilizing' and Christianizing) also shaped the relationship. With time, the settlement ambitions of Europeans led to a growing interest in land and, thus, to the displacement and control of the Aboriginal population. To a large extent, the history of Aboriginal–white relationships involves the transfer of land from Native to non-Native control. Whenever land is needed by the white population – whether for settlement, natural resources, fishing (commercial or recreational), or golf courses – the transfer process from Native to non-Native ownership and/or control is set in motion (Valentine 1980).

Recent decades have been characterized by an attempt on the part of Native peoples to change this process so that the transfer becomes an equitable exchange. As a result, Native communities have been in regular conflicts with governments, business and industrial corporations, and white communities, who likewise depend on land and the exploitation of natural resources for their vitality and well-being.

Improving the Condition of Aboriginal Women
The socioeconomic and political situation of Aboriginal women was even worse than that of Aboriginal men. 'Indian women come close to matching their male counterparts in educational attainment – only to fall lowest with respect to labour force involvement and income ... In addition ... Indian women who are young suffer especially low labour-force participation and high unemployment ... Native females suffer multiple jeopardy on the basis of a number of objective indicators of social and economic well-being' (Gerber 1990: 80).

Significant remedies to these conditions will come about primarily if women organize themselves to deal with them. The general political mobilization of the 1960s and 1970s, especially the women's movement had a major impact on Aboriginal women. These consciousness-raising movements made Aboriginal women increasingly aware that they could do something to improve their condition and that improvements would not be the initiative of men, including Aboriginal men.

They were also prompted to organize as a political force in their own right. By the mid-1970s, Native Women's Associations had been formed in virtually all the provinces and territories as well as at the national level, the first one having been established in 1969 in British Columbia. These regional and national associations included both status and non-status Indians, in contrast to the main male-dominated organizations that were based on legal criteria.

Two national organizations were established, the Native Women's Association of Canada and the National Committee on Indian Rights for Indian Women. The first is primarily a grassroots organization concerned with issues such as 'women's employment opportunities, economic development of Aboriginal communities, alcohol and drug abuse, and child welfare ...'; that is, with general community development and, in particular, with those aspects of community life that affect women most directly' (Krosenbrink-Gelissen 1993: 344). The objective is also to promote the assumption by women of active roles within their communities. The second is externally oriented: it seeks to combat the sex-discriminatory status regulations in the Indian Act.

Being Recognized as Legitimate Political Actors
Native peoples assumed that by identifying such goals and working towards them through their organizations and leaders, they would

come to be accepted as rightful participants in the policy-making process itself, that is, in the exercise of power. No longer would white governments and corporations devise policies and programmes for them. They wanted more than simply being peripheral pressure groups to whom those in power respond once in a while. They wanted to be full-fledged participants in the polity. To achieve this, for example, to be represented at constitutional conferences, they applied pressure of various kinds: demonstrations, social disruption (e.g., roadblocks), violence, and appeals to the international community.

This last-mentioned tactic has been a critical strategy pursued by Native groups. Relationships between Canadian Indians and foreign governments and organizations are not a new phenomenon, but such relations have expanded considerably in the past few decades. This 'internationalization' of their affairs has taken many forms. Ponting (1990: 2–4) identified a number of them: (a) the emergence of the concept of 'The Fourth World' and the associated reaching out on the part of Canadian Aboriginal people to indigenous groups around the world in similar situations; (b) the cultivation of U.N. bodies as allies and their involvement as monitors and lobbyists; (c) appeals to the Queen and to the British Parliament and court; (d) participation in international fact-finding missions and research projects; and finally, (e) drawing international figures to Canada to observe Indian conditions firsthand and to obtain their moral support (e.g., the Pope).

In the case of Aboriginal women, there is a 'double jeopardy' with regard to the political process – just as there is with regard to their socio-economic situation. Indeed, the issue for them is to be recognized as rightful participants in the policy-making process itself not only by white institutional leaders but also by male Aboriginal leaders. 'Male-dominated national Aboriginal organizations – the National Indian Brotherhood and the Native Council of Canada – appeared not to be concerned with Aboriginal women's views' ... and to make it difficult for women to attain leadership in these organizations' (Krosenbrink-Gelissen 1993: 343, 347). For example, an effort by Aboriginal women to change the sex-discriminatory provisions of the Indian Act did not get the wholehearted support of the male-dominated organizations. Thus, in their political fight for changes, Native women had to lobby the National Indian Brotherhood and the Native Council of Canada, as well as the federal government.

The Transformation of the Institutions of the Larger Society
As already noted, Native peoples are pulled in two directions at the same

time: towards as much participation as possible in distinct, autonomous communities, on the one hand, and towards integration in the larger social structure, on the other. The pull is not the same for all individuals. Some are in situations that limit and even make virtually impossible extensive participation in an indigenous community, while others experience conditions that facilitate such an involvement. For the former, the issue becomes the responsiveness of the institutions of the larger society to their specific needs and cultural distinctiveness, whether these be businesses and industries, labour unions, schools, hospitals, welfare agencies, and so on. For the latter, the issues pertain to the social, economic, and political conditions of community development.

Circumstances Impinging on the Reversal Process

Many social forces, internal and external to the Aboriginal collectivity, act on the processes of change. Among the internal factors are the size of the population, its diversity, and its widespread distribution across the country. First, the Aboriginal population includes status or registered Indians,[5] non-status Indians, Métis, and Inuits. In 1991 there were 511,791 status or registered Indians in Canada compared with 230,902 in 1967 (Canada, Department of Indian Affairs and Northern Development, DIAND 1995: 5). This significant increase is partly due to natural increase but also to a change in the legal definition of a status Indian. Indeed, in 1985 the Indian Act was amended to reinstate Indians who had lost or were denied status in the past, many of whom were Indian women who had married men who were not legally Indian. Many of the eligible have applied for reinstatement and as a result, the number of registered Indians jumped from 332,178 in 1982 to 415,898 in 1987.

It is difficult to estimate the number of non-status North American Indians and their increase in the past thirty years. This is partly because of the self-designated ethnic affiliation allowed by the census as well as the new possibility of declaring both single and multiple origins.[6] The census enumerated 220,100 people with Aboriginal ancestries in 1961 and 312,800 in 1971 (single male-line origins only). This is no doubt an underestimate since DIAND's Register included 264,680 status Indians in 1972, leaving less than 50,000 for non-status Indians, Métis, and Inuits. In 1986 the census allowed single and multiple origins, and the total number of people with Aboriginal ancestries increased to 711,725 (from 491,500 in 1981 – an increase of 220,225) (Norris 1990: 37). In 1991, the total Aboriginal population enumerated in the census was 1,002,670, that is, 3.7 per cent of the Canadian population. But, 'depending on the criteria employed, estimates of the non-status and Métis population for the country as a whole range from a low of 400,000 to over two million' (Morrison and Wilson 1995: 610).

The Inuit population, on the other hand, has been administered and counted separately, and there is less disagreement on their numbers which are estimated to have been 36,215 in 1991 (ibid.: 610), an increase from 11,800 in 1961 (when multiple origins were not allowed in the census enumeration).

Unlike the population of French origin, the Aboriginal population is not concentrated in one part of the country: it is distributed across all of the provinces and territories. In 1992 status Indians, for instance, were distributed as follows: 3.9 per cent in the Atlantic provinces, 9.9 per cent in Quebec, 22.9 per cent in Ontario, 15.2 per cent in Manitoba, 15.3 per cent in Saskatchewan, 12.4 per cent in Alberta, 17.0 per cent in British Columbia, and 3.5 per cent in the Yukon and Northwest Territories.

There is also considerable ethnocultural and linguistic diversity in the Aboriginal population. There are twelve distinct linguistic families, each with fifty-four or more dialects. Cultural variations more or less related to ecological regions also exist. Thus, six cultural regions have been identified: the Eastern Woodlands, the Plains, the Pacific Coast, the Cordillera, the Mackenzie and Yukon river basins, and the Arctic barren grounds (Valentine 1980: 55–6).

Such a differentiation – legal, territorial, and cultural – does not facilitate sociopolitical mobilization for the pursuit of common goals in relation to the larger society. Indeed, such differentiation is frequently associated with a fragmentation of economic and political interests. There are also variations in the ecological conditions and in their distance from centres of economic activity that affect the potential for community development (Gerber 1979) and for self-government (Little Bear 1984; Gibbins and Ponting 1986). The size of bands is also important for the economic viability of Indian communities. In 1981 only 10.2 per cent of the 578 Indian bands had a population of 3,000 or more, while 56 per cent had a population of less than 1,000 (Siggner 1986: 62).

Differences in interests and conditions for community organization are particularly pronounced between those who have status under the law and those who do not. Those who benefit from legally established prerogatives tend to want to exclude all but those considered genuine members of the group, however defined. In contrast, a pan-Aboriginal organization would require an emphasis on inclusion rather than exclusion.

Finally, there appears to be an increasing gap between leaders and their communities, the younger generation in particular. For instance, the national chief of the Assembly of First Nations said recently that younger militants 'say all the chiefs, including myself, are really collaborators with the system. And from their point of view we have lost the right to lead since we have not created any reforms that have brought about substantial changes in their lives' (*Globe and Mail*, 2 March 1996: D5). The distance between leaders and the young generation is particularly significant in view of the large proportion of young people in the Aboriginal population: indeed, the 1991 census reports 54.7 per cent of the total population with Aboriginal origins as under 25 years of age (Canada, Statistics Canada 1995). In the country as a whole, this age category is 20 per cent smaller: 34.8 per cent (Canada, Statistics Canada, 1992).

The Aboriginal population is becoming more educated. For instance, the number of status Indian students completing high school increased from 4.3 per cent in 1961–2 to 62.6 per cent in 1992–3. Registrations in post-secondary programs have increased from 2,684 in 1976–7 to 21,566 in 1992–3 (Canada, DIAND 1995: 39, 41). These gains represent a considerable asset for political and economic organization, but they also constitute a challenge for Aboriginal leaders as well as for the larger society, since a more educated population tends to have higher aspirations.

There are also external factors that impinge on the reversal of the traditional relationship between Natives and the larger society. Resistance is found among those whose interests are affected by Native claims for change. Some of them are powerful and can deploy very effective strategies to maintain their traditional position of dominance. Some of the land claims have been settled. But the question of land and the protection of prerogatives with regard to matters such as hunting, fishing, and monetary compensation continue to generate resistance in certain categories of non-Natives. Together with the demands for administrative autonomy or self-government, they all have a potential impact on the interests of non-Aboriginal groups, whether these be economic, political, or social.

Those affected are corporations in resource extraction, governments interested in the revenues from resource exploitation, workers and labour unions interested in the jobs it can generate, politicians and bureaucrats who wish to maintain control in particular domains of activity, commercial fishermen and anglers concerned with the Natives' fishing prerogatives (especially since stocks appear to be shrinking fairly rapidly), and so on.

Public opinion surveys show moderate support for Native aspirations and for measures aimed at community development and autonomy. For instance, a 1986 survey showed that 42 per cent of Canadians agree strongly or moderately that 'it is important to the future well-being of Canadian society that the aspirations of Native people for self-government be met.' The study found that the level of sympathy for Indians decreased slightly from 1976 to 1986, but that on the average, 'Canadians do not tend to be markedly hostile nor markedly supportive in their attitudes toward Indians.' However, possible policies and programs to assist Native people encounter more resistance and antagonism from non-Natives when the word 'special' is incorporated in the question (Ponting 1988: 12–14).

English–French Relations

The dynamics of English–French relations have changed over the past few decades. There has been an evolution in three main areas. First, there has been a movement on the part of Francophones from social and institutional isolation to economic and social participation, and to the acquisition of power. Second, the politics of identity and recognition has acquired considerable importance in shaping the relationship between the two collectivities. Third, there has been a change in the dynamics of identification with and attachment to the larger Canadian entity.

In considering English–French relations in Canada, it is important to keep in mind that the composition of both collectivities has changed. Indeed, the British and French groups 'negotiating' in 1991 are somewhat different from those in contact in 1961. In 1961, 43.8 per cent of the population was of British origin. In 1991, census counts were by single and multiple origins: 20.8 per cent were of single and 7.3 per cent of multiple British origins (multiple including combinations such as English and Irish), and 16.5 per cent had multiple origins involving non-British ancestries. The total percentage with some British ancestry remained about the same – 43.8 and 44.6, but the Britishness of more than a third is blended with other origins. Since the number with multiple origins in 1961 is not known, it is impossible to assess this specific aspect of the change, but it appears that people of British origin are becoming more integrated with other ethnic categories.

A similar but less-pronounced pattern occurred among the French component of the population. In 1961, 30.4 per cent were of French origin. By 1991 this percentage had declined to 22.8 if single origins only are considered. It remained essentially the same if those with multiple origins that involve French are included. The population of French origin is largely concentrated in Quebec where it constituted 80.6 per cent of the population in 1961 and 80.1 per cent in 1991, if both single origins (74.7) and multiple origins (5.4 per cent) are included.

In addition, as will be seen in the next section, the non-British, non-French component of the population is becoming more diversified ethnically and racially. The proportion of immigrants in the country is significant and fairly stable since 1951: 14.7 per cent in 1951 and 16.1 per cent 1991. In Quebec the percentage of immigrants was 8.7 per cent in 1991[7] (Badets 1993: 8).

Since the relationship is largely between the English- and French-speaking collectivities – between Anglophones and Francophones – it is important to consider mother tongue and home language in addition to ethnic origin. The number of Anglophones is increasing all the time as people of non-British origins adopt English as their language. In 1991 while the population included 28.1 per cent with British ancestry (single or mixed), English was the mother tongue for 77.1 per cent and the home language for 86.7 per cent. A similar but less pronounced phenomenon is occurring in Quebec: while 74.6 per cent are of French origin, 81.6 per cent have French as mother tongue and 82.3 per cent use French at home. But the situation is different with Francophones outside Quebec among whom there is a decline as one moves from French origin (5.3 per cent) to French mother tongue (4.7 per cent) to French home language (3.0 per cent).

Another important contextual factor is the fact that the population of Quebec is declining as a percentage of the total population of the country: from 28.8 in 1961 to 25.3 in 1991.

From Social and Institutional Isolation to Economic and Social Participation to the Acquisition of Power

The control of institutions has always been at the centre of the conflicts and accommodations between English- and French-speaking Canadians. Canada is a society segmented into two parallel, linguistically different institutional systems. To a large extent, the material well-being of English- and French-speaking Canadians depends on the opportunities and services provided by their linguistic subsocieties. Their individual identities tend to be constructed in relation to the cultural features of their respective institutions and nourished by their symbolic activities. Their self-esteem is determined by the societal status of the linguistic group with which they identify.

Both English- and French-speaking Canadians have established and controlled and continue to establish and control separate systems of institutions, each with a distinctive character. Both want their organizational domains to expand so as to provide more opportunities as the size and aspirations of their populations grow. Both want institutions that embody their culture and religion and operate in their language. The history of English–French relations in Canada has been and continues to be characterized by recurrent power struggles for the control of the means required for society building in its economic, cultural, and linguistic dimensions (Breton 1978, 1988; Horowitz 1985: Chapter 1).

Accordingly, intergroup clashes have taken place and continue to occur. Initially, these were political, but they took place primarily over the control of the institutional means to maintain language, religion, and cultural practices. The conflicts entailed clashes between divergent ideas, sociopolitical philosophies, and values with regard to the organization of society and different interpretations of history.

The Quebec Act of 1774, adopted by the British colonial administration, was perhaps the first critical accommodation to the fact that there were two societal projects competing not only for a social space but also for ascendancy in the same territory. 'The Act was a final abandonment of the efforts at a uniform system of colonial government based on English institutions' (McInnis 1969: 160). While preserving several English institutions, it accepted French civil law, reaffirmed freedom of Catholic worship, and reinforced the foundations of the Church and seigniorial system by extending their privileges.

The British North America Act of 1867 represented a further institutionalization of this accommodation. That arrangement gave to the provinces the powers pertaining to social, civil, family, education, prisons, hospital, charitable institutions, and municipal organization. Protestants were given constitutional protection in Quebec, and Catholics were given similar protection in the other provinces that existed at the time. In short, the provinces received the powers with cultural relevance and that involved direct contact with individuals and families.

During this phase, the British colonial administration was seeking to establish a society in their own cultural image, and the conquered French were attempting to maintain sufficient institutional control so as to be able to protect their religious and cultural life. What was involved was a *dominant* British nationalism in opposition to a French *survival or protectionist* nationalism, both having to accommodate to each other through regular struggles over institutional control.

The Pressure for Integration in Common Institutions
For an extensive period, English and French were segregated in the economic sphere. With the expansion of Anglo-Canadian and American enterprises in Quebec, however, the French became progressively part of an economic system constructed by Anglophones who occupied a position of dominance in it. The federal governmental system was also largely under the control of Anglophones (as were the Quebec government and the city of Montreal for a considerable period of time).

Studies carried out by the Royal Commission on Bilingualism and Biculturalism in the 1960s showed that Francophones were not only disadvantaged in the economic sphere, but they were also largely absent from the higher levels of decision making in the federal bureaucracy (Beattie 1975). (The first separatist organization, Le Rassemblement pour l'Indépendance Nationale, was established in the late 1950s by a disgruntled federal civil servant.)

Several reasons for the economically disadvantaged position of French Canadians have been offered by Porter and other authors. First and perhaps the most frequently mentioned is the clergy-controlled educational system which was not 'geared to the provision of industrial skills at the managerial or technical level' (Porter 1965: 91–2). Related to this is the 'rigidity of French-Canadian class structure, and the authoritarian character of French-Canadian institutions' (ibid.: 91). Clark, however, pointed out that Porter may have exaggerated the difference between English- and French-speaking Canada in this regard: 'Members of the British Charter group were admittedly very much on top ... [But] in truth, the rural and working class masses of French Canada were caught up in a social system denying them opportunities for advancement not essentially different from the social system in which the rural and working masses of English-speaking Canada were caught up' (Clark 1975: 28).

Second, the domination by the British charter group placed restrictions on the mobility of French Canadians, partly through the imposition of English as the language of work (Porter 1965: 92).

Third, the competition of the large Canadian and American firms reduced the size of the Francophone-controlled industries. Contrary to the commonly accepted view, Francophones in Quebec were at the outset active participants in the process of industrialization. For instance, there were 23,000 small and medium-size manufacturing enterprises in Quebec in 1890, but their number had fallen to 6,948 by 1929 (Bovey 1936). An important reason was that they were too small to withstand the competition by larger Canadian and American firms that benefited from large capital investments.

Porter noted that the disadvantage did not exist in other spheres: 'French-Canadian political leaders have ruled Quebec, and, by entering into a series of coalitions with British political leaders within Confederation, have been able to exert a very powerful influence on federal government policy' (Porter 1965: 92). 'This seeming contradiction between being a large deprived minority within Canada and having representatives in the structure of power can be explained in terms of the class structure of French Canada which until recently had been premodern ...' (Porter 1975: 269). Although the cultural characteristics of the educational system were no doubt a factor, the structure of control of industry and of the governmental bureaucracy must occupy a central place in explaining the pattern of ethnic stratification.

The unfavourable situation of Francophones began to be felt particularly strongly after the Second World War. The Quiet Revolution of the 1960s accelerated processes of social and political changes that could already be observed for some time (Guindon 1964, 1968; Behiels 1985). In a few decades, the level of education of the French-origin population 25 years of age and older increased enormously: from 3.4 per cent with at least some post-secondary education in 1961 to 37.7 per cent in 1991. The corresponding figures for the total population of the country are 3.4 and 44.4 per cent, showing that a 'quiet revolution' was also going on in the country as a whole (Clark 1975).

This 'revolution' was a 'revolution of rising expectations' in terms of economic and political participation. A new set of expectations emerged, namely, to have access to the opportunities and resources available in Anglo-controlled institutions, economic enterprises, and government bureaucracies. Demands were expressed for new linguistic 'rules of the game' in government, business, and industry – rules that would facilitate Francophone socioeconomic mobility. It also implied recruitment through different sets of social networks. The traditional dominance of clergy and Anglophones was challenged.

The Quiet Revolution added grievances concerning barriers to mobility to already existing linguistic and cultural anxieties. Since it consisted largely in the expression of grievances and the affirmation of expectations and rights, it could be said to be a *protest* nationalism. Needless to say, this led to severe conflicts as Anglophones were not readily willing to change drastically the linguistic and other rules of the game that placed them in a situation of advantage.

Building and Expanding Institutional Domains

The Quiet Revolution had economic as well as political and cultural manifestations. The idea that Quebec had to build and expand its own power base beyond the sociocultural and religious spheres began to be felt and articulated politically. The revolution of rising expectations also included a desire to conquer or reconquer certain institutional spaces, a process that generated confrontations with those who already were in control: the traditional French-Canadian elites, the clergy, and the groups represented by the Duplessis regime; the English-speaking groups dominating the Quebec economy; and the politico-bureaucratic groups controlling the federal government (Pelletier 1990).

The agenda of this category of contending groups was to gain control of the means necessary for organization building, particularly political power and capital, and to displace, partly or completely, those who had traditionally controlled them. This is expressed in the agendas cast in terms of province building, 'Quebec Inc.,' provincial autonomy, sovereignty, or independence. In the 1960s began a process of acquiring increasing control of business and industry. Enterprises under the control of Francophones increased from 47.1 to 61.6 per cent between 1961 and 1987. The increase, however, was larger in certain sectors than in others: from 6.5 to 35.0 in mining, from 33.4 (in 1978) to 92.3 in forestry, from 25.8 to 58.2 in finance, from 50.7 to 75.5 in construction, from 21.7 to 39.3 in manufacturing, and from 51.8 to 67.2 in public administration (Vaillancourt 1993: 412). The state took an active role in economic development through the creation and expansion of state enterprises, the most prominent and economically important being Hydro-Québec, and through policies and programs aimed at reinforcing Francophone-owned enterprises (Bernier 1993).

Thus, for a segment of the Quebec elite and population, integration in institutions controlled by Anglophones is either not sufficient or irrelevant. For many of them, Canadian institutions are necessarily controlled by Anglophones since they constitute a majority of the population – and a growing majority at that. What is sought is an increasing control of the means of economic production and of the centres of political power within (Francophone) Quebec. The issue is institution building and control. This is clearly the objective of sovereignty, whether in its pure form as 'sovereignty-association' or some other. This orientation and process could be referred to as *entrepreneurial* nationalism. It is entrepreneurial in the sense of taking advantage of opportunities for institution building and control and for gaining sovereignty. But it is also *strategic* in the sense that entrepreneurial ambitions are partly pursued through the mobilization of primordial ethnic attachments (that were prominent in survival nationalism) and of past or present grievances (that characterize protest nationalism). It is the strategic use of ethnicity with its cultural and experiential baggage in the achievement of economic and, especially, political goals.

In short, there has been over the years, a progressive shift from a survival, to a protest, to an entrepreneurial and strategic nationalism. It is not that there are no longer any concerns about cultural survival or that there are no more grievances, but rather that institution building and control (a 'projet de société') are now the central themes of nationalism.

Recent Changes: From Accommodation to Confrontation
During the 1960s and 1970s, elites throughout the country and a significant segment of the population seemed to agree that Francophones in general and Québécois in particular had *legitimate grievances* that needed to be rectified. There was considerable disagreement and debate as to *what* should be done, but a fairly widespread consensus that something ought to be done.

In recent years, the prevailing perception is that, by and large, grievances have been dealt with by shifts of some powers from Ottawa to Quebec City, through language legislation adopted by different levels of government, by economic development policies and programs, by the promotion of bilingualism in the federal civil service, and by the increasing control over sources of capital for institution building within Quebec. In this context, further claims made by Quebec are seen as attempts to grab more and more power to the detriment of the rest of the country rather than to deal with inequities.

Much of the response in the rest of Canada is cast in a power framework: no more concessions to Quebec – anything Quebec gets must also be granted to the other provinces. The principles of the equality of the provinces must be maintained. The self-interpretation of Quebec as a 'distinct society' is seen by those outside of Quebec as a claim for special status and, thus, for more power in the federation. There is also a significant status dimension to this response: it is felt that, even without more constitutionally entrenched power, the recognition of Quebec as a distinct society (or a founding people) would represent a failure to recognize the distinctiveness of other regions and their contribution to the construction of the country.

This is felt also among some ethnic minorities who seek to have their historical participation in the formation and evolution of Canadian society recognized. Some claim that they are also, like the Québécois, 'founding peoples'; they also played a critical role in the settlement of a particular region and in its institutional development (Breton 1984: 136).[8]

Attitudes have changed in Quebec as well. Claims are less and less made on the basis of injustices or violation of rights but rather in terms of being distinct and not like the other provinces, especially not like the small provinces; in terms of the potential for economic development and organizational efficiency; and in terms of the legitimate aspiration of nations to self-determination. Also, as indicated above, status and recognition are quite central to the dynamics of the relationship between Quebec and the rest of Canada. Even the threat to the language and culture brought about by the fact of being 'drowned in a sea of Anglophones' has become less prominent in the political discourse surrounding sovereignty or independence, although it is not absent from the debate. Rather, the central elements in that discourse have to do with the failed attempts to modify the constitution in order to enhance Quebec's power to manage its own affairs and to accord it the status it deserves in the country.

Underlying these different positions are two different conceptions of Canada that could be called respectively 'segmentalist' and 'pan-Canadian.' The segmentalist approach advocates strengthening the sociopolitical boundaries between the two linguistic communities. It is based on the premise that Quebec is the homeland of the French in North America; that Francophone resources and energies should be oriented towards the development of that society. It sees as unrealistic any expectation that the French language and culture can survive and develop elsewhere in Canada in present-day circumstances (except, perhaps, for one or two exceptions such as New Brunswick). Political power is to be built in Quebec through the accumulation of economic, political, and sociocultural resources. Territorial bilingualism (i.e., unilingualism in each territory) is favoured.

The pan-Canadian approach, by contrast, promotes the view that both the Francophone and Anglophone communities exist in all regions of the country. Thus, it is important that in all regions, whenever numbers warrant it, services be provided for the education of children in the language and culture of the family; that other cultural facilities, such as radio and television stations, be available; and that individuals be able to use, in their own language, the services of at least the federal government – but preferably those of the other levels of government as well. Institutional bilingualism is what is advocated.

The structural component of this ideological cleavage is that the proponents of each view see their advantages (either economic, political, or cultural-symbolic) as being rooted primarily in the Quebec or in the Canadian institutional system. Most French Quebecers want changes, but different groups favour different programs of change. Also many are ambivalent as both the provincial and the federal spheres of policy making and activity are relevant for them in some regard or other. 'Sovereignty-association' and 'partnership,' even if these terms mean somewhat different things to different people, are striking expressions of this ambivalence. They are the affirmation of interests in the two social and institutional domains.

The Evolution of Support for Sovereignty
The consensus among Quebec's elite with regard to the desirability of sovereignty seems to be increasing. There are, however, variations in the extent to which association with the rest of Canada should or should not be part of the sovereignty project. Support for sovereignty is widespread in the political, bureaucratic, and labour elites as well as in the intelligentsia (e.g., media people, artists, teachers, professors). In the 1980 referendum, 67 per cent of intellectuals, 61 per cent of other semi-professionals and technicians, and 56 per cent of those in liberal professions voted 'Yes,' in contrast to 38 per cent of managers and proprietors, 39 per cent of farmers, and 45 per cent of workers. The federalist vote, or rather neo-federalist, since the intention was 'to set in motion negotiations for a renewed federalism,' was more likely to come from managers and proprietors (36 per cent were neo-federalists and only 10 per cent status quo 'No's) (Pinard and Hamilton 1984: 22–30). Since then, it seems that support for sovereignty has increased among business-industrial elites, especially those in small and mid-size enterprises.

Popular support for independence[9] has also increased. In the early 1960s, it was 8 per cent. It had increased over 40 per cent in the early 1990s (with the exception of the two polls in November and December 1990), which showed support at 56 per cent. Sovereignty-association was always more favoured (the question began to be asked in the 1970s). In 1970 the support was at 32 per cent, and it climbed to between 53 and 61 per cent in early 1990s (65 per cent in the November and December polls of 1990) (Pinard 1992).

The terminology used in public opinion surveys has a significant influence on the results. Pinard's analysis of a number of surveys carried out since 1989 revealed that the term 'sovereignty' yields the greatest number of positive responses and 'separation' the smallest, with 'independence' in-between. On the average, the difference between sovereignty and separation is +11 per centage points (Pinard 1994).

Fragmentation and Competition in the Francophone Collectivity
A fragmentation occurred among Francophones in different parts of the country. Francophones outside Quebec began to think of their communities not as extensions of Quebec but as distinct sociopolitical entities. To a certain extent, they also began to see themselves as facing regionally specific circumstances. In the process, regional identities became more salient (e.g., Acadian, Franco-Ontarian, Franco-Manitoban) and superseded the self-conception as 'French Canadian,' at least in the younger generations (Juteau-Lee and Lapointe 1982).

This was the result of several phenomena. First, the Quebec-centredness of the independentist movement had much to do with the fragmentation. This was symbolically reflected in the very name of the association that represented 'Francophones *outside* Québec,' a denotation that is striking by its negative form (it was changed a few years ago). Second, several of the institutions seen as critical by Francophone communities (education, culture, welfare, and municipal administration) are under provincial jurisdictions. The massive expansion of activity in those areas that began in the 1960s oriented the attention and the action of community groups and leaders towards provincial governments. Finally, the changing attitudes in some segments of English Canada, language policies, and government programs for official language minorities contributed to a new sense of power among Francophone minorities and to the emergence of new elites determined to increase the organizational capacity of Francophone communities outside Quebec.

Thus, demands for change were also articulated in provincial arenas. Gains were made. There were, however, considerable variations among the provinces as governments faced varying degrees of political difficulty in giving increased recognition and institutional services to Francophones. Institutional recognition and services are legitimated in reference to the larger pan-Canadian context, but not without meeting much resistance. In all provinces except Quebec and New Brunswick, Francophones constitute a small percentage of the total population (frequently smaller than that of other ethnic groups), many of whose members do not see why the French should receive special treatment.

Status Anxieties and the Politics of Recognition

Another dimension of recent changes has been a shift from a concern with cultural survival to a preoccupation with recognition and status. This is a question of emphasis, not an all-or-none matter. It is the quest for respect and endorsement that, almost automatically, accompanies the pursuit of institutional control.

Recognition and a sense of group worth are important for members of a collectivity because self-esteem is in good measure a function of the esteem accorded to one's collectivity – the more so if membership in that collectivity is central to one's personal identity (Horowitz 1985: 143). This would be the case, for instance, in 'institutionally complete' groups[10] such as Quebec Francophones. There is a yearning for a favourable evaluation of the social, cultural, and moral worth of one's group. It is to be expected, then, that people will have an interest in the status bestowed upon their group, its culture and language by the public institutions of the larger society and by those that they regard as their 'significant others' (Mead 1934).

This yearning generates processes of social comparison. Members of groups, minority groups in particular, pay regular attention to how well 'we' are doing compared with 'them'; how well the system is favouring 'them' as opposed to 'us.' Federal policies, programs, and expenditures in Quebec are compared with those in the rest of the country. The media frequently compare the situation with regard to indicators of economic well-being, social policy, educational achievement, and arts and culture in Quebec with what is happening in Ontario or in the rest of Canada.

The salience of social evaluations and recognition by others is accentuated by factors such as intervention by the central state in various domains of activity, integration in larger Canadian and continental economic systems, and intergroup communication through the media. Indeed, all increase the opportunities for intergroup comparisons in terms of economic well-being, political power, and social status (which are, of course, interconnected).

One of the important manifestations of this concern for status is the claim in recent years for recognition as a distinct society and for sovereignty or sovereignty-association. It also underlies the refusal to be given the same status as other ethnic minorities and for Quebec to be treated like any other province. Correspondingly, many members of other ethnic minorities and of other provinces consider the recognition of distinctiveness as establishing an inequality in status or a 'pecking order' (Kallen 1988) and, accordingly, reject the claim.

But many Quebec Francophones experience more than the sense of a simple refusal. There is the perception of a withdrawal of a historically based status in the federation, namely, that of a 'founding people.' This is important if one considers that losing something is probably more painful than the failure to acquire it. Similarly, the independentist aspiration is partly motivated by the wish to be recognized by the international community, something that would force the rest of Canada to deal with Quebec, at least formally, on an equal basis.

The concern for status is also manifest in the theme of 'humiliation' that comes up regularly in the current political discourse. It was prominent during recent dealings with the question of the Constitution. The vocabulary denouncing the opposition to recent attempts at constitutional change included terms such as 'humiliation,' 'rejection,' 'isolation,' and 'being put in one's place.' In addition, many of the economic arguments against independence are cast in a framework that exacerbates the status anxieties of many Quebeckers. The idea is to show that remaining in Canada is economically advantageous; but the underlying, and frequently the explicit message is 'look, you can't make it on your own; you need the rest of Canada.' Such a campaign perhaps has – for the status-sensitive segment of the population – an effect *opposite* to the one intended.

Thus, while in English-speaking Canada, as noted above, the constitutional claims of Quebec are perceived as a quest for more power, in French-speaking Quebec they have as much to do with recognition and status as with power (although these two elements may not be given the same weight by institutional elites and by average citizens). The questioning of and opposition to constitutional change on the part of English Canadians is perceived as a refusal to recognize Quebec's distinctiveness in terms of culture and institutions.

The Dynamics of Identification and Attachment

Two issues have become salient with the rise and growth of the independentist movement: the nature of the identification with or attachment to Canada and to Quebec and the possibility of the coexistence of partly different identifications and attachments. What is the basis of identification and attachment to a society? Is it based on economic advantages? on a sense of interdependence and therefore of mutual obligations? on commonalities, such as common descent, historical experience, or cultural traits? or on a shared sociopolitical philosophy to guide the construction and evolution of the society?

In 1991 an Angus Reid national survey asked respondents about their attachment to Canada. Twenty-two per cent of French-origin Quebeckers said they have 'a deep emotional attachment to Canada, that they love the country and what it stands for.' In contrast, 37 per cent said they were attached to Canada, but only as long as it provides a good standard of living. Another 38 per cent said they were not attached to Canada and would prefer to see the country split up into two or more smaller countries or joined to the United States. The corresponding per centages are 64, 24, and 10 in the rest of the sample (non-French origin respondents in Quebec and all respondents in the rest of Canada).

Why is the attachment of Quebeckers to Canada primarily utilitarian, if it exists at all? More generally, what are the sources of identification to a collectivity in a society that is culturally heterogeneous, that is, where commonalities of descent and culture do not exist? Three can be identified. First, the collectivity provides the conditions and opportunities for the realization of *individual* aspirations and goals. Second, the collectivity provides the conditions and opportunities for the realization of *collective* goals, specifically, organizational, cultural, and status goals. And, third, people invest themselves and their resources and, as a result, sense that they are contributing to the construction of the society, to the creation and maintenance of its institutions, of its social and material infrastructure, of its networks of communication, and to the realization of collective projects (political, social, economic, or technological).

In recent decades at least, it seems that the public discourse has been appealing primarily to utilitarian motives or to a sense of interdependence (or, as indicated earlier, to a sense of dependence). Is this because there is no other source of identification with Canada to which one can appeal in the case of the Québécois? Or is it the dominant values of our market-oriented culture that make it difficult to perceive any other human motivation except utilitarian? Or both?

Does the public discourse in Canada include references to the contribution of each region to the well-being and development of the society as a whole? Or does it tend to emphasize how each region is being disadvantaged by being part of the federation? (Public opinion polls suggest that a substantial proportion of the population in *each* region of the country feels that their region or province is getting a bad deal.)

Is there a historical role in the building and evolution of the society played by the various collectivities that constitute the country? If so, why do the institutional elites not celebrate it when it is appropriate? Perhaps there is not enough on which to build a convincing mythology; the prevailing view was that English and French would each build their own society and compete for the economic and political power necessary for their attainment of their societal ambitions. As a result, the boundaries of 'participatory' identification and attachment and of corresponding obligations would coincide with the linguistic boundaries.

Immigrants and Ethnic Minorities

The dynamics of the relations between immigrants, ethnic minorities, and the larger society have also changed since the publication of *The Vertical Mosaic*. Three demographic changes should be underscored. First, the non-British, non-French component of the population has become more diversified: the proportion of European origin declined from 22.6 per cent of the total population in 1961 to 15.4 per cent in 1991 (single origins only), while the Asian proportion increased from 0.7 to 6.0 per cent, and the proportion of other origins increased from 1.3 to 4.5 per cent. This is due to a change in the source countries of immigration. While before 1961 about 95 per cent of immigrants came from Europe and the United States, it was about 30 per cent in the 1981–91 period. Asia, the Middle East, the Caribbean, South and Central America, Africa, and other parts of the world have become the main regions from which immigrants come to this country now.

Second, the relative size of visible minorities increased significantly. They constituted less than 3 per cent of the total population in 1961 (including the Aboriginal groups). 'In 1991 the 1.9 million adults in a visible minority in Canada represented 9 per cent of the population aged 15 years of age and over, doubling the 1981 proportion' (Kelly 1995: 3). However, the non-white population was still overwhelmingly foreign-born: between 72 and 94 per cent for all visible minority groups in 1991, except the Japanese (23 per cent) and the Pacific Islanders (63 per cent) (Kelly 1995: 4).

Third, as noted above, the proportion of the total population born outside Canada is significant: 16.1 per cent in 1991 (about twice the proportion in the United States). Immigrants, however, are far from being evenly distributed across the country. For instance, in 1991, 23.7 per cent resided in Ontario, 22.3 in British Columbia, 15.1 in Alberta, 11.0 in the Yukon, 8.7 in Quebec, and 6 per cent or less in each of the other provinces. There are as well important differences among metropolitan areas: 38 per cent in Toronto, 30 per cent in Vancouver, thirteen cities showing per centages between 13 and 24 per cent,[11] four with 7 or 8 per cent,[12] and the rest having less than 5 per cent (Badets 1993: 10).

Four aspects of the relationship between these groups and mainstream society will examined: (a) the evolution of ethnic stratification; (b) the tension between universalism and particularism; (c) the extent and modalities of state intervention; and (d) the reactions of 'majority Canadians.'

The Evolution of Ethnic Stratification

Ethnic stratification was one of Porter's main preoccupations, not only in terms of the overall distribution of groups across occupational and income categories, but also in terms of inclusion in the economic and political elites.

As a result of urbanization, the rise in the levels of education, economic growth, and a combination of growing tolerance and of pressure towards Anglo-conformity, minorities have progressively been integrated into the social structure. The institutional rigidities that existed at the time *The Vertical Mosaic* was published were already breaking down as a result of forces unleashed by the Second World War and by increasing foreign, especially American, investments in the Canadian economy. A 'quiet revolution' took place not only in Quebec but also in English-speaking Canada: 'What emerged after the war was a new Canadian society' (Clark 1975: 29). The educational and industrial institutions that Porter blamed for the lack of mobility opportunities changed: facilities were expanded at all levels of the educational system, and 'new and expanding types of business enterprises emerged ... offering opportunities for rapid economic advancement.' These were accompanied by massive shifts of population from rural areas to cities, by an increase in the number of women in the labour force, and by an expansion of the middle class (Clark 1975: 29).

These transformations also facilitated the integration of immigrants. If integration was usually partial in the immigrant generation, by the second and especially the third generation, minorities reached and sometimes surpassed the level of socioeconomic attainment of Canadians of British origin (Darroch 1979; Brym and Fox 1989: 103–13; Boyd 1992; Reitz and Breton 1994: 97). This is the case not only at the mass level but also at the level of elites (Ogmundson and McLaughlin 1992).

In his analysis of the determinants of a person's position in the social structure, Porter, like other social scientists at that time, paid little attention to gender or to the interaction of ethnicity and gender. The women's movement that emerged in the late 1960s and 1970s was one of the main forces that focused attention on the ways in which and extent to which women are disadvantaged with regard to employment, occupational status, and income, and on the patterns of gender concentration in different occupational categories. Focusing on occupation, Lautard and Guppy observed that the 'gendered division of labour is more marked than is the ethnic division of labour; that men and women tend to be clustered in "sex-typed" jobs more often than members of specific ethnic groups are concentrated in "ethnic-linked" jobs ...' Also, 'typically women in the labour force are paid less but have higher levels of schooling than men' (1990: 204; see also Reitz 1990).

Many women are subjected to 'multiple jeopardy' in seeking to improve their socioeconomic condition. That is, whatever negative impact age, ethnicity, race, or immigrant status might have on socioeconomic disadvantage, it is compounded by the fact of being a woman (Gerber 1990; Labelle 1990; Billson 1991; Boyd 1992). However, just as members of different ethnic or racial groups are not equally advantaged or disadvantaged in labour market, the degree of jeopardy experienced by women varies depending on their particular ethnic or racial affiliation. For instance, Gerber observed that Indian women suffered a greater economic disadvantage than Inuit and Métis women (1990: 80). The constraints are also greater for 'visible minorities' than for white ethnic groups, although such broad categories may conceal more than they reveal. Indeed, Stasiulis noted that 'the combined liability of race and gender in the Canadian labour market varies considerably from one non-white group to another' (1987: 7, quoted in Labelle 1990: 74). Ethnicity or race may be more or less of an asset or more or less of a liability depending on the group with which one is affiliated (Breton et al. 1990: Chapter 1), a proposition that would apply to women as well as to men.

Such variations are partly due to the ways in which those who control resources, especially white men, react to different categories of women. It may also be the result of the ways in which gender identity and roles are defined in different ethnocultural groups. But, as Billson pointed out, little attention has been given to 'the direct impact of culture on the relative power of men and women ... [to] what it means to be male or female in each culture, in terms of roles, power, permitted versus restricted behaviours, or self-concept' (1991: 52). This underscores the importance, whether for theoretical or policy purposes, of examining patterns of culture-specific gender inequalities.

An important change since the publication of *The Vertical Mosaic* has been the increased number of visible minorities in the Canadian population. A number of these minorities have been in Canada for a long time, but the size of these groups has increased considerably in recent decades, and new ones have been added. This change was brought about by the fact that the supply of labour from European countries was diminishing, many of them having become themselves importers of labour. Changes in Canadian immigration policy were another factor. Indeed, the point system introduced a significant degree of universalism in the selection of immigrants, a process that had up to then been largely geared to the recruitment of white immigrants.

Whether or not the overall pattern of socioeconomic mobility for minorities of European origin will repeat itself for visible minorities is not clear. Among immigrants, especially immigrant women, in some visible minorities, socioeconomic achievement is not as high, but neither was it among white immigrants who came in earlier periods (Boyd 1992; Reitz 1990; Reitz and Breton 1994: 97). This is not the case in all visible minorities, some attaining high levels of occupation and income, even in the immigrant generation (Kelly 1995).

The large proportion of members of visible minority group that are foreign-born raises the question of the long-term effects of 'visibility' in ethnic stratification. By and large, 'Anglo-conformity' is the model of incorporation of immigrants that has prevailed in Canada. The implicit understanding was that conformity was expected, indeed demanded, and that compliance would increase one's chances of making it in the socioeconomic structure. This model assumes that individuals have considerable choice over the social salience of their cultural traits, that is, over what distinguishes them from Anglos and from what are the expected patterns of appearance and behaviour. The choice is, of course, greater in the second than in the first generation, but it exists to some degree even among immigrants (Palmer 1976). In spite of the rhetoric about the valuation of diversity in Canadian society, this model still prevails today (Reitz and Breton 1994).

Will this model operate when colour is involved, that is, when individuals have no choice in keeping or shedding a distinguishing trait? Of course, they may emphasize or play it down in social interaction (Lyman and Douglass 1973), but they have limited control over whether or not others will take it into account in their interaction with them. In other words, are racial boundaries as permeable as ethnic ones? The experience of blacks and of Native people, on the one hand, and of Asian minorities, on the other, suggests a differential application of the 'Anglo-conformity' model.[13] But this was likewise the case for immigrants of European origin and their descendants: the model worked better for some than for others. It is only with data over generations and for different groups that it will be possible to answer these questions in the Canadian context.

Another issue concerns the impact of language differences on ethnic stratification – an issue that is of particular significance in Quebec. In recent decades, public policy, with strong public support, has moved to promote and institutionalize the same model that has prevailed in the rest of North America, except that in this instance it is 'Franco' rather than 'Anglo-conformity' that is expected – both linguistically and culturally. However, state intervention is more critical in Quebec than it was and continues to be in the rest of the country. Indeed, the linguistic assimilation of newcomers in English-speaking Canada can be taken for granted. It takes more or less time, but it is virtually inevitable as the demographic, economic, cultural (e.g., mass media), and social forces operating in Canada, in North America, and indeed in the world all motivate individuals to learn English.

In Montreal (the rest of Quebec is largely ethnically and linguistically homogeneous), the situation is significantly different. The economic, demographic, and sociocultural forces promoting English operate there as well. But part of this context is the ethnic composition of Montreal. The proportion of persons of French origin in the census metropolitan area was 64.2 per cent in 1961; in 1991 58.9 per cent were of single French origin and 6.7 per cent of multiple origins involving French. Those with French as mother tongue increased from 64.8 to 66.9 per cent (70.2 if those with multiple mother tongues are included). In 1991, 68.2 per cent used French only as a home language, and 2.3 per cent used it and another language – a total of 70.5 per cent (home language data are not available for 1961).

Thus, the non-Francophone population is not negligible. However, as in other cities, it tends to be concentrated in certain neighbourhoods where, in a number of instances, Francophones constitute the minority.

This demographic situation is not favourable to the adoption by non-Francophones of French as their daily language. This predicament of the French language in Montreal has been accentuated in recent years by the movement towards the suburbs (a phenomenon observed in many North American cities).

Thus, in response to these pressures, special measures have been adopted to promote the learning and use of French. Some consist of requirements such as the obligation for immigrants to send their children to French schools and the specifications concerning the language of work. Others are climate creating such as requirements with regard to commercial signs.

Still others are aimed at creating job opportunities that reward the learning and use of French. Indeed, French-controlled institutions – the provincial and municipal civil services and, as noted elsewhere, a growing Francophone-controlled private sector – contain a significant segment of the Quebec labour market.

Programs have been established for the recruitment of non-Francophones in the public service and to fight discrimination. However, it is not clear that the bargain implicit in the Anglo-conformity – a bargain that, as noted, seems to have worked to a considerable extent for white ethnic minorities – is an integral part of the Franco-conformity expected of minorities in Quebec. For instance, some research indicates that the incorporation of minorities in the provincial and municipal public services appears to be quite slow (McAll 1991: 24).

In addition, there is a 'widening socioeconomic gap between the Francophone and immigrant populations' a gap that 'is even more evident in the school system ... 31 per cent of Francophone schoolchildren on the Island of Montreal are now placed in private schools' (McAll 1991: 15). Public pressures to open up opportunities for minorities may not be as strong in Quebec as they are in other parts of the country. For instance, a survey conducted in 1993 found that 57 per cent of Quebec respondents and 38 per cent of those in the rest of Canada feel that 'there is nothing wrong in giving advantages to people from the same ethnic groups as yourself.'[14]

Universalism versus Particularism: De-ethnicizing or Ethnicizing Public Institutions

Porter was quite concerned with the question of whether or not societal resources should be allocated on an ethnic or non-ethnic basis. This question appears in several of his writings (1965, 1972, 1975, 1979). His central concern was that 'ethnic differentiation in social structure always creates a high risk of ethnic stratification' (1975: 289). This issue continues to be part of academic concerns and of the public debate about multicultural policies and programs.

Traditionally, a central proposition in the theory of equality of opportunity and in the formulation of related rights has been that individuals should have access to societal resources and should be treated by societal institutions *irrespective* of their ethnicity, race, and national origin. This, it should be noted, was to neutralize the effect of ethnicity: it was to prevent or make it more difficult for ethnic groups advantaged in terms of the historical position in the social structure, in terms of social networks, and in terms of access to centres of decision to use their ethnic ties against other groups. Because of this, the hypothesis maintained by Porter, among others, was that the maintenance of ethnic or racial boundaries almost inevitably leads to inequality and conflict.

In policies based on the treatment of individuals irrespective of their ethnicity or race, the incorporation strategy is to 'multiculturalize' institutions, that is, to define them as common spaces in which all individuals participate on an equal basis. It is to institutionalize mechanisms such that decisions are made on the basis of professional, economic, artistic, and such standards – not on an ethnic basis.

The underlying view in this approach is that ethnicity is a potentially perverse phenomenon. Ethnicity and ethnic affiliations are viewed by those who belong to dominant groups as strategic resources in the competition for power, wealth, status, and, therefore, advantage. They are means to gain and/or retain control over jobs, positions of power and influence, and decision making. Ethnicity is seen as a basis of social exclusion, invidious social comparisons, and conflict.

The appropriate strategy, then, is to suppress its operation in social life as much as possible. Otherwise, it will tend to have negative consequences for certain categories of individuals, for communities, the society, and the functioning of institutions. Similarly, the allocation of recognition, influence, and material resources by the state must be opposed. Such allocations invite intergroup comparisons and status competition. They encourage groups to organize in order to influence institutional decisions. The result is to accentuate the social salience of ethnic boundaries and to foster ethnic competition.

In contrast, the social logic of intervention on an ethnic basis is that the distribution of opportunities and resources and of public services will be carried out by *taking into account* ethnic origin and race. In other words, the organization of society becomes progressively institutionalized on an ethnic basis.

The incorporation strategy that flows from taking ethnic boundaries into account can take many forms: (a) the formation of ethnic enclaves within institutions such as school programs and curricula, and even entire schools, welfare agencies, or cultural organizations designed for specific ethnic or racial groups; (b) basing personnel decisions on ethnic representation; (c) encouraging the persistence of ethnic solidarity and cultural expression in as many institutional spheres as possible; and (d) a process that tends to follow automatically from such schemes, the creation of official ethnic categorizations in order to be able to take into account ethnic diversity in the administration of the various public programs.[15]

In this approach, ethnicity and ethnic affiliations are treated as socially benign phenomena. They constitute an anchorage for individual identity and self-esteem; a basis for social inclusion, community cohesion, and cooperation; and a locus for cultural life and expression. Because ethnicity has such value for individual identity, cultural expression, and social cohesion, the argument is made that it should be supported and even enhanced.

One of the concerns underlying this issue, strongly expressed by Porter, was that fighting discrimination with strategies based on ethnicity or race may have the unintended consequence of reinforcing the very ethnic and racial boundaries that the policy aims at removing or reducing. The risk is the institutionalization rather than the reduction of ethnic and racial competition which, in turn, risks increasing the chances of conflict and of inequalities. On the other hand, the 'irrespective of ...' strategy is seen as leading to strategies and programs aimed at all disadvantaged people in some particular respect, whatever their ethnic or racial affiliation.

Porter observed that 'for some, the revival of ethnicity has come about precisely because of the failure of universalistic and achievement values to take hold, and thus create a society of equality of opportunity and condition' and that it is understandable that because of this failure 'minorities have had to organize to obtain some measure of distributive justice when deprivation remained concentrated within particular groups' (1975: 295). But he emphasized that 'the new instruments focused as they are on groups, and providing what might be called group rights – say, to proportional representation within all institutional hierarchies – constitute a radical departure from a society organized on the principle of individual achievement and universalistic judgments, towards one organized on group claims to representation on the basis of particular rather than universal qualities' (1972: 193–4). The dilemma with regard to the kind of society Canada is to become is still very much on the public agenda.

In concluding her analysis of this societal choice, Burnet (1979) argued that neither alternative can be fully accepted: arrangements that represent compromises between the two sets of principles must be worked out. This would be part of a Canadian tradition. Indeed, even though the principles of universalism and the practices of 'irrespective of ethnicity, race religion' are deeply rooted in our sociopolitical culture, they have not been applied uniformly in our society.

On the contrary, there are several instances of group-based organization or practices in Canadian society. The segmentation of the society into French and British was constitutionally established with the BNA Act, with the Official Languages Act, and through a number of public programs. The segmentation on the basis of Aboriginality was legally established with the Royal Proclamation of 1763, the Indian Act of 1850 and its subsequent modifications, and the maintenance of a separate government department. The right to public support for denominational schools is established in the Constitution. Employment equity legislation seeks to assure a certain representation of groups in the workforce of different institutional sectors. Not surprisingly, given the coexistence of two sets of principles in the culture, all these are more or less strongly contested by some groups and supported by others.

Thus, Canadians have been proclaiming two principles which are contradictory in some of their institutional implications: the right of all to be treated equally *irrespective* of their ethnicity and the right of some to be treated differentially *because* of their ethnicity.

The State and Ethnic and Racial Groups

The state has always intervened in the management of diversity in Canada. It has dealt with the amount and composition of immigration and to some degree with immigrants' integration in Canadian society. At different points, it has been actively involved in their settlement. It has taken measures for their linguistic and cultural assimilation. It has kept an eye on the ethnic press and other community organizations. It has segregated and deported members of some groups during war periods.

But in recent decades, beginning at the time of the publication of *The Vertical Mosaic*, state intervention has increased considerably not only in the provision of services but also in the structuring of civil society, ethnicity being one of the areas in which this has taken place. Recent decades have witnessed, at all levels of government, the creation of structures for the management of the social organization of ethnicity and of intergroup relations.

The control of immigration remains an important area of government activity. Four areas are relatively new for state intervention or, if not new, the modalities of intervention are somewhat different.

The Internal Organization of Ethnic Collectivities

Interventions in this area have to do with the institutional bases of linguistic and cultural maintenance and expression and organization for the exercise of political influence. The interventions might be intended to strengthen some dimension of the group's culture or structure, to weaken it, or to control its development or evolution.

By legitimizing ethnically based activities and claims on the state, the multiculturalism policy of the federal government (proclaimed in 1971) provided positive symbolic capital for ethnic mobilization and organization. Furthermore, governmental programs, administrative structures, budgets, and various initiatives (e.g., conferences, ethnic chairs in universities, research programs) provided an opportunity structure for ethnically based action and organization. Third, subsequent years saw other levels of government and school boards adopt their own policies with regard to ethnocultural diversity.

The Pursuit of Socioeconomic Equality

There are also interventions aimed at the distribution of income, goods, and services (jobs, education, housing, welfare services, police protection). The main objective is usually to attain greater equality, either of opportunity or of outcome in market and state institutions.

The conception of equality underlying public policies also changed in recent decades, raising at least two issues. First, should public policy pursue equality of opportunity or equality of results/outcomes? This is the issue underlying the debate on employment equity (or affirmative action/positive discrimination). Second, does equality of treatment mean the same treatment applied to all groups or different but equivalent treatments to groups who differ in their historical, political, demographic, and socioeconomic situation? This is the issue underlying the debate over the public funding of denominational schools; the recognition of Quebec as a distinct society; self-government for Aboriginal communities; special programs for the French outside Quebec; and special programs for visible minorities.

The pursuit of equality, however defined, seems to have acquired a new urgency in recent years. Indeed, immigrants seem to have new expectations. This has been suggested by West Indian poet Cecil Foster who said that 'the myth of the immigrant experience: first generation immigrants must willingly put up with self-denial for the benefit of their children. This myth does not hold for West Indians like me. While we hope that our kids reap the benefits of our labour, we also want the harvest to start during our lives' (Foster 1994).

The rise in immigrant expectations may be due to the changing higher levels of education of immigrants. It may also be the result of government policies such as multiculturalism and employment equity and to the entitlement culture of the providential state. These expectations, however, should be seen in the larger context of individuals and groups pursuing their interests and making claims on society and its institutions – a phenomenon far from being restricted to ethnic and racial minorities. (This is discussed further below.)

Finally, some authors have pointed out that claims for social benefits in Western societies are increasingly made on the basis of status as a victim rather than on status as a citizen. To the extent that one can expect less and less redistribution because of poverty or disadvantage, claims are made for compensation for being a victim of past injustices or present maltreatment. It is not that compensation for injustices is not part of our moral culture. It is. Nor is it that such compensation is not deserved in many instances. The point is that being a victim seems to be acquiring importance for the justification of redistribution, while one's social rights as a citizen seem to carry less weight (Rosanvallon 1995).

The Distribution of Recognition and Status
Government intervention also has an impact on the distribution of status among groups. The interventions may be to establish the status of a group, to increase that of another, or to change the relative statuses of different groups. The dynamics of the distribution of symbolic resources is different from that of goods and services (although they are related to each other).

The Prevention and Management of Conflict
Measures aimed at the prevention and management of conflict include measures aimed at shaping intergroup attitudes, the expression of hos-

tility (e.g., hate propaganda), and the control of intergroup confrontations. Several initiatives have been taken in schools and communities for the mediation of conflicts and for negotiations over issues dividing communities. The active promotion of the ideology of multiculturalism through education and public relations campaigns has been undertaken to encourage positive attitudes towards diversity.

Symbolic Restructuring

The definition of the country as 'multicultural in a bilingual context' was officially proclaimed and formally established in government organization and programs following the Royal Commission on Bilingualism and Biculturalism. This provided a new framework for interpreting events and their implications for the value attached to different ethnic backgrounds in the cultural-symbolic order. It was a resource for mobilization on an ethnic basis. By legitimizing ethnically based activities and claims on the state, state policies and programs provided positive symbolic capital for ethnic mobilization and organization. It has been pointed out that the multiculturalism budget has always been quite small. Although this is no doubt true, it is reasonable to suggest that the main capital provided by the state was not financial, but symbolic (Breton 1984, 1986).

The Creation of an Ethnic Structure of Opportunity

Support to a network of voluntary groups is one of the structural mechanisms through which government mobilizes citizen participation in the implementation of policy, attempts to legitimize its intervention, and seeks to expand its domain of activity. Indeed, groups that obtain government support become 'effective constituencies demanding program expansion in their area' (Pal 1993: 14).

   Government support to voluntary groups is not limited to ethnic and racial groups. It is a pattern found in a wide range of governmental departments such as Health and Welfare, Environment, Agriculture, Justice, Sports, Consumer and Corporate Affairs, Fisheries and Oceans, Indian Affairs and Northern Development, and Labour. But it included ethnic groups: in 1974–5 the number of grants awarded to ethnic organizations was 648; in 1987–8 it was 2,073. Some grants go to multicultural organizations and others to organizations of specific ethnic groups. By providing an opportunity structure, such support can expand considerably the potential for ethnic community organization and collective action. Indeed, several authors have pointed out that the formation of new groups is one of the *consequences* of legislation, not one of the *causes* of its passage (Pal 1993).

What has emerged in recent decades is an ethnocultural policy community, that is, an interorganizational network that includes, in addition to ethnic and multi-ethnic organizations, academic researchers, private consulting firms, and other agencies with an interest in the field. It includes as well, of course, the governmental and other bodies whose policies and practices they wish to influence or from which they seek to obtain benefits. These organizations interact over the definition of issues, the structuring of the policy field, and the pursuit of common objectives – one of these objectives being to maintain and, if possible, expand the field of ethnocultural action (Pross 1986).

It has been hypothesized (and in some instances documented) that an effect of this evolution has been a certain distancing of ethnic leaders and their governance structures from the rank and file of the collectivity (Savas 1987; Ponting and Gibbins 1980: 208–9). This pattern is suggested by results for two related questions addressed to respondents in the late 1970s Toronto study. The first asked how concerned leaders of their ethnic group were with the problems and interests of the ordinary members of the community, and the second enquired about the effort leaders made to get approval from members for their decisions. The fraction who said their leaders were very interested or made an effort to get approval was never higher than one-third in the seven groups included in the study (Breton 1991: Chapter 4).

The Secretary of State's report for the fiscal year 1974–5 mentioned above indicates that '14 per cent of all funded groups are not effectively controlled by the membership.' In addition, of the 83 per cent that hold annual elections of officers, over 80 per cent had less than 300 individual members, the average being 84 members ('45 per cent of the time, organizations funded by multiculturalism which report individual citizens as members have from 20 to 85 members') (Secretary of State 1976: 14). Thus, ethnic leaders become somewhat more responsive to the significant actors in the interorganizational network than to their community.

Reactions of 'Majority Canadians'

The expression 'majority Canadians' is in quotation marks because it is an ambiguous denotation in contemporary Canada. Who constitutes the 'majority'? Insofar as minorities of European origin are concerned, the majority may still be those of British origin (or of French origin in Quebec). But do visible minorities make a distinction between British origin and other white ethnic groups, or are they all 'whites' and therefore all part of the 'majority?' This is not a conceptual but a social ambiguity no doubt due to significant demographic and social change.

Ambivalence *vis-à-vis* Diversity

Canadians are ambivalent *vis-à-vis* diversity: they find that it has the potential of adding to the cultural richness of Canada, but that it also harbours potential dangers for its cohesion. One manifestation of this ambivalence is the continuing concern about the extent to which and the ways in which multiculturalism ought to be institutionalized. Another is that the public debate seems at times to focus on its positive features, while in other periods the emphasis is on its problematic aspects.

The latter is the situation today. In contrast to a few years ago, multiculturalism tends to be seen by many as a source of problems. Because the sociopolitical context has changed in significant ways, multiculturalism is now seen and interpreted differently, that is, as adding to or accentuating the problems confronting our society.

Several contextual changes have taken place: the integration of Canada in a continental and global economy; the critical role of 'single issue' interest groups in the political process; the mobilization of collectivities previously at the periphery of the political process (e.g., women, Native peoples, and visible minorities); systematic province building in most regions and the accompanying confrontations with the federal government; the magnitude of the providential state and the related 'culture of entitlement'; and the continuing presence of the Quebec independentist movement. One of the many impacts of these trends and phenomena is to have created the feeling among many people that hardly anyone is concerned for the state of the society as a whole; that each group is out for the pursuit of its own interest and goals, without much concern for its impact on the larger polity, economy, and society.

A related feeling is that the country is being slowly fragmented; that its cohesion is being undermined; that its capacity to act as a nation is reduced. In this context, multiculturalism is seen as the program of another set of groups seeking their own interest and goals, making claims on the society and its institutions, and accentuating the fragmentation.

In addition, there appears to be confusion as to the ways of interpreting the claims made on society and its institutions. Bellah et al. (1985) have noted the difficulty of understanding the complexity of modern social relations; that people they talked to 'had real difficulty piecing together a picture of the whole society and how they relate to it.' They comment that 'since we lack a way of making moral sense of significant cultural, social, and economic differences between groups, we also lack means for evaluating the different claims such groups make. The conflict of interest is troubling when we do not know how to evaluate those interests' (ibid.: 207).

All these changes have contributed in one way or another to the 'devalidation' of the traditional cultural paradigms in our society. There is considerable ambiguity as to how one should think about moral issues, religion, family, social rights, authority, and, of course, ethnicity and its place in the organization of society and public institutions. There is a fair amount of confusion, not to say disorientation, among many segments of the population. It seems to exist as well among intellectuals (academics, university professors, teachers, and media people), among institutional managers and their advisers, and among political leaders.

There is ambivalence about the value of ethnic diversity. A Decima survey (sponsored by *Maclean's* magazine), carried out in 1989, asked respondents in Canada and the United States the following question: 'What do you think is better for Canada / the U.S. for new immigrants to be encouraged to maintain their distinct culture and ways, or to change their distinct culture and ways to blend with the larger society?' The overall results showed, first, that in both countries less than a majority of respondents favour cultural retention: 47 and 34 per cent of the American and Canadian samples respectively and, second, that the results are *opposite* to what one would have expected on the basis of the prevailing Canadian system of belief: 13 per cent more Americans than Canadians favour the maintenance of 'distinct cultures and ways' (Reitz and Breton 1994: Chapter 2).

Other studies revealed a similar attitude. For example, a variation of the following question was included in surveys carried out in 1976, 1986, and 1988: 'People who come to Canada should change their behaviour to be more like us' (Berry et al. 1977: 141). In 1976, 50 per cent agreed with the statement in comparison with 60 per cent and 62 per cent in 1986 and 1988 respectively. Other items, however, suggest the opposite: that Canadians tend to favour cultural maintenance. For instance, in 1976, 64 per cent agreed that 'it would be good to see that all the ethnic groups in Canada retain their cultures.' And in both 1976 and 1986 about half disagreed that 'the unity of this country is weakened by ethnic groups sticking to their old ways.' The surveys also explored the question of the private versus public manifestations of ethnic cultures: should members of ethnic groups who want to keep their own culture keep it to themselves and not bother other people in the country? In 1976, 49 per cent agreed with the item. In 1988 the item was somewhat different: it concluded with 'should not display it publicly.' The results are accordingly different: 34 per cent agreed. These results suggest that some Canadians support cultural maintenance provided that it 'fits' well with the ways of other groups. If it is to generate any interference in society, then it should remain private.

There may be a tendency to favour cultural maintenance, but also to wish that people who come here should change their behaviour to be like Canadians; that people retain their culture and be allowed to display it publicly, but not if this is to 'bother' others. There appears to be a rejection of assimilation, but also of outright pluralism. In other words, there is a twofold expectation presented to ethnic minorities, an expectation perhaps best captured with the term 'integration': on the one hand, become fully part of the society, fit in, adopt our ways of doing things; on the other, do not abandon your cultural background, retain and express your culture, but only if this fits well in the Canadian sociocultural matrix.

There is also ambivalence and confusion concerning the matter of individual and collective rights. Part of the difficulty in interpreting the claims of ethnic groups is that some are made in terms of individual rights, while others are made in terms of collective rights (and some in terms of both). Four kinds of issues generate confusion on this question.

First, individual and collective rights may come into conflict as the above discussion of 'irrespective of ...' and 'taking into account ...' principles suggests. Second, there is the question of the boundaries of the collectivity that possesses rights. Who is included in (and excluded from) a particular group? To whom do the group rights apply? On what basis is the categorization of the population with specific rights established?

Third, when individual rights are discussed, it is usually in relation to specific rights, whether these are political, civic, or social. What specific rights are to be recognized when collectivities are concerned? Does the notion of collective right include only the right to maintain the group language, or does it extend beyond that? Do all ethnic or racial collectivities have the rights to language maintenance, or is it a right for some but not for other groups? More generally, do all ethnic collectivities have the same rights, or do specific rights vary from one group to another?

Fourth, who is obligated by the recognized collective rights? What obligations can the leaders of an ethnic collectivity impose on its own members for the attainment of the goals underlying the group rights? In other words, what are the costs for individual members of the implementation of collective rights? How are those costs imposed? And what obligations and costs do ethnic collective rights impose on the rest of the society and through what kinds of institutional mechanisms are these obligations to be met? For the implementation of individual civil, political, and social rights, T.H. Marshall (1965) identified three corresponding sets of institutions (e.g., the courts of law, the electoral system, Parliament, public education, and the social safety net). What would be the public institutions for the implementation of collective rights? And would they agree with those for individual rights?

Status Anxieties and Relative Deprivation

Harney has noted that 'the two founding nations, the Prairie ethnic blocs, and the new immigrant *ethnies all* thought their piece of the pie and the survival of their cultures were threatened' (Harney 1988: 71). There are two sides to the perceived threat. First, these feelings are a natural reaction to a sense of social displacement, to economic insecurity, declining political power and influence, and/or the erosion of one's cultural world. Second, these social and cultural anxieties are frequently accompanied by envy, resentment, and anger. The anxieties and resentments are, if anything, even more generalized than they were when Harney wrote the above lines. As Spicer said, we live in 'an archipelago of envies and anxieties' (quoted by Wilson 1993). These tend to be accompanied by feelings of relative deprivation which, as research has shown, are related to subjective dissatisfaction, support of particular political candidates and movements, and attitudes towards outgroups (Dion 1986: 176).[16]

There are, first, groups who feel that they are being displaced. These include groups of people of British origin who feel they are no longer the main definers of the cultural make-up of the society and the main interpreters of events, situations, and problems requiring public action. They also include whites who increasingly feel that they are in the process of being marginalized by the growing number of visible minorities, at least in certain community settings, if not in the society as a whole.

Second, there are those in the middle of the class structure who feel that they are paying a disproportionate share of the societal burden and thus resent the 'special interest groups.' They see the rich as taking care of themselves and the poor as being taken care of by government. They feel relatively deprived in relation to those classes, especially those on welfare whom they perceive as being better off even though they have the same or lower educational backgrounds than theirs and certainly do not match them in work ethic. They resent paying taxes to support such groups or seeing them advantaged by government legislation and programs.

Included in this category are those whose economic situation has declined as shown by stagnant if not declining wages, the threat of unemployment, underemployment, or part-time work, and the absence of benefits. Many people in this predicament resent those whom they see as enjoying special privileges such as those on welfare; new immigrants and refugees getting special attention in getting a job, housing, and access to other public services; and minorities seen as advantaged by employment equity programs. Also part of this category are members of established ethnic groups who (or their parents) came to Canada without the government programs now available to new immigrants: resentment that newcomers now have advantages they did not have.

Third, there are those who experience a particular kind of status inconsistency. The traditional image of the immigrant is of one who starts at the bottom of the class structure and works hard to climb the socioeconomic hierarchy. The expectation is that they will, in general, occupy a status lower to that of the members of the receiving society.[17] But some immigrants, especially Chinese, appear to be starting quite high up in the structure. So, many middle-class people, workers, small business entrepreneurs, and unemployed workers resent the fact that immigrants are economically more successful than they are. Some white parents 'complain that school honour rolls are dominated by new immigrants' children, making it difficult for their own, less bookish children to get into the increasingly choosy [universities].' Some are offended by 'the Asian kids who have better cars than the teachers do' (Cernetig 1995: D2).

Fourth, there is a generalized fatigue with 'special interest groups' as revealed in a recent survey: 77 per cent of respondents were fed up with interest groups and governments whining about getting their 'fair share' from the federal purse – Ontarians being the most fed up (Ekos Research Associates 1995). A 1991 Angus Reid survey found that 50 per cent agree with the statement: 'I am sick and tired of some groups complaining about racism being directed at them,' and 41 per cent with the statement: 'I'm tired of ethnic minorities being given special treatment.'

Finally, over the past few years, nativistic ideologies have been propounded by political parties and other organizations. These have made it increasingly possible and legitimate to express the status anxieties, sense of relative deprivation, and resentment felt by individuals who feel displaced or threatened in some way. Indeed, nativism is a belief system and a set of attitudes 'most likely held by people in social groups that have the same racial, ethnic, and/or religious characteristics as the dominant class, but not the economic or political power ... [They] generally arise among previously dominant social elements during times of social, political, and economic crisis, suggesting a possible link with relative deprivation. The demand of nativist groups is for increased conformity to the historically based traditions and customs common to the territory' (Harrison 1995: 7, 164).[18]

Nativistic tendencies exist in all parts of the country, although their specific manifestations vary, the main differences being between Quebec and English-Canadian nativism. Ultra-nationalists in Quebec perceive such realities as the English language, federalism, and immigration as threatening the culture and survival of the Quebec 'people.' Similar groups and individuals in English-speaking Canada see threats to the Canadian identity and character as stemming from immigration and especially the multiculturalism ideology and policy.

Conclusion

Canada has clearly been in a state of transition, during the few past decades, with regard to all axes of ethnic differentiation. The direction in which it is evolving is still uncertain. This change has been taking place in the context of rapid change in many other areas of economic, political, and social life.

Profound changes have been taking place in the relationship between Native peoples, Quebec, and Francophones elsewhere, immigrants, white ethnic groups, and visible minorities, on the one hand, and relevant segments of the larger society, on the other. In various ways, these groups or categories of people have initiated the process of transforming and even of reversing their traditional condition and status in the society.

The amount of change in the different dimensions of the social structure may be why a relatively low consensus seems to exist in the country with regard to diagnoses and/or remedies around questions of ethnic and racial relations. There is considerable disagreement in Quebec: independentists, federalists, autonomists all have a certain base of support in the population. Native peoples do not agree on the particular political and administrative arrangements that would be acceptable.

Members of other ethnic groups hold different views on whether public institutions should incorporate ethnicity or should be de-ethnicized as much as possible.

Inter-ethnic relations turned out to be somewhat different from what Porter anticipated in *The Vertical Mosaic*, although his basic theoretical postulates proved to have validity. Porter saw the power structure as dominated primarily by the British charter group with the other groups located in lower strata. This pattern, however, was partly due to the historical British dominance, but it was also the result of institutional rigidities, that is, of educational and industrial institutions unable to produce opportunities for mobility. Immigration was a substitute for institutional reforms.

But a quiet revolution brought about institutional reforms in English-speaking Canada as well as in Quebec. The educational and industrial institutions that Porter blamed for the lack of mobility opportunities changed. These transformations facilitated the integration of immigrants and of their descendants. In short, the social order that existed at the time of Porter's analysis has changed, and as a result the mosaic is not as vertical as it used to be. Whether or not this will occur for non-white immigrants and their descendants is not clear. It may for some of the minorities, but not for others as their situations differ significantly (Kelly 1995) and as attitudes of whites are not the same *vis-à-vis* all visible minorities and neither are those of visible minorities *vis-à-vis* each other.

An examination of the contemporary socioeconomic order that adopted Porter's perspective would focus on the possible impact on ethnic stratification of phenomena such as the globalization of capital, labour and commodity markets, free trade agreements, and the technological transformations in industry, since these are clearly having an impact on the opportunity structure. Thus, the analysis would consider the changes in the occupational structure and in the functioning of labour markets, in the types of jobs and careers being created, and in the distribution of income. Patterns of socioeconomic competition appear to be changing, and this may well have an impact on ethnic stratification. This would be the case for resources distributed by either privately or publicly controlled institutions.[19]

Theory and research by sociologists and other social scientists has also evolved during the past decades, and these have tended to be along the lines of evolution of ethnic and racial realities in the society. It is impossible to summarize all the developments that have taken place in a few pages. However, it is possible to identify a few themes that seem to have received a fair amount of attention.

Ethnicity and Social Inequality

The theme that was prominent in Porter's writings – ethnicity and social inequality – continued to be at the centre of research preoccupations. As noted, the mosaic reflecting inequalities among ethnic groups of European origin seems to have faded considerably over time, a phenomenon that is consistent with part of Porter's analytic framework.

This does not mean, however, that ethnicity has no impact on patterns of inequality. First, birthplace remains a factor in socioeconomic attainment – immigrants, on the average, doing less well than native-born Canadians. Second, ethnic networks and concentrations in occupational niches can be assets as well as liabilities in socioeconomic mobility. There seems to be no simple relationship between the maintenance of ethnic identity and ties and lower chances of socioeconomic mobility: sometimes ethnicity is an asset, sometimes a liability (Reitz 1990). Third, contrary to the mosaic vs melting pot ideology, patterns of socioeconomic integration and of acculturation have been largely the same in Canada and in the United States. The same structural (e.g., the functioning of the labour market) and cultural forces (e.g., the 'Anglo-conformity' expectations) appear to be operating in both societal contexts (Reitz and Breton 1994).

Fourth, while ethnicity has decreased in importance, race has become critical in accounting for patterns of inequality. As noted, the colour difference may be of greater significance since it makes ethnic boundaries more visible. Accordingly, it may lead to more persistent patterns of social exclusion and discrimination than is the case when culture is the prime factor of differentiation. However, earlier immigrants of European origin were also subject to prejudice and discrimination. In fact, even among whites some minorities used to be seen as racially different and inferior.

During recent years, studies of ethnic inequalities have also paid more attention to the interaction of gender, ethnicity, and immigrant status. Research shows that immigrant women, particularly if they are members of visible minorities, experience multiple jeopardy in terms of socioeconomic attainment.[20] This is also the case for Aboriginal women (Gerber 1990).

An issue that has drawn some attention concerns the impact of employment equity programs on inequality along racial lines. This issue has generated a lot of research, mostly in the United States, but in Canada as well.[21] A key theoretical and empirical point is whether 'programs designed to improve the employability of various minority groups will end up with ... a reinforcement of the existing occupational distribution structure' (McAll 1991: 26).

Ethnic Identity and Cultural Maintenance

The study of ethnic identity and retention has been influenced by the concept of 'symbolic ethnicity' (Gans 1979) or 'affective ethnicity' (Weinfeld 1981). These concepts do not assume that identity and cultural retention necessarily go together; acculturation can take place while ethnic identity remains, although transformed. A related line of research has been on the selective character of ethnic cultural retention (Isajiw 1990). In these developments, the idea is that acculturation is not an all-or-none phenomenon, but one that takes place selectively depending on the ethnic group and perhaps especially on the social context. What is retained is a function not only of what is valued by the group itself, but also of what is seen as acceptable or legitimate in the larger cultural context. Ethnicity is largely 'situational' (Nagata 1974). It is 'not a constant inherited from the past, but the result of a process which continues to unfold.' It has relatively little to do with the culture of origin, but much more 'with the exigencies of survival and the structure of opportunity' in the adopted country (Yancey et al. 1976: 400).

Ethnicity and the State

Recent decades have witnessed massive state intervention in society generally and in the management of ethnicity and inter-ethnic relations in particular. Given this reality, it is not surprising that the preoccupation with its impact has also gained importance. A basic theoretical concern has to do with the extent to which and the ways in which government intervention shapes the organization of ethnic communities, either directly or indirectly; affects the saliency of ethnic boundaries and the significance of their role in social relationships and in the functioning of institutions; and stimulates the politics of identity and recognition. The effects could stem directly from the policies of programs themselves or through the ethnic/racial categorizations produced for the administration of programs, for the distribution of resources, and for public recognition practices.

As a result, political power and influence seem to have acquired greater salience than economic issues in shaping intergroup relations. Identity, status, and their symbolic expression – the politics of identity and recognition – have also acquired considerable significance. To a large extent, intergroup competition and tensions are over the allocation of symbolic resources among groups by larger society and its institutions, particularly the state.

Primordialism versus Mobilization

Perhaps one of the most important theoretical developments in recent decades is the counterbalancing of the ascriptive conception of ethnicity with the view of ethnicity as a socially constructed phenomenon. This dual view influenced the study of many aspects of ethnicity, race, and intergroup relations. It is not really that new since it originates with Weber, who saw ethnic identities and affiliations as mobilizable resources for the control of resources such as jobs, institutional domains, and state policies (Neuwirth 1969). But beginning about the time of the publication of *The Vertical Mosaic*, this perspective was developed and applied more systematically than it had been up to then (Lyman and Douglass 1973; Cohen 1974; Bell 1975; McKay 1982; Breton 1991).

Indeed, this view – that ethnicity is not only a matter of primordial ties and identity but also a base on which to build in social 'networking,' in organizing for social purposes, in mobilizing in order to influence government or other institutional policies, and generally to be used strategically in improving one's situation in the community or society – is present, as seen above, in the research on social inequality, employment equity, ethnic maintenance, the politics of identity and recognition, and the analysis of state policies with regard to language, race, and ethnicity.

Notes

1 I wish to thank Professors Rick Helmes-Hayes, James Curtis, Harold Troper, and Jeffrey Reitz for their valuable comments on an earlier version of this chapter.
2 For an excellent summary and analysis of Porter's views on ethnicity and stratification, see Vallee (1981).
3 Some of Porter's ideas are discussed further in what follows.
4 The Friends of the United Nations commissioned a panel of advisers to

choose fifty model communities: 360 communities were considered and of the fifty winners three were in Canada: Walpole Island First Nations community near Windsor, Ontario, Sanikiluaq Inuit community in eastern Hudson Bay, and the community of the Oujé-Bougoumou Crees of Northern Quebec (Valpy 1995).

5 The Indian Register is a list of all persons legally entitled to be registered as status Indians rather than just those who may be ethnically defined as status Indians (e.g., a non-Indian woman who marries a status Indian man is legally entitled to be registered as a status Indian, even if she is not of North American Indian ethnic origin) (Ponting 1988: 15).

6 The counts of status Indians presented above come from the register maintained by the Department of Indian Affairs and Northern Development and not from the census. In fact, the census enumerated only 380,900 status or registered Indians in 1991, a count that is much lower than the 511,791 included in the register.

7 Throughout this century, immigrants have constituted less than 10 per cent of the Quebec population (Badets 1993: 9).

8 An illustration is the title of a book on the history of the Finnish Organization of Canada: *Builders of Canada* (Eklund 1987).

9 Questions varied from poll to poll, referring to either 'separation' or 'independence' (Pinard 1992: 3).

10 The concept was developed to examine ethnic minorities consisting of immigrants and their descendants (Breton 1964), but it is eminently applicable to Quebec Francophones – a collectivity that shows a degree of institutional completeness by far higher than that of any other minority in the country.

11 They are Hamilton, Kitchener, Windsor, Calgary, Victoria, St Catharines–Niagara, London, Edmonton, Winnipeg, Oshawa, Montreal, Ottawa-Hull, and Thunder Bay.

12 They are Regina, Saskatoon, Sudbury, and Halifax.

13 For an interesting overview of recent developments on this question, see Agocs and Boyd (1993).

14 The survey was conducted by Decima Research for the Canadian Council of Christians and Jews; the total sample size was 1,200.

15 On the impact of social categorization on intergroup relations, see Billig and Tajfel (1973). For an interesting analysis of official ethnic categorizations, see Fontaine and Shiose (1991), and Shiose and Fontaine (1995).

16 This is the case for what Runciman (1966) has labelled 'fraternalistic relative deprivation' which refers to feelings of deprivation not with one's position as an individual but with the position of one's ingroup in society (Dion 1986: 167).

17 On the social impact of the violation of status expectation, see Hughes (1958) and Kemper (1979).
18 See Barrett (1987) on extremist groups promoting racist ideologies.
19 I am grateful to Jeffrey Reitz for alerting me to this dimension of Porter's analysis.
20 For a review of the literature, see Labelle (1990).
21 For a brief review of the literature on this issue, see McAll (1991: 25–7).

References

Agocs, Carol, and Monica Boyd. (1993). 'The Canadian Ethnic Mosaic Recast: Theory, Research and Policy Frameworks for the 1990s'. Pp. 330–52 in James Curtis, Edward Grabb, and Neil Guppy (eds.), *Social Inequality in Canada: Patterns, Problems and Policies* (2nd ed.). Scarborough: Prentice-Hall.

Badets, Jane. (1993). 'Canada's Immigrants: Recent Trends.' *Canadian Social Trends* Summer: 8–11.

Barrett, Stanley R. (1987). *Is God a Racist? The Right Wing in Canada*. Toronto: University of Toronto Press.

Beattie, Christopher. (1975). *Minority Men in a Majority Setting*. Toronto: McClelland and Stewart.

Behiels, Michael. (1985). *Prelude to Quebec's Quiet Revolution*. Montreal: McGill-Queen's University Press.

Bell, Daniel. (1975). 'Ethnicity and Social Change.' Pp. 141–74 in Nathan Glazer and Daniel P. Moynihan (eds.), *Ethnicity: Theory and Experience*. Cambridge: Harvard University Press.

Bellah, Robert N., Richard Madsen, William M. Sullivan, Ann Swidler, and Steven M. Tipton (1985). *Habits of the Heart: Individualism and Commitment in American Life*. New York: Harper and Row.

Bernier, Luc. (1993). 'State-Owned Enterprises in Quebec: The Full Cycle, 1969–1990.' Pp. 243–58 in Alain-G. Gagnon (ed.), *Quebec: State and Society* (2nd ed.). Scarborough: Nelson.

Berry, John W., Rudolf Kalin, and Donald M. Taylor. (1977). *Multiculturalism and Ethnic Attitudes in Canada*. Ottawa: Supply and Services Canada.

Billig, Michael, and Henri Tajfel. (1973). 'Social Categorization and Similarity in Intergroup Behaviour.' *European Journal of Social Psychology* 3: 27–52.

Billson, Janet Mancini. (1991). 'Interlocking Identities: Gender, Ethnicity, and Power in the Canadian Context.' *International Journal of Canadian Studies* 3: 49–67.

Bovey, Wilfrid. (1936). *Canadien: étude sur les Canadiens français* (3rd ed.). London: Dent (English version).

110   Raymond Breton

Boyd, Monica. (1992). 'Gender, Visible Minority, and Immigrant Earnings Inequality: Reassessing an Employment Equity Premise.' Pp. 279–321 in Vic Satzewich (ed.), *Deconstructing a Nation: Immigration, Multiculturalism and Racism in the 1990s in Canada*. Toronto: Fernwood.

Breton, Raymond. (1964). 'Institutional Completeness of Ethnic Communities and the Personal Relations of Immigrants.' *American Journal of Sociology* 70: 193–205.

– (1978). 'Stratification and Conflict between Ethnolinguistic Communities with Different Social Structures.' *Canadian Review of Sociology and Anthropology* 15 (2): 148–57.

– (1984). 'The Production and Allocation of Symbolic Resources: An Analysis of the Linguistic and Ethnocultural Fields in Canada.' *Canadian Review of Sociology and Anthropology* 21(2): 123–44.

– (1986). 'Multiculturalism and Canadian Nationbuilding.' Pp. 27–66 in Alan Cairns and Cynthia Williams (eds.), *The Politics of Gender, Ethnicity and Language in Canada*. Toronto: University of Toronto Press.

– (1988). 'English-French Relations in Canada.' Pp. 557–86 in Lorne Tepperman and James Curtis (eds.), *Understanding Canadian Society*. Toronto: McGraw-Hill Ryerson.

– (1991). *The Governance of Ethnic Communities: Political Structures and Processes in Canada*. Westport, CT: Greenwood.

Brym, Robert, with Bonnie J. Fox. (1989). *From Culture to Power: The Sociology of English Canada*. Toronto: Oxford University Press.

Burnet, Jean. (1979). 'Separate or Equal: A Dilemma of Multiculturalism.' Pp. 176–83 in A.W. Rasporich (ed.), *The Social Sciences and Public Policy in Canada*. Calgary: Faculty of Social Sciences, University of Calgary.

Canada, Department of Indian Affairs and Northern Development (1969). *Statement of the Government of Canada on Indian Policy*. Ottawa: Indian Affairs.

– (1995). *Basic Departmental Data – 1994*. Ottawa: Supply and Services.

Canada, Statistics Canada. (1963). *Population: Ethnic Groups by Age Groups*. Bulletin 1.3–2. Ottawa: Queen's Printer.

– (1995). *Profile of the Aboriginal Population of Canada*. Ottawa: Ministry of Industry, Science and Technology. Cat. no. 94–325.

Cernetig, Miro. (1995). 'White Flight, Chinese Distress.' *Globe and Mail*, 30 September: D1.

Clark, S.D. (1975). 'The Post Second World War Canadian Society.' *Canadian Review of Sociology and Anthropology* 12(1): 25–32.

Cohen, Abner. (1974). 'Introduction: The Lessons of Ethnicity.' Pp. 1–36 in Abner Cohen (ed.), *Urban Ethnicity*. London: Tavistock.

Connor, Walker. (1972). 'Nation-Building or Nation-Destroying?' *World Politics* 24: 319–55.

Darroch, Gordon A. (1979). 'Another Look at Ethnicity, Stratification and Social Mobility in Canada.' *Canadian Journal of Sociology* 4(1): 1–25.

Dion, Kenneth L. (1986). 'Responses to Perceived Discrimination and Relative Deprivation.' Pp. 159–79 in James M. Olson (ed.), *Relative Deprivation and Social Comparison*. Ontario Symposium, vol. 4. Hillsdale, NJ: Erlbaum.

Eklund, William. (1987) *Builders of Canada: History of the Finnish Organization of Canada, 1911–1971*. Toronto: Finnish Organization of Canada.

Ekos Research Associates. (1995). *Rethinking Government '94*. Ottawa: Ekos Research Associates.

Fontaine, Louise, and Yuki Shiose. (1991). 'Ni Citoyens, ni Autres: la Catégorie Politique "Communauté culturelle."' Pp. 435–43 in C. Emeri et al. (eds.), *Citoyenneté et Nationalité: Perspectives en France et au Québec*. Paris: Presses Universitaires de France.

Foster, Cecil. (1994). 'The Mood has Soured.' *Maclean's*. 7 February, p. 33.

Frideres, James S. (1993). *Native peoples in Canada: Contemporary Conflicts* (4th Ed.). Scarborough: Prentice-Hall.

Gans, Herbert. (1979). 'Symbolic Ethnicity: The Future of Ethnic Groups and Cultures.' *Ethnic and Racial Studies* 2: 1–20.

Gerber, Linda. (1979). 'The Development of Canadian Indian Communities: A Two-Dimensional Typology Reflecting Strategies of Adaptation to the Outside World.' *Canadian Review of Sociology and Anthropology* 16(4): 123–50.

– (1990). 'Multiple Jeopardy: A Socioeconomic Comparison of Men and Women among the Indian, Métis, and Inuit Peoples of Canada.' *Canadian Ethnic Studies* 22(3): 69–84.

Gibbins, Roger, and J. Rick Ponting. (1986). 'An Assessment of the Probable Impact of Aboriginal Self-Government in Canada.' Pp. 171–245 in Alan Cairns and Cynthia Williams (eds.), *The Politics of Gender, Ethnicity and Language in Canada*. Toronto: University of Toronto Press.

Guindon, Hubert. (1964). 'Social Unrest, Social Class, and Quebec's Bureaucratic Revolution.' *Queen's Quarterly* 70: 150–62.

– (1968). 'Two Cultures: An Essay on Nationalism, Class, and Ethnic Tension.' Pp. 33–59 in Richard H. Leach (ed.), *Contemporary Canada*. Toronto: University of Toronto Press.

Harney, Robert F. (1988). '"So Great a Heritage as Ours" – Immigration and the Survival of the Canadian Polity.' *Daedalus* 117: 51–97.

Harrison, Trevor. (1995). *Of Passionate Intensity: Right-Wing Populism and the Reform Party of Canada*. Toronto: University of Toronto Press.

Hawthorn, H.B. (ed.). (1966-7). *A Survey of the Contemporary Indians of Canada: Economic, Political, Educational Needs and Policies*, 2 vols. Ottawa: Department of Indian Affairs.

Horowitz, Donald L. (1985). *Ethnic Groups in Conflict*. Berkeley: University of California Press.

Hughes, Everett C. (1958). *Men and Their Work*. New York: Free Press.

Isajiw, Wsevolod W. (1990). 'Ethnic-Identity Retention.' Pp. 34–91 in Raymond Breton, Wsevolod W. Isajiw, Warren E. Kalbach, and Jeffrey G. Reitz, *Ethnic Identity and Equality: Varieties of Experience in a Canadian City*. Toronto: University of Toronto Press.

Juteau-Lee, Danielle, and Jean Lapointe. (1982). 'From French Canadians to Franco-Ontarians and Ontarois: New Boundaries, New Identities.' Pp. 173–86 in Jean Elliott (ed.), *Two Nations, Many Cultures*. Scarborough: Prentice-Hall.

Kallen, Evelyn. (1988). 'The Meech Lake Accord: Entrenching a Pecking Order of Minority Rights.' *Canadian Public Policy* 14: S107–20.

Kelly, Karen. (1995). 'Visible Minorities: A Diverse Group.' *Canadian Social Trends* 37 (Summer): 2–8.

Kemper, Theodore D. (1979). 'Why Are the Streets So Dirty? Social Psychological and Stratification Factors in the Decline of Municipal Services.' *Social Forces* 58: 422–42.

Krosenbrink-Gelissen, Lilianne Ernestine. (1993). 'The Native Women's Association of Canada.' Pp. 335–64 in James S. Frideres (ed.), *Native peoples in Canada: Contemporary Conflicts*. (4th Ed.) Scarborough: Prentice-Hall.

Labelle, Micheline. (1990). 'Femmes et Migrations au Canada: Bilan et Perspectives.' *Canadian Ethnic Studies* 22(1): 67–82.

Lautard, Hugh, and Neil Guppy. (1990). '*The Vertical Mosaic* Revisited: Occupational Differentials among Canadian Ethnic Groups.' Pp. 189–208 in Peter Li (ed.), *Race and Ethnic Relations in Canada*. Toronto: Oxford University Press.

Little Bear, Leroy, Menno Boldt, and J. Anthony Long (eds.). (1984). *Pathways to Self-Determination: Canadian Indians and the Canadian State*. Toronto: University of Toronto Press.

Lyman, Stanford M., and William A. Douglass. (1973). 'Ethnicity: Strategies of Collective and Individual Impression Management.' *Social Research* 40: 344–65.

Marshall, T.H. (1965). *Social Policy in the Twentieth Century*. London: Hutchison.

McAll, Christopher. (1991). *Beyond Culture: Immigration in Contemporary Quebec*. Ottawa: Economic Council of Canada, Working Paper No. 25.

McInnis, Edgar. (1969). *Canada: A Political and Social History*. Toronto: Holt, Rinehart, and Winston.

McKay, James. (1982). 'An Exploratory Synthesis of Primordial and Mobilizationist Approaches to Ethnic Phenomena.' *Ethnic and Racial Studies* 54: 395–420.

Mead, George Herbert. (1934). *Mind, Self and Society*. Chicago: University of Chicago Press.

Miller, James R. (1989). *Skyscrapers Hide the Heavens: A History of Indian–White Relations in Canada* (2nd ed.). Toronto: University of Toronto Press.

Morrison, Bruce R., and C. Roderick Wilson (eds). (1995). *Native peoples: The Canadian Experience* (2nd ed.). Toronto: McClelland and Stewart.

Nagata, Judith. (1974). 'What Is a Maly? Situational Selection of Ethnic Identity in a Plural Society.' *American Ethnologist* 1: 331–50.

Neuwirth, Gertrud. (1969). 'A Weberian Outine of a Theory of Community: Its Application to the "Dark Ghetto."' *British Journal of Sociology* 20: 148–63.

Norris, Mary Jane. (1990). 'The Demography of Aboriginal People in Canada.' Pp. 33–60 in Shiva S. Halli, Frank Trovato, and Leo Driedger (eds.), *Ethnic Demography: Canadian Immigrant, Racial and Cultural Variations*. Ottawa: Carleton University Press.

Ogmundson, R., and J. McLaughlin. (1992). 'Trends in the Ethnic Origins of Canadian Elites: The Decline of the BRITS?' *Canadian Review of Sociology and Anthropology* 29(2): 227–38.

Pal, Leslie A. (1993). *Interests of State: The Politics of Language, Multiculturalism, and Feminism in Canada*. Montreal: McGill-Queen's University Press.

Palmer, Howard. (1976). 'Mosaic versus Melting Pot? Immigration and Ethnicity in Canada and the United States.' *International Journal* 31: 488–528.

Pelletier, Réjean. (1990). 'Social Transformation and Political Change in Quebec: Political Parties and the State.' Pp. 297–322 in Raymond Breton, Gilles Houle, Gary Caldwell, Edmund Mokrzycki, and Edmund Wnuk-Lipinski (eds.), *National Survival in Dependent Societies*. Ottawa: Carleton University Press.

Pinard, Maurice. (1992). 'The Quebec Independence Movement: A Dramatic Resurgence.' Montreal: McGill University, Department of Sociology, Working Paper No. 92-06.

– (1994). 'De Meech et Charlottetown au ... Québec.' *Opinion Canada* 2(3).

Pinard, Maurice, and Richard Hamilton. (1984). 'The Class Bases of the Quebec Independence Movement: Conjectures and Evidence.' *Ethnic and Racial Studies* 7:19–54.

Ponting, J. Rick. (1988). 'Public Opinion on Aboriginal Peoples' Issues in Canada.' *Canadian Social Trends* 11 (Winter): 9–17.

– (1990). 'Internationalization: Perspectives on an Emerging Direction in Aboriginal Affairs.' *Canadian Ethnic Studies* 22(3): 85–109.

Ponting, J. Rick, and Roger Gibbins. (1980). *Out of Irrelevance: A Socio-Political Introduction to Indian Affairs in Canada*. Toronto: Butterworths.

Porter, John. (1965). *The Vertical Mosaic: An Analysis of Social Class and Power in Canada*. Toronto: University of Toronto Press.

– (1972). 'Dilemmas and Contradictions of a Multi-Ethnic Society.' *Transactions of the Royal Society of Canada*, Series 4, vol. 10: 193–205.

114   Raymond Breton

- (1975). 'Ethnic Pluralism in Canadian Perspective.' Pp. 267–304 in Nathan Glazer and Daniel P. Moynihan (eds.), *Ethnicity: Theory and Experience*. Cambridge: Harvard University Press.
- (1979). 'Melting Pot or Mosaic: Revolution or Reversion?' Pp.139–62 in J. Porter, *The Measure of Canadian Society*. Toronto: Gage.
Pross, Paul. (1986). *Group Politics and Public Policy*. Toronto: Oxford University Press.
Reitz, Jeffrey G. (1990). 'Ethnic Concentrations in Labour Markets and Their Implications for Ethnic Inequality.' Pp. 135–86 in Raymond Breton, Wsevolod W. Isajiu, Warren E. Kalbach, and Jeffrey G. Reitz, *Ethnic Identity and Equality: Varieties of Experience in a Canadian City*. Toronto: University of Toronto Press.
Reitz, Jeffrey G., and Raymond Breton. (1994). *The Illusion of Difference: Realities of Ethnicity in Canada and the United States*. Toronto: C.D. Howe Institute.
Rosanvallon, Pierre. (1995). *La Nouvelle Question Sociale*. Paris, Seuil.
Runciman, W.G. (1966). *Relative Deprivation and Social Justice*. Berkeley: University of California Press.
Savas, Daniel J. (1987). 'Interest Group Leadership and Government Funding,' PhD thesis, University of British Columbia.
Secretary of State, Canada. (1976). *Multicultural Program Granting Activity, Fiscal 1974–1975*. Ottawa.
Shiose, Yuki, and Louise Fontaine. (1995). 'La Construction des Figures de l'"Autre": les Communautés Culturelles au Québec.' *Revue Canadienne de Sociologie et d'Anthropologie* 32(1): 91–110.
Siggner, Andrew J. (1986). 'The Socio-Demographic Conditions of Registered Indians.' Pp. 57–83 in J. Rick Ponting (ed.), *Arduous Journey: Canadian Indians and Decolonization*. Toronto: McClelland and Stewart.
Stasiulis, Daiva. (1987). 'Rainbow Feminism: Anti-Racist Politics and the Canadian Women's Movement.' *Resources for Feminist Research* 16: 1–10.
Vaillancourt, François. (1993). 'The Economic Status of the French Language and Francophones in Québec.' Pp. 407–21 in Alain-G. Gagnon (ed.), *Quebec: State and Society* (2nd ed.). Scarborough: Nelson.
Valentine, Victor. (1980). 'Native peoples and Canadian Society: A Profile of Issues and Trends.' Pp. 45–135 in Raymond Breton, Jeffrey G. Reitz, and Victor Valentine, *Cultural Boundaries and the Cohesion of Canada*. Montreal: Institute for Research on Public Policy.
Vallee, Frank G. (1981). 'The Sociology of John Porter: Ethnicity as Anachronism.' *Canadian Review of Sociology and Anthropology* 18(5): 639–50.
Valpy, Michael. (1995). 'Three Award-Winning Communities.' *Globe and Mail*, 26 September.

Weinfeld, Morton. (1981). 'Myth and Reality in the Canadian Mosaic: "Affective Ethnicity."' *Canadian Ethnic Studies* 13: 80–100.

Wilson, V. Seymour. (1993). 'The Tapestry Vision of Canadian Multi-Culturalism.' *Canadian Journal of Political Science* 26: 645–69.

Yancey, William B., Eugene Ericksen, and Richard Juliani. (1976). 'Emergent Ethnicity: A Review and Reformulation.' *American Sociological Review* 41: 391–403.

Missing Women: A Feminist Perspective on *The Vertical Mosaic*

PAT ARMSTRONG

Fitting Women In

My first idea about how to address the problem of the missing women was to begin by fitting women into *The Vertical Mosaic*. But this did not work for two important reasons.

The first reason is that women were indeed missing from the elites Porter described. In fact, Porter (1965: 264) made it quite clear that 'there are no women' in his economic elite and that Diefenbaker 'broke new ground bringing a woman into Cabinet' (1965: 396). He wrote about 'Dr Clark's Boys' (1965: 425) and 'C.D. Howe's Men' (1965: 430) in the federal bureaucracy, without feeling the need to point out women's absence. Porter assumed we will all know that women are not among the high clergy, the 'men of science,' or among those owning the media. He noted that there were a few women in the labour elite and four women in Section II of the Royal Society, adding that 'although this was a small number of women it was a greater proportion than appeared in the other elite groups' (1965: 501).

Some things have changed since Porter wrote *The Vertical Mosaic*. For one, there are more women in these elites, especially in the academic and labour ones (Marshall 1987). It must be recognized, however, that it would be virtually impossible to have fewer of them. For another, we have a great deal of research from the decade or so following *The Vertical Mosaic* on the role of women in the economy (Agocs 1985), in politics (Vickers 1978), in the bureaucracy (Archibald 1970), in the clergy (Wallace 1976), in the media (Fournier and Diamond 1987), in unions (White 1980), and in academe (McDonald and Lenglet 1973). But, as Margrit Eichler (1975: 475) pointed out in her 1975 review of the research on women, 'Without exception, these studies always find the same syndrome: women are poorly (if at all) represented in the upper echelon occupations, they are paid less than men in comparable positions, and they are vastly overrepresented in lower echelon occupations.' And while this research both reflected and promoted change, women are still mainly missing from the seats of power that Porter described (Armstrong 1989; Armstrong and Armstrong 1992). For those concerned about women, then, it makes more sense to look at where women are rather than focus primarily on where they are not.

Women are not simply missing from *The Vertical Mosaic* in the sense of what Porter called the absence of 'elite roles for women.' The second reason I could not begin by putting women into Porter's book is that women are also missing from the theory that guides his analysis. They are missing from the theory in a way that makes it very difficult to use that theory to include them. Porter told us that 'few women occupy positions of power because it is not "appropriate" that women should' (1965: 264). However, he offered no further explanation for women's exclusion or even of what he meant by "appropriate"; indeed he made very little comment on the missing women after this point about the economic elite. Earlier, he told us that women and men who immigrated to fill the lower level jobs did quite different kinds of work (1965: 57). He even noted that 68 per cent of the female labour force was concentrated in just three occupational categories (1965: 81) and that 'a high proportion of low-income recipients in the income tax statistics were married women and their husbands' (1965: 111).

Yet Porter's analysis rested on a notion of class primarily based on characteristics of the male labour force. However, beginning with Margaret Benston (1969: 14) in the years shortly after *The Vertical Mosaic* appeared, feminists have been demonstrating that 'women as a group do indeed have a definite relation to the means of production and that this is different from that of men.' Equally problematic is Porter's way of establishing classes; a way that leaves the impression that class is primarily about distributive categories rather than about what Dorothy Smith called the 'relations of ruling' (see Clement and Myles 1994). By conceptualizing class in this manner, Porter left out of the theory the many significant ways power is used to ensure male dominance in class relations and the ways these relations shift over time. Conceptualizing class in this manner means both looking at how relations change over time, often through struggle, and also at how classes are constructed as relations.

Porter's notion of class also assumes that what male owners and workers do in the market determines class position. This approach not only fails to problematize the specific ways women relate through the formal market, but it also fails to take the household into account, except through the marriages that tie male elites together. Porter had a great deal of company in making these assumptions. Indeed, theorists from all perspectives tended to treat class as a male category based on male employment in the labour force. This was as true for political economists as it was for traditional stratification theorists (Maroney and Luxton 1987).

In 1973, in one of the first Canadian publications addressing the issue of how to conceptualize class to include women, Dorothy Smith (1973: 17–18) argued:

Questions of how the mode of production determines features of the social structure cannot be treated as if they were questions about the interaction between economic and other institutional orders. The differentiation of economic and other institutional orders is itself a feature of a specific mode of production, and the underlying determinations of the relations between differentiated institutional modes are to be found only by viewing them as part of a total organization of productive activity. We have to characterize the mode of production at a more fundamental level, a level which determines not just the character of the economy and the family, but their separation; not merely that they are separate, but how their separation separates women from the locus of 'where history is made to happen.'

Some feminists looked for the roots of women's inequality in ideas learned in the socialization process and reflected in male discrimination against women; to what Porter may have meant by notions of 'appropriate' female work. Others looked to biology as an explanation of ideology and inequality (see Armstrong and Armstrong 1990b). These theories helped expose both the ideas that are a central component in inequality and the fundamental power differences between women and men. But feminists taking these approaches were not focused on understanding class.

Those who were primarily concerned with figuring out how to reconceptualize class in order to understand gender inequality struggled through a variety of ways to use marxist analytical tools to not only redefine class but also to expand the notion of political economy to include the household. What came to be called the "domestic labour debate" raged among feminists over the next decade. Through these debates, feminists explored the complex connections between domestic and wage labour, and their significance for class relations (Armstrong and Armstrong 1983). While these debates did not produce a definitive way of conceptualizing class, they did make it clear that women have a different relationship to production and reproduction than do men. Moreover, they also revealed significant differences among women in terms of their reproductive and productive work, making class differences among women more visible. They explored the interpenetration of household and formal economy, exposing the permeable and shifting boundaries that helped shape class relations. After these debates, it was evident that collapsing class into distributive categories based on male labour force work failed both to capture class differences and to reveal how class relations work.

Empirical studies drawing on these feminist theories led to new ways of viewing class. Based on their attempts to understand class relations in fishing communities from the broader perspective called for in the domestic labour debates, Patricia Connelly and Martha MacDonald (1983: 46), for example, argued 'that working class households have always required more than the male wage and that women have always contributed to the maintenance of the family household either by intensifying their domestic labour in the home, by earning money through the informal economy, or by participating in the labour force and earning a wage themselves.'

A notion of class that includes both household and formal economy, they argued, allows us not only to take differences among women into account but also to better understand the class relations of men. 'In the fishing community, there was a complementarity between inshore fishing for men and plant work for women. The female labour reserve was activated and was a major element in the survival of the "independent" producer and the underdevelopment of the industry' (Connelly and MacDonald 1983: 67). Research such as that done by Bettina Bradbury (1993) on Montreal families in the nineteenth century and by Joy Parr (1990) on Ontario households early in the twentieth century supports the argument that class theory must consider work both in and out of the household, and must make differences between and among women central to that account.

The need to theorize women's subordination, then, led many feminists away from a notion of class as a category and towards a view of class as a relation. This relation encompassed both the formal economy and the household, along with their continually shifting boundaries and interpenetration. Class was viewed as a relation that developed through struggle and daily interaction, rather than simply through structured inequality. As we put it more than a decade ago (Armstrong and Armstrong 1983: 30): 'Theories that are blind to sex differences obscure not only divisions fundamental to all classes, but also the structure of capitalism. The working class, as well as the ruling class, has two sexes. Without acknowledging these divisions – without integrating them into a class analysis – neither capitalism nor households can be understood.' Other theorists have made it clear that relations among women related to race, immigration status, and disability must also be an integral part of analysis related to power and inequality (see, e.g., Brand 1991; Henry et al. 1995; and Ng 1988a).

Of course, it is one thing to call for a different approach to class and another thing to do it in practice. This is a very large, and difficult, project; one that feminists are far from accomplishing. Neverthless, it is still a necessary one if we are to not only understand how classes form but also how they make change. As Patricia Connelly and I (1992: ix) put it more recently:

Class has to be reconceptualized through race and gender within regional, national, and international contexts. The static categorizing of class that has been used in so much class analysis does not capture the experience of gender, race, ethnicity or class. Class is dynamic and relational and it is a fundamental basis for change. While gender, race, ethnic and national identities are never absent, they interact with class in various ways with one being more salient than another at different points in time.

While Porter's analysis of class did look at how the elites used their power to ensure the dominance of white, Anglo-Saxon men, his approach to class was based on a category derived almost exclusively from the market. Although it would be easy enough to count the women the way he counted men, it is much more difficult to integrate the complex character of women's subordination, especially as it related to race and region, into this approach.

It is difficult to understand women's subordination by relying on Porter's ideas about skill and equal opportunity, and his view of the role of the state. For Porter, skill was a category primarily related to objective criteria. Although he did recognize that there are subjective and relational elements to the evaluation of skills, he nevertheless assumed that the main determinants of skill could be found in the characteristics of the job or the worker. He challenged the assumption that a shift from manual to white-collar work was necessarily evidence of upward mobility on the grounds that clerical workers 'are more akin to unskilled workers from the point of view of both their training and their earnings' (1965: 51). For Porter, this explained why 'workers in the highly skilled trades' assigned to office work 'medium or very low ratings both in terms of social prestige and as a desired occupation for their sons' (Porter 1965: 52). As Jane Gaskell (1986) and others have pointed out, however, skill is more socially constructed than it is objectively determined, and the sex of the workers plays an important part in this social construction (Armstrong and Armstrong 1991).

In her study of clerical work, Gaskell (1986: 378) concluded:

The time and form that training for a job take are created through a process of political struggle between workers and capital ... [S]ome male workers have been able to retain relatively lengthy apprenticeships with restricted access while women in clerical work are trained in programmes that are short and widely available. While one might argue that neither job is actually very difficult to learn, or that both are quite difficult, there is little basis for arguing that one is significantly more difficult to acquire than the other. The differences arise in the power of organized male workers, their ability to monopolize access to their skills and the unwillingness of employers to invest in training women.

For many feminists, then, it is not only the skill rating but also the evaluation of training itself that must be understood as fundamentally linked to the gender of the worker and the struggle over what gets defined as skill. Unlike Porter, who saw skill as primarily attached to the workers and largely separated from the workplace and conditions of work, they saw skills as negotiated and as a reflection of power.

Many feminists would also find Porter's stress on assimilation and equal opportunity problematic. When speaking of the association between 'ethnic affiliation and social class,' Porter said that 'a democratic society may require a breaking down of the ethnic impediment to equality, particularly the equality of opportunity' (1965: 73). He recognized what would today be called structural or systemic discrimination and advocated 'structural assimilation,' a condition that exists 'when ethnic origin is not a relevant attribute in the allocation of people to positions in the social system or in the distribution of rights' (1965: 72). Equal treatment in school and work was the logical way of addressing inequality understood in these terms.

However, as Rosalie Abella (Canada 1984) pointed out in her report for the Royal Commission on Equality in Employment, to treat everyone the same is to offend the principle of equality precisely because women, the disabled, visible minorities, and Aboriginal peoples are differently located. These groups start from different, and unequal, positions and thus require different, rather than the same, treatment if they are to have similar opportunities. Moreover, as Mary O'Brien so eloquently explained in *The Politics of Reproduction* (1981), women's unique reproductive capacity makes it extremely difficult to think of equity as assimilation. While women certainly vary in terms of whether or not and how they experience reproduction, their reproductive capacities make them distinct from men. Certainly the consequences of this capacity are socially constructed and evaluated, and thus need not lead to subordination, but they cannot easily be assimilated away.

For Porter, the main key to assimilation and equality of opportunity was the education system. He analysed the social, psychological, and economic barriers to equality in education and showed how they limit access. While he failed to mention gender barriers, it would be easy enough to add women in if the theory was to be left unchallenged. Indeed, like some feminists, Porter later did just that (Porter, Porter, and Blishen 1973). But his notion of equity leaves little room for an understanding of the profound sexism in the education system that feminists like Susan Russell (1986) have revealed or the reproduction of the relations of ruling that Smith (1973, 1987) theorized. Moreover, a multitude of feminists have demonstrated that the different, and unequal, conditions women face from birth lead to ideas and practices too difficult to overcome by the time they reach school. It is the conditions of their lives and the relations of ruling, as much as what happens in school, that shape their opportunities.

The focus on education as the solution leads to my final problem with fitting women into Porter's theory. In his approach, the state remains largely unexplained. It is primarily in terms of the education system that Porter discussed state intervention, although he did document the role the state plays in perpetuating racial inequality. He was much more concerned with who is in politics and in the government bureaucracy than with what the state does. Yet, as Carolyn Andrew (1984), for example, made clear, the state in all its manifestations plays a critical role in women's lives and in turn is shaped by women's demands. Through its regulation of the household and formal economy, through the provision of services, and through its employment practices, the state has an enormous impact on women's possibilities. It is the state that structures, to a large extent, what is public and private in the market economy and where the distinction between the private household and the formal economy is drawn (Armstrong and Armstrong 1990b: Chapter 7). And it is the state that can mediate the distribution of wealth and power (Calvert 1984). Without a theory that incorporates a broader notion of the state, it is very difficult to assess women's position today.

Using *The Vertical Mosaic* for Women

To argue that women cannot easily be fit into the theory and reality of *The Vertical Mosaic* is not to argue that the book has had little impact on the analysis of women's conditions or that it has little relevance today. In providing such a rigorous and thoroughly documented account of class and power, John Porter did more than any other Canadian academic to make the study of inequality legitimate. After *The Vertical Mosaic*, it was beyond dispute that Canada is a fundamentally unequal society, with a segregated labour force based more on what sociologists have called ascribed rather than achieved attributes. Equally important, Porter made this analysis accessible to a wide audience, while basing it on recognized academic practices. Although he had little to say about women, he did help set the stage for an analysis of gender inequality.

Indeed, as I reread *The Vertical Mosaic* in the context of the neo-conservative agenda sweeping the country, I was struck by how much we need the book today. We are experiencing a revolution that calls for a return to family values and to community responsibility, a return to a market economy through privatization and deregulation, a return to less government and lower taxes, and a return to a more flexible labour force. It is a revolution that is nostalgic for the good old days that Porter described; days characterized by enormous inequalities based on class, race, sex, region, and immigration status.

Women have made some important gains since the publication of *The Vertical Mosaic*. These gains are now under threat. In fact, women are the major targets in much of the neo-conservative agenda. So instead of trying to fit women into Porter's analysis, I want to outline some of these gains and some of these threats. It is an analysis that draws on the different approach I have already described. From my feminist political economy perspective, an analysis of class and power begins with a recognition of fundamental divisions based on sex and with an examination of where women are rather than with where they are not. It includes an analysis of struggles over power and of the changing conditions in and out of the household under which such struggles take place. It views the state both as a contested terrain and as a player that has a profound impact on the structure of private and public spheres.

Although it does not build on Porter's categories, mine is an analysis that is very much in keeping with Porter's concerns. In the first chapter of *The Vertical Mosaic*, Porter (1965: 6) lamented that 'There is scarcely any critical analysis of Canadian social life upon which a conflicting image could be based.' He went on to say that 'very little' of what intellectuals 'write could be considered social criticism. Their contribution therefore to dynamic dialogue is minimal' (1965: 500). What I want to do here is contribute to the dynamic dialogue by outlining how women's gains are being undermined by the neo-conservative and neo-liberal practices in Canada. I want to do this in the Porter tradition of social criticism, a tradition that encourages intellectual enquiry written in accessible language.

Where Women Fit

In the years since Porter wrote *The Vertical Mosaic*, Canada has changed fundamentally. During this period the economy has continued to grow – albeit less quickly and less consistently than in the years immediately before Porter wrote his famous book. Unions have continued to expand, and the women's movement has gained strength. The welfare state has reached maturity. No aspect of women's lives has remained untouched by these developments and some parts have altered dramatically.

Paid Work

The most obvious change has been in women's participation in the labour force. Although Porter was writing of a time when women made up less than a third of the labour force, they accounted for nearly half by the 1990s. Forty years ago, three-quarters of women did not work for pay; now nearly three-quarters of them do (Armstrong and Armstrong, 1994). Various forces contributed to this growth, but the most important were economic.

The Fordist regime of the postwar period was characterized by stable, full-time employment for men, especially in the relatively highly paid and highly unionized, male-dominated production workplaces in central Canada. 'In the fifties, stable prices and a strong economy gave wage earners their largest gains this century in purchasing power' ('Perspectives on Labour and Income' 1993: 5). For the first, and perhaps only, time in Canadian history, a large number of women were able to rely primarily on their husband's labour force income for economic support. The image of the full-time and fully supported housewife matched reality for a significant proportion of women for only that very short period. As Porter himself (1965: Chapter 1) made clear, full support often did not include the entire range of products associated with the good life. Moreover, even in the booming 1950s many low-income families achieved high consumption levels only 'through having more than one income earner in the household' (Porter 1965: 5). Many immigrant and Aboriginal families never shared in the boom, and neither did most families that included the disabled. For the single, widowed, and divorced women in the labour force, high consumption was rarely a possibility, given that during the 1950s women averaged half the male wage.

Even as Porter was writing, however, a growing number of men could not support a family on one income, as cracks in the postwar boom began to appear. The male unemployment rate was 2.5 per cent in 1951, and it had reached 8.4 per cent by 1961 (Statistics Canada 1993: Series D223–35). The rate has climbed even higher in recent years. Male wages no longer stayed ahead of prices, and, by the 1990s, the real average male wage actually fell (Rashid 1993: 18). As more and more men brought home less and less money, a growing number of married women entered the labour force, although economic need was not the only reason they had for taking paid work. In 1951 just over one in ten married women was counted as having paid work. By 1991 this was the case for more than six in ten (Armstrong and Armstrong 1994: Table 20). The flood into the labour force began with married women whose children were in school, but they were quickly followed by those with preschool children as well. By the 1990s the majority of women with children under six years of age were in the labour force (Statistics Canada 1994: Table 6.4).

For a time the wages of these women helped sustain the household income and, in some cases, even meant that its collective income increased (Armstrong and Armstrong 1978). However, by 1990, average family incomes were falling regardless of women's employment. 'The decline in real income was widespread among various types of families ... Among non-elderly families, the most notable losses were for those with family heads less than 25 years of age (down 12.8 per cent, to $31,499), for female lone-parent families (down 7.6 per cent to $21,086), and two-parent families with one income earner (down 7.4 per cent to $40,515)' (Statistics Canada 1992: 9).

Of course, not all women worked because they needed the income. Women, especially highly educated ones married to men with high incomes, also entered the labour force during this period. Indeed, their employment helped increase inequality among households (Chawla 1992; Duffy, 1988). Meanwhile, there were many women who could not take paid work even though they desperately needed the income. The scarcity of affordable and good day care meant many had little alternative but to stay home with their children. Hard-won state support for day care, particularly for single mothers, helped some with child care and thus improved their opportunities to take paid work. But their participation remained lower than that of other women, in part because they did not have other kinds of support and in part because welfare conditions often prevented them from taking paid work. Although there was variation among women in terms of pressures and possibilities, most women entered the labour force in order to provide necessary support for their households.

At the same time as women's need for income was increasing, so too was the demand for female labour. A major source of this demand was the state sector. Guided by Keynesian economic theory, pushed by strong labour and community groups, and without strong resistance from major employers, the state had expanded rapidly. Public health care, pensions, and new welfare services were introduced, while education services were extended considerably (Armstrong 1996a, 1996b; Yalnizyan 1994). There was a new emphasis on shared responsibility and shared risk. A notion of public responsibility for individual problems became increasingly common. These programs both reflected and reinforced ideas about collective rights while redefining what was public and what was private in the market. In many areas, the public was defined as both the logical and the best provider.

This provider was not always experienced as benevolent. For example, as the authors of *The Colour of Democracy* (Henry et al. 1995: 105) pointed out, an 'analysis of racism in policing, the justice system, and human services shows how the policies, programs, procedures and delivery systems of these major institutions discriminate against people of colour.' Women, too, had many complaints (Brodie 1996). Nevertheless, the state, as provider, did extend services enormously and in a more democratic manner than the largely private service system in the United States.

Women were hired to do most of this public sector work because they were available, because they had what were defined as the necessary skills, because they were cheap, and because this had traditionally been women's work. Besides, the majority of the men had found employment elsewhere, and the labour force remained highly segregated along male/female lines. In 1951 just over 260,000 women were employed in education, health, welfare, and public administration, accounting for a little less than a quarter of the entire female labour force. By 1981 there were nearly one and a half million women with jobs in these industries. Thirty per cent of employed women were being paid mainly by the state (Dominion Bureau of Statistics 1966: Table 12b; and Statistics Canada 1988: Table 2).

Demand, especially for clerical workers, also grew rapidly in the finance, insurance, and real estate sectors. The number of women working in these industries grew from 64,000 in 1951 to well over 400,000 in 1981. Demand grew even more rapidly in the accommodation and food services industries, where close to a half million women found paid work in 1981 (Dominion Bureau of Statistics 1966: Table 12b; Statistics Canada 1988: Table 2). Many of the new jobs in these and other areas were part-time or part-year. This kind of work was not attractive to adult men and attracted many married women who had another job at home.

Not only did more women enter the labour force, more of them stayed there permanently. Concentrated in large workplaces and in the job for the long haul, women increasingly joined unions and women's groups that fought for changes in their conditions of work. Given the distribution of women's employment, it is not surprising that the majority of unionized women were in public sector unions (White 1993). These and other unions successfully fought for vacations, paid maternity leave, and better benefits and hours of work, as well as for better pay and for the right to say no, especially to harassment. They also fought for a change in legislation to make it easier to organize those doing women's work in the labour force.

The Royal Commission on the Status of Women (Canada 1970), itself a manifestation of demands from women's groups (Pierson et al. 1993) and unions, set the stage for major changes in pay and employment legislation that made it easier for many women to get, and to keep, decent work. An assessment of the report's impact (Canadian Advisory Council on the Status of Women 1979) indicated that, while not all recommendations had been implemented, the government had taken significant steps to improve women's possibilities. The Royal Commission on Equality in Employment (Canada 1984) played a similar role, although it highlighted differences among women more than was the case with the previous Commission. The state regulation of business practices that emerged as a result of these commissions and more generally of women's struggles did not ensure equality either among women or between women and men. State contributions to women's groups did not ensure an equalization of power either. Indeed, more than one feminist has argued that the result has simply been state patriarchy (see Brodie 1996). State actions did, however, improve opportunities for many women. Equally important, they redrew the distinctions between the public and private, legitimating public intervention in private business as a means of protecting collective interests.

Writing at the end of the 1980s, Norene Pupo (1988: 212) saw the state as critical to women's progress:

The welfare state may prove to be one of the greatest contradictions of capitalism. Perhaps within women's cultural and historical tradition, the welfare state may be representative of empowerment, struggle, resistance, and change much like the trade union within the working-class male cultural and historical tradition. While it would be inaccurate to over-emphasize the possibility of empowerment and change through welfare state politics, especially in light of the nature and role of the state under capitalism, it is important to highlight women's resistance and participation in the struggle for equity and justice.

Some of these interventions by the state and through collective agreement provisions required that women be treated in the same way as men. However, in order to put them in a position equal to that of men, some required different treatment for women. Many women's groups began by demanding equal treatment along the lines Porter suggested, but many eventually moved towards strategies that took women's particular position and limited power into account. The struggle around pay provides just one example.

Initially, women demanded pay equal to that of men doing the same work. Yet it quickly became obvious that few women did work that was exactly the same as that of men. Moreover, when they did, it was easy for the employer to change the work in ways that escaped the legislation. After a series of attempts to get at the problem, groups like the Ontario Equal Pay Coalition were finally successful in demanding equal pay for work of equal value (Armstrong and Armstrong 1990a; Fudge and McDermott 1991). Equal value legislation, in Ontario at least, required employers to compare jobs in terms of the required skill, effort, responsibility, and working conditions. Employers were then to pay women on the same basis as men, rather than to strictly match jobs in order to assess whether or not the pay was equal. This kind of legislation brought to the fore the issues Gaskell had raised about skill. Increasingly it became clear that skill was not a fixed category, but rather a socially constructed one that was fundamentally biased against women. Anticipating this problem, the legislation called for evaluations of jobs that were free of gender bias. Under the interpretation provided by the Ontario Equal Pay Tribunal, this means that the particular characteristics of women's jobs must be taken into account and appropriately valued. Difference, rather than assimilation, is built into the legislation.

The pay equity legislation recognized that women and men did different work in different places for different rewards. Federal human rights legislation also recognized the fundamental division within the labour force. This was made clear in a landmark case against Canadian National Railway.[1] A women's group, Action travail des femmes, successfully charged the corporation with discriminating against women in the way it structured work. At issue was much more than hiring practices and the conditions of work. The very way work was organized was determined to be discriminatory against women, given women's particular position in and out of the labour force. Schedules, for example, often made it difficult to allow women to be at home at night with their families, but these schedules were not necessary for the work. Such practices recognized that women did not have to choose between sameness and difference, as Porter suggested. Rather, different situations call for different approaches, and sometimes require recognizing both difference and similarity at the same time.

State intervention and union victories helped improve the situation of women. Women did not benefit equally from these processes, however. Differences related to class, race, immigration status, and disability remained. Aboriginal women, for example, are less likely to have paid work than are other women. When they do, they are more likely to have part-time jobs and are less likely to be in managerial or professional positions. Moreover, their wages, on average, are $2,000 a year less than those of non-Aboriginal women (Statistics Canada 1995a: 152). In some instances, state policies perpetuated segregation into the least attractive work. This was the case for foreign domestic workers (Macklin 1994) and for those Patricia Daenzer (1993) has called 'immigrant servants.' For many other women, the victories have had quite contradictory results. As Christina Gabriel (1995: 192) explained in her study of Ontario multicultural policy, the outcomes are 'marked by advances and setbacks that are not necessarily predictable. Positive outcomes or gains, however, are often very fragile, given the marginal status of groups advancing claims of "difference" and the strength of forces resistant to them.'

Furthermore, the labour force remained highly segregated along male/female lines. In 1991, of the 200 occupations listed by Statistics Canada, 35 were at least 70 per cent female, and two-thirds of the employed women worked in these 35 jobs (Armstrong 1992b). Nevertheless, women did move into some traditionally male jobs, they did become less concentrated in traditionally female work, and they did gain more benefits and protections. The wage gap declined, especially for unionized women. In Ontario, where pay equity legislation applied most broadly, women's wages have increased from 65.4 per cent of the male wage in 1987, the year the legislation was introduced, to 71.2 per cent in 1991 (Statistics Canada 1994: Table 4.2).

Collective rights, then, aided many individual women, even if all women did not equally benefit. Access to decent employment helped shift the power balance for many women and helped many households survive. State intervention demonstrated the virtues of a level playing field established through rules of the game.

Women's participation in the labour force grew dramatically in the years after *The Vertical Mosaic*. So did their participation in post-secondary education. In the early 1950s three times more men than women received a bachelor or first professional degree, six times more men received a master's degree, and only 11 women compared with 191 men, were granted doctorates. Few community colleges of the kind we know today existed at the time, so women's numbers were negligible there as well (Statistics Canada 1990: 47). Guided by a philosophy that saw investment in human capital as necessary for economic growth, and pushed by employers who wanted an educated labour force and by other groups that wanted access, states expanded public, post-secondary educational institutions enormously. Strong and active student groups successfully demanded better bursaries and loans along with low tuition fees. Women's groups successfully demanded that the quotas on females that existed for many professional schools be removed and that services such as day care be provided. In the wake of all these developments, women flooded into the new universities and colleges. By the 1990s women accounted for the majority of those enrolled in bachelor and first professional degree programs, almost half of those in master's programs, and just over a third of those doing doctoral work (Statistics Canada 1994: 6).

While differences among women related to class, region, and race certainly remain, and while the impact was frequently contradictory, women from all groups have benefited in some ways from the expansion in state-supported post-secondary education.

Aboriginal women are still the most disadvantaged in terms of higher education, with 6 per cent of Aboriginal women compared with 13 per cent of non-Aboriginal women having university degrees. Women with disabilities are also significantly less likely than other women to have graduated from university (Statistics Canada 1995b). Differences are much less evident with other groups. Indeed, visible minority women are significantly more likely than other women in Canada to have a university degree or some post-secondary education, but they are less likely to have a post-secondary diploma. Many of the visible minority women are immigrants, so it is not surprising to learn that immigrant women under age 65 are somewhat more likely to have a university degree than are Canadian-born women, and a similar proportion have some other form of post-secondary education. It is difficult to tell, however, whether this reflects an immigration policy that gives preference to those with higher education or whether it reflects access to education in Canada. That visible minority women and immigrant women are less likely than their male counterparts to have university degrees suggests that immigration practices play an important role. In the case of Aboriginal women and women with disabilities, they are somewhat more likely than men but less likely than other women to have a university degree (Statistics Canada 1995b).

Training and apprenticeship programs also have had their bias against women exposed. Pressure helped make them more accessible, although men were still significantly more likely to receive on-the-job or language training. Some special counselling and employment services were opened, especially for immigrant women. Roxana Ng (1988b) has shown how these often served to perpetuate inequality, even as they helped find employment. Yet women still needed these services in order to find work.

Public education, state financial support, and new regulations reduced inequalities in access to education. Women did not equally benefit, and victories sometimes turned into losses. But state intervention, itself a response to democratic and collective efforts by women, shifted the power balance and made it more possible for many more women to acquire post-secondary degrees or certificates. This, in turn, helped more of them gain access to some jobs, although this was mainly the case in areas such as law and medicine where certification is the main criterion for entry. Many barriers still remain, especially in the business world and among Porter's economic elite, but some have been successfully battered.

While all these dramatic changes were happening in the labour force, things were changing much more slowly in the household. Research in the early 1970s (Clark and Harvey 1976) and in the early 1990s (Ornstein and Haddad 1991) demonstrated that the work of cleaning, cooking, and child care in the home is women's work. This is the case whether or not the research is done in Vancouver (Meissner et al. 1975), Sudbury (Wilkinson 1992), or the Great Northern Peninsula of Newfoundland (Sinclair and Felt 1992). And it is the case whether or not the woman works for pay outside the home. Male contributions to household work have increased somewhat over time, and they do vary somewhat with education. Unemployed men do help more than some others, as men take on especially more of the child care tasks, while their wives work for pay. But most of the regular household work is still women's work.

Although women may not be getting much more help from their spouses, they do have more help from labour-saving devices. When Porter wrote, less than 15 per cent of households had automatic clothes washers and dryers or home freezers. 'Less than 5 per cent had automatic dishwashers' (1965: 130). By 1994 close to 90 per cent of two-spouse households had an automatic washer and dryer, over 70 per cent had a freezer, and close to 60 per cent had a dishwasher. Women who parented alone were less likely to have these appliances. But nearly 70 per cent of them had washers and dryers, though less than a third had a dishwasher (Statistics Canada 1995a: Table 3.3). This technology became both possible and necessary as women entered the labour force at the same time as it helped women take on labour force work. Meanwhile, the introduction of these labour-saving devices meant that women had fewer opportunities to earn money at home through the provision of such services to other households.

The last thirty years have witnessed significant changes in other aspects of what is often called women's private lives. While Porter was writing, women's groups were demanding that the personal be made political. Battles against restrictions on access to abortion and birth control resulted in legislative and programmatic changes that helped women make choices about when, and if, to have babies (Pierson et al. 1993). New pharmaceutical products and new technologies also helped, although like the other forms of technology they often had contradictory affects on women (Overall 1992). These processes all contributed to the decline in the birth rate, a decline that both reflected and promoted women's participation in the labour force. Individually and collectively women also challenged doctors' powers over birth control, pregnancy, and delivery. As a result of their struggles, not only midwives but also birthing centres came on the agenda.

At the same time, study after study and government report after government report demonstrated the need for and value of day care. Demonstrations and petitions demanded affordable, non-profit, and state-supported and -regulated care for children. The state response was limited and far from adequate. Moreover, state policy encouraged many women to rely on the low-paid services of foreign-born domestics who were often required to work in quite poor conditions (Macklin, 1994). Nevertheless, the number of day care spaces grew significantly, largely through state initiative. And pay equity, in Ontario at least, helped some of the women who worked in these centres get decent wages. Unionization helped some get decent conditions as well.

The state provided much more help in terms of support for those who were old, ill, had disabilities, or faced abusive relationships. The expansion of public medical care, social services, pensions, and community services not only provided decent jobs for women. They also kept much of this work out of the home and improved the position of many women, especially in terms of access to services. These services were not without their own contradictions and inadequacies. By providing them through the paid employment of formally educated women, however, the state was encouraging the notion that this was skilled work that should be collectively supported and paid.

Mainly as a result of universal pensions and their supplements, poverty declined significantly among elderly women (Townson 1996). Moreover, an increasing number of elderly women had access to state-supported nursing homes and homes for the aged. Women were able to seek shelter from abusive households, and disabled women gained access to some transport and care. These and other measures were rightly criticized for their quality and character, but they did help many women survive (Carty 1992).

Research and protest also led to new state policies concerning property and relations in the home (Mossman 1995). Women were recognized as equal contributors to household economies and gained the legal right to half the marital home. At the same time, legislative change meant women were no longer considered the property of their spouses. Spousal abuse and wife rape were recognized as crimes. These developments, combined with new divorce legislation, made it easier for women to leave marriages. However, both the low support payments assigned by the courts and the lack of enforcement of these court-ordered payments left many divorced women in poverty. Welfare helped, especially after the old 'spouse in the house' rule that assumed any male living with a woman supported her financially, was removed (Evans, 1996). Legal aid helped many women fight for these rights.

Of course, none of these developments was free from faults. Indeed, some even reinforced women's inequality and restricted their power at the same time as they allowed women to survive. As was the case with women's paid work, some of the state legislation remained unenforced or was poorly enforced. Some victories were turned into losses or simply had a quite contradictory impact. Other legislation, and other programs, had an impact far from their stated intent. Some areas, like the rights of lesbian spouses, were left unprotected. Nevertheless, the state increasingly intervened in the private sphere in ways that protected many women and relieved others of heavy burdens of work. The personal became political and the public responsible, and the focus shifted somewhat from the individual and the market to the collective. In opening up these areas as public concerns, women were opening them to the possibility for democratic process and for a shift in power from the economically privileged, mainly male, elites.

Refitting Women

It is difficult to believe that so much has changed for women in thirty years. I find it difficult to believe, and I lived through this period as an adult. Equally difficult to contemplate is the speed with which many of these gains are being swept away. These have proven to be truly fragile victories, as Christina Gabriel (1996) explained and Norene Pupo (1988) predicted. Governments and businesses are restructuring and downsizing. Deregulation in the market is radically changing what is public and what is private, while more and more of what has been considered public enterprise is being shifted to the home. Work and skills are being redefined and so are union activities.

Some of this transformation is the result of technological innovation. Much of this innovation, however, is itself a response to the gains of workers in general, and of women in particular. Business, and governments under pressure from business, are using both technology and new methods of work organization to discipline workers. In health care, for example, computer programs are used both to count how long workers spend carrying out specific tasks and to develop formulas to control how long workers are allowed to spend at these tasks (Choiniere 1993). Investors who are running out of places to make profits are demanding, quite successfully, that what have been public sector services be open to private sector development for profit. For example, home care services are increasingly being provided by for-profit firms. These changes are fuelled by a new economic philosophy (or is it an old one?) that stresses a 'level playing field,' where the rules are determined by the market. This playing field is defined as one free of government intervention that would not in any way restrict business interests. The only line is the bottom line as what O'Connor (1973) called the legitimation and accumulation functions of the state are collapsed into one. Only accumulation is legitimate. While no household or individual remains untouched by these fundamental changes, women in particular suffer from the impact, mainly because they gained most from state intervention.

The impact is already evident in the official statistics on the labour force. For the first time since the year *The Vertical Mosaic* was published, women's labour force participation rates have declined in consecutive years. An increasing proportion of the women with paid jobs have part-time or short-term work with irregular, and often quite limited, hours. Indeed, only 40 per cent of the women with paid jobs have full-time, full-year work. Those with these full-time jobs are facing very long hours and work intensification, as fewer and fewer women are hired to do the jobs that remain, and work is reorganized (Armstrong 1996b). As a result, the differences among women are increasing.

We are seeing the harmonizing down among many workers in the labour force. Men's jobs too are being casualized, and more and more men are moving into traditional female areas of work, especially in the service sector. In other words, men's jobs are becoming more like women's jobs. And this is especially the case for young men. By the 1990s nearly 40 per cent of the men over age 25 did not have full-time, full-year work. And men were competing much more directly with women for both the full- and part-time work that remains (Armstrong 1996b).

Take clerical work, for example. Jobs are rapidly disappearing in this female-dominated sector. A recent study (de Wolff 1995: 2) revealed that 'the number of clerical workers receiving general social assistance more than tripled between 1989 and 1994 in Metropolitan Toronto.' A third of those who still have clerical jobs work part-time or part-year. As is the case throughout the economy, work is being restructured to intensify labour and eliminate jobs. In one payment centre, the 'most recent work redesign focussed on the speed-up of the work. It was preceded by the introduction of team work, which added scheduling and interpersonal and work process problem solving to clerical jobs' (de Wolfe 1995: 3). More and more work is done through temporary employment agencies, and an increasing proportion is done at home. Clerical work is still very much female-dominated, although far fewer women find jobs here, and they now compete more directly with men for the increasingly limited number of jobs.

The harmonizing down of men's jobs is also evident in wages. The wage gap declined in the 1990s. However, it declined mainly because male wages declined as fewer men worked in the highly unionized, goods production fields, and more found jobs in the female-dominated service sectors (Armstrong 1995). Men still make significantly more money than women, even when they work in female-dominated jobs. But their declining wages put even more pressure on women to work for pay. So do their continuing high levels of unemployment and the increasing length of their periods of unemployment.

This restructuring of work began in the private sector as employers developed strategies to avoid collective agreements, reduce reliance on labour, and create a more flexible labour force. Just-in-time production means the hiring of just-in-time workers. Team work is promoted as a way to get around unions and encourage workers to discipline each other. Hierarchies are being flattened, reducing promotion ladders, and increasing the distance between the top and the bottom. Work is increasingly designated as multi-skilled, too often with the result that all skills are devalued, and none are protected. In the process, women's traditional ways of working in teams and new ways of working their way up the promotion ladder are eliminated (see, e.g., Mackay 1995; Richardson 1994).

States are supporting these developments by deregulating the private sector. In Ontario, for instance, employment equity legislation has been withdrawn, and pay equity legislation is under threat. Minimum labour and health standards are being relaxed, and these too often constituted the only protection non-unionized women had. Labour legislation is being redesigned to make it more difficult to organize and negotiate or enforce collective agreements. Public sector unions in particular are under attack, and women constitute a majority here.

In the name of fighting the deficit and making services more efficient as well as more effective, the state is privatizing many services, downsizing others and applying private sector practices to those that remain (Armstrong et al. 1996). In education, cutbacks are leading to reductions in wages and jobs as well as to direct private sector involvement in education. Because women form the overwhelming majority of those employed in primary education and of those most recently hired into faculty positions at universities, they are the most likely to suffer. Moreover, while almost all those who teach in the public sector are unionized, this is not the case in private education. Thus, the more the private sector becomes involved in education, the less likely women are to be covered by collective agreements.

The cutbacks in education also have an impact on access to higher education. The federal government has proposed to shift more financing to students through loans rather than financing institutions. Students will pay for more of their education, but they will be eligible for government-backed loans to cover the costs. The loans will be paid back as a per centage of income. Given women's lower earnings and more limited access to resources, women will be paying loans over a much longer period than men. The strategy will undoubtedly increase the importance of class and sex in terms of access to post-secondary education as an individual's personal finances become more important.

Similarly, health care is being dramatically restructured and downsized. The female-dominated registered nursing jobs provide just one example. In Alberta alone, 2,000 registered nursing jobs have disappeared in the 1990s (Richardson 1995). Some parts of their paid work have been eliminated; other parts have been transferred to workers with less formal training. Professions are being deregulated as a way of reducing the monopolies on skills and of allowing less expensive, and less formally trained, people to do the work. In the process, women's nursing work is being devalued.

The reductions in services mean not only job loss for women. They also mean there is increasing pressure on women to do the job as unpaid workers in the home (Armstrong 1992a). The new technologies and techniques introduced in the market have not eliminated all the necessary labour. Rather, as is the case with banking machines and gas pumps, much of it simply transfers the work to individuals unpaid and untrained for the job (Glazer 1993). The process is increasing women's workload at the same time as it is redefining the skill involved in the work. The transfer of health care work in particular is promoted as increasing choice and increasing choice and as returning work to the home. But much of this work has never been done there. Women have not traditionally done intravenous feedings, changed surgical bandages, cleaned catheters, or attached oxygen masks. Moreover, now most women are in the labour force and few have a choice about being there (Armstrong and Armstrong 1994). The state-supported services that are available in the home are provided in ways that reduce the privacy of those who live there, in the process regulating the private in a manner that reduces women's power.

Other supports for women in their unpaid work are also disappearing. In Ontario, welfare is not only being reduced. It is also becoming increasingly regulated as more rigid qualification criteria are introduced. Legal aid is under attack, as are counselling services, centres for abused women, and financial support for women's groups. Meanwhile, homes are increasingly becoming workplaces where minimum wages and minimum standards do not apply. Employment benefits are also non-existent. Hazards from the workplace are transferred to the homes where an increasing number of women find their paid work. One of the reasons they work at home is that the state is withdrawing support for child care and kindergarten.

In these ways the conditions and relations of the market are invading the household more than ever, making the private public in a manner different from the past and changing class relations as well. While business is regulated less, citizens in general and women in particular have fewer opportunities and less protection.

Conclusion

In the period since *The Vertical Mosaic* was written, women have made significant gains in terms of access to education and paid jobs; in terms of the recognition of their skills and their economic contributions; in terms of power. Through their collective action, they have won significant rights as individuals. A combination of conditions and relations made it possible to win significant concessions from the state and from employers. By changing conditions, they opened up opportunities, albeit too often unequal ones. Much of this was supported by state intervention either through the provision of services or the regulation of practices in the private sector. Unions also played a critical role. Certainly there was a great deal that was problematic and contradictory about the practices of unions, employers, and states. Equally certainly, we cannot go back to the past, even if we wanted to do so. I would not advocate another kind of nostalgia to replace that advocated by those in power.

However, the revolutionary changes under way in the state and business sectors are rapidly eliminating women's collective gains. New combinations of conditions and relations are undermining many past victories and turning some into losses. Increasingly, access to education and services is based on money. Increasingly, collective protections are being dismantled in the name of returning to a free market. Work is being intensified at the same time as it is becoming more precarious. Women, and especially immigrant and visible minority women, and women with disabilities, have benefited most from these changes, even as they have suffered from some of them. The more markets are allowed to dominate, the more those in the weakest positions lose. Women are in the weakest position because of the systemic discrimination they face rather than as a result of their individual characteristics. We are back to the notion of equality based on an individual race to the top.

As *The Vertical Mosaic* made clear, we start from very unequal conditions. Without intervention to alter these conditions, we will end up with an unequal race to the bottom, especially for women. We are being pushed to a past, a past Porter's research clearly established was dominated by white men in suits pursuing their own interests at the expense of women, and of women from minority groups in particular. If Porter were writing *The Vertical Mosaic* today, I have no doubt that he would produce an analysis that started from some different assumptions, an analysis that takes women into account. I have no doubt that he would be critical of the policies and practices now being put in place, policies that are more likely to promote inequalities than reduce them. Such critical analysis is essential to the development of new strategies for equality.

Notes

1 *Action Travaille des Femmes* v *Canadian National Railways*, [1987] S.C.R. 1114.

References

Agocs, Carol. (1985). 'Missing Persons: Perspectives on the Absence of Women from Canada's Corporate and Bureaucratic Elites.' *Organizational Behaviour* 68: 689–718.

Andrew, Carolyn. (1984). 'Women and the Welfare State.' *Canadian Journal of Political Science* 17(4): 667–83.

Archibald, Kathleen. (1970). *Sex and the Public Service.* Ottawa: Queen's Printer.

Armstrong, Pat. (1989). 'Is There Still a Chairman of the Board?' *Journal of Canadian Studies* 8(6): 6–16.

– (1992a). 'Closer to Home: More Work for Women.' Pp. 95–110 in Pat Armstrong, Hugh Armstrong, Jacqueline Choiniere, Gina Feldberg, and Jerry White (eds.), *Take Care: Warning Signals for Canadian Health Care.* Toronto: Garamond.

– (1992b). *Equal Pay for Work of Equal Value.* Report prepared for the Public Service Alliance of Canada.

– (1995). 'The Feminization of the Labour Force: Harmonizing Down in a Global Economy.' Pp. 368–92 in Karen Messing, Barbara Neis, and Lucie Dumais (eds.), *Invisible.* Charlottetown: Gynergy Books.

– (1996a). 'From Caring and Sharing to Greedy and Mean?' Pp. 251–68 in Andre Lapierre, Patricia Smart, and Pierre Savard (eds.), *Language, Culture and Values in Canada at the Dawn of the 21st Century.* Ottawa: Carleton University Press.

– (1996b). 'Unravelling the Safety Net: Transformations in Health Care and Their Impact on Women.' Pp. 129–50 in Janine Brodie (ed.), *Women and Canadian Public Policy.* Toronto: Harcourt Brace.

Armstrong, Pat, and Hugh Armstrong. (1978). *The Double Ghetto: Canadian Women and Their Segregated Work.* (1st ed.) Toronto: McClelland and Stewart.

– (1983). 'Beyond Sexless Class and Classless Sex: Towards Feminist Marxism.' *Studies in Political Economy* 10 (Winter): 7–44.

– (1990a). 'Lessons from Pay Equity.' *Studies in Political Economy* 32 (Summer): 29–54.

– (1990b). *Theorizing Women's Work.* Toronto: Garamond.

– (1991). 'Limited Possibilities and Possible Limits for Pay Equity: Within and beyond the Ontario Experience.' Pp. 110–21 in Judy Fudge and Patricia McDermott (eds.), *Just Wages: A Feminist Assessment of Pay Equity.* Toronto: University of Toronto Press.

– (1992). 'Sex and the Professions in Canada.' *Journal of Canadian Studies* 27(1): 118–25.

– (1994). *The Double Ghetto: Canadian Women and Their Segregated Work* (3rd ed.) Toronto: McClelland and Stewart.

Armstrong, Pat, et al. (1996). *Medical Alert: New Work Organization in Health Care.* Toronto: Garamond.

Benston, Margaret. (1969). 'The Political Economy of Women's Liberation.' *Monthly Review* 21: 13–27.

Bradbury, Bettina. (1993). *Working Families*. Toronto: McClelland and Stewart.

Brand, Dionne. (1991). *No Burden to Carry: Narratives of Black Working Women in Ontario 1920s to 1950s*. Toronto: Women's Press.

Brodie, Janine (ed.). (1996). *Women and Canadian Public Policy*. Toronto: Harcourt Brace.

Calvert, John. (1984). *Government Unlimited: The Corporate Takeover of the Public Sector*. Ottawa: Canadian Centre for Policy Alternatives.

Canada, Royal Commission on Equality in Employment. (1984). *Equity in Employment*. Ottawa: Supply and Services Canada.

Canada, Royal Commission on the Status of Women. (1970). *Report*. Ottawa: Information Canada.

Canadian Advisory Council on the Status of Women. (1979). *10 Years Later*. Ottawa: Canadian Advisory Council on the Status of Women.

Carty, Linda (ed.). (1992). *And Still We Rise*. Toronto: Women's Press.

Chawla, Raj. (1992). 'The Changing Profile of Dual-Earner Families.' *Perspectives on Labour and Income* 4(2): 20–9.

Choiniere, Jacqueline. (1993). 'A Case Study Examination of Nurses and Patient Information Technology.' Pp. 59–88 in Pat Armstrong, Jacqueline Choiniere, and Elaine Day (eds.), *Vital Signs: Nursing in Transition*. Toronto: Garamond.

Clark, Susan, and Andrew Harvey. (1976). 'The Sexual Division of Labour: The Use of Time.' *Atlantis* 2(1) (Fall): 46–55.

Clement, Wallace, and John Myles. (1994). *Relations of Ruling: Class and Gender in Post-Industrial Societies*. Montreal: McGill-Queen's University Press.

Connelly, M. Patricia, and Pat Armstrong. (1992). 'Introduction.' Pp. ix–xix in M. Patricia Connelly and Pat Armstrong (eds.), *Feminism in Action*. Toronto: Canadian Scholars' Press.

Connelly, M. Patricia, and Martha MacDonald. (1983). 'Women's Work: Domestic and Wage Labourers in a Nova Scotia Community.' *Studies in Political Economy* 10 (Winter): 45–72.

Daenzer, Patricia. (1993). *Regulating Class Privilege*. Toronto: Canadian Scholars' Press.

de Wolff, Alice. (1995). 'Job Loss and Entry Level Information Workers.' Summary Report of the Metro Toronto Clerical Workers, Adjustment Committee.

Dominion Bureau of Statistics. (1966). *1961 Census of Canada, Labour Force*. Ottawa: Trade and Commerce. Cat. no. 94–551.

Duffy, Ann. (1988). 'Struggling with Power: Feminist Critiques of Family Inequality.' Pp. 111–42 in Nancy Mandell and Ann Duffy (eds.), *Reconstructing the Canadian Family: Feminist Perspectives*. Toronto: Butterworths.

Eichler, Margrit. (1975). 'Sociological Research on Women in Canada.' *Canadian Review of Sociology and Anthropology* 12(4) (Part 1): 474–81.

Evans, Patricia. (1996). 'Single Mothers and Ontario's Welfare Policy: Restructuring the Debate.' Pp. 151–72 in Janine Brodie (ed.), *Women and Canadian Public Policy*. Toronto: Harcourt Brace.

Fournier, Francine, and Bonnie Diamond. (1987). *Equality and Access: A New Social Contract*. Montreal: National Film Board.

Fudge, Judy, and Patricia McDermott (eds.). (1991). *Just Wages*. Toronto: University of Toronto Press.

Gabriel, Christina. (1996). '"One or the Other?" Race, Gender and the Limits of Official Multiculturalism.' Pp. 173–98 in Janine Brodie (ed.), *Women and Canadian Public Policy*. Toronto: Harcourt Brace.

Gaskell, Jane. (1986). 'Conceptions of Skill and the Work of Women: Some Historical and Political Issues.' Pp. 361–80 in Roberta Hamilton and Michèle Barrett (eds.), *The Politics of Diversity*. Montreal: Book Centre.

Glazer, Nona. (1993). *Women's Paid and Unpaid Work*. Philadelphia: Temple University Press.

Henry, Frances, Carol Tator, Winston Mattis, and Tim Rees. (1995). *The Colour of Democracy*. Toronto: Harcourt Brace.

Mackay, Bouni. (1995). 'Work Restructuring and Privatization in the Education Sector.' Paper prepared for Conference on Service Sector Revolutions: Dilemmas and Opportunities for Labour, Port Elgin, Ontario.

Macklin, Audrey. (1994). 'On the Inside Looking In: Foreign Domestic Workers in Canada.' Pp. 13–40 in Wenona Giles and Sedef Arat-Koç (eds.), *Maid in the Market*. Halifax: Fernwood.

Maroney, Heather Jon, and Meg Luxton (eds.). (1987). *Feminism and Political Economy*. Toronto: Methuen.

Marshall, Katherine. (1987). *Who Are The Professional Women?* Ottawa: Supply and Services Canada.

McDonald, Lynn, and Marcia Smith Lenglet. (1973). 'The Status of Women at McMaster University.' Pp. 117–44 in Marylee Stephenson (ed.), *Women in Canada*. Don Mills: General Publishing.

Meissner, Martin, et al. (1975). 'No Exit for Wives: Sexual Division of Labour and the Culmination of Household Demands.' *Canadian Review of Sociology and Anthropology* 12, 4, Part 1 (November): 424–39.

Mossman, Mary Jane. (1995). 'The Paradox of Feminist Engagement with the Law.' Pp. 211–44 in Nancy Mandell (ed.), *Feminist Issues: Race, Class and Sexuality*. Scarborough: Prentice-Hall.

Ng, Roxanna. (1988a). 'Immigrant Women and Institutionalized Racism.' Pp. 184–203 in Sandra Burt, Lorraine Code, and Lindsay Dorney (eds.), *Changing Patterns: Women in Canada*. Toronto: McClelland and Stewart.

– (1988b). *The Politics of Community Services*. Toronto: Garamond.

O'Brien, Mary. (1981). *The Politics of Reproduction*. London: Routledge Kegan Paul.

O'Connor, James. (1973). *The Fiscal Crisis of the State*. New York: St Martin's Press.

Ornstein, Michael, and Tony Haddad. (1991). *About Time: An Analysis of the 1986 Survey of Canadians*. North York: Institute for Social Research, York University.

Overall, Christine. (1992). 'Feminist Philosophical Reflections on Reproductive Rights in Canada.' Pp. 240–50 in Constance Backhouse and David H. Flaherty (eds.), *Challenging Times*. Kingston: McGill-Queen's University Press.

Parr, Joy. (1990). *The Gender of Breadwinners*. Toronto: University of Toronto Press.

Perspectives on Labour and Income. (1993). *Highlights* 5(2): 1–7.

Pierson, Ruth Roach, Marjorie Griffin Cohen, Paula Bourne, and Philinda Maters (eds.). (1993). *Canadian Women's Issues*, vol. 1: *Strong Voices*. Toronto: Lorimer.

Porter, John. (1965). *The Vertical Mosaic: An Analysis of Social Class and Power in Canada*. Toronto: University of Toronto Press.

Porter, Marion R., John Porter, and Bernard Blishen. (1973). *Does Money Matter?* Toronto: York University, Institute for Behavioural Research.

Pupo, Norene. (1988). 'Preserving Patriarchy: Women, the Family and the State.' Pp. 202–39 in Nancy Mandell and Ann Duffy (eds.), *Reconstructing the Canadian Family*. Toronto: Butterworths.

Rashid, Abdul. (1993). 'Seven Decades of Wage Changes.' *Perspectives on Labour and Income* 5(2): 9–22.

Richardson, Trudy. (1994). *Total Quality Management Programs: More Work for Less Pay*. Edmonton: United Nurses of Alberta.

– (1995). 'Total Quality Management Programs.' Paper prepared for Conference on Service Sector Revolutions: Dilemmas and Opportunities for Labour, Port Elgin, Ontario.

Russell, Susan. (1986). 'The Hidden Curriculum of Schools: Reproducing Gender and Class Hierarchies.' Pp. 343–60 in Roberta Hamilton and Michèle Barrett (eds.), *The Politics of Diversity*. Montreal: Book Centre.

Sinclair, Peter R., and Lawrence F. Felt. (1992). 'Separate Worlds: Gender and Domestic Labour in an Isolated Fishing Region.' *Canadian Review of Sociology and Anthropology* 29(1) (February): 55–71.

Smith, Dorothy. (1973). 'Women, The Family and Corporate Capitalism.' Pp. 14–49 in Marylee Stephenson (ed.), *Women in Canada*. Don Mills: General Publishing.

– (1987). *The Everyday World as Problematic*. Toronto: University of Toronto Press.

Statistics Canada. (1988). *1986 Census, Industry Trends 1951–1986*. Ottawa: Supply and Services Canada. Cat. no. 93–152.

- (1990). *Women in Canada* (2nd ed.). Ottawa: Supply and Services Canada. Cat. no. 89–503E.
- (1992). *Family Incomes, Census Families 1990*. Ottawa: Supply and Services Canada. Cat. no. 13–208.
- (1993). *Historical Statistics of Canada* (2nd ed.). Ottawa: Supply and Services Canada. Cat. no. S11–516E.
- (1994). *Women in the Labour Force* (1994 edn.). Ottawa: Supply and Services Canada. Cat. no. 75–507E.
- (1995a). *Labour Force Annual Averages 1989–1994*. Ottawa: Minister of Industry, Science and Technology. Cat. no. 71–529.
- (1995b). *Women in Canada*. (3rd ed.). Ottawa: Supply and Services Canada. Cat. no. 89–503E.

Townson, Monica. (1996). *Our Aging Society: Preserving Retirement Incomes into the 21st Century*. Ottawa: Canadian Centre for Policy Alternatives.

Vickers, Jill. (1978). 'Where Are the Women in Canadian Politics?' *Atlantis* 3(2), Part II: 40–51.

Wallace, Cecilia. (1976). 'Changes in the Churches.' Pp.92–128 in Gwen Matheson (ed.), *Women in the Canadian Mosaic*. Toronto: Peter Marten.

White, Julie. (1980). *Women and Unions*. Ottawa: Canadian Advisory Council on the Status of Women.

- (1993). *Sisters and Solidarity*. Toronto: Thompson.

Wilkinson, Derek. (1992). 'Change in the Household Division of Labour Following Unemployment in Elliot Lake.' Paper presented at Learned Societies Meetings, CSAA, Charlottetown, Prince Edward Island.

Yalnizyan, Armine. (1994). 'Securing Society: Creating Canadian Social Policy.' Pp. 17–72 in Armine Yalnizyan, T. Ran Ide, and Arthur Cordell (eds.), *Shifting Time*. Toronto: Between the Lines.

Three Decades of Elite Research in Canada: John Porter's Unfulfilled Legacy[1]

MICHAEL ORNSTEIN

The empirical studies of elites in *The Vertical Mosaic* represent John Porter's most important intellectual legacy. This work was, and remains, a challenge to English-Canadian sociology, directing attention to the systematic study of power and wealth, situating capital at the centre of power, and laying a claim to the sociological study of the state. In joining analysis of education and occupational mobility to the study of elites in one volume, Porter set the broad, probabilistic associations between parental background, ethnicity, education, and jobs, which describe the patterns of social stratification in the population, against the deep inequalities of economic and political power and wealth, and vice versa. In Porter's words, 'It is the interplay between social class and elite structure which is the subject of this book' (1965: 28).

I begin with a discussion of the theoretical and empirical terrain of elite theory, locating *The Vertical Mosaic* in this context. Then, in cataloguing and assessing elite research of the past three decades, I will show which themes from Porter's work have been addressed and which neglected, in the context of broader developments in English-Canadian sociology. This essay is a critical appreciation of Porter's work, which is used to reflect on issues in economic and political sociology and to make suggestions for future empirical research. In a nutshell, my argument is that only corporate elites have attracted serious and sustained scholarly attention and that, despite the enormous attention paid to the state in the past twenty years, the relative neglect of state elites seriously impairs our understanding of power and inequality in Canadian society.

I consider the economic, labour, political, and bureaucratic elites, but not what Porter identified as the 'ideological elites' in the mass media, the universities, and the clergy. In *The Vertical Mosaic,* the discussion of the mass media is concerned mainly with describing the corporate ownership of the major mass media and with the impact of ownership on media content. But, if the media elites are no more than their corporate owners, understanding them is only a minor element in the analysis of corporate elites. As Clement (1975: Chapter 8) demonstrated, the mass media are well integrated in Canadian corporate capital. What distinguishes the media from other corporate elites is its particular, ideological 'product,' which provides a basis for a *distinct* elite of commentators, editors, producers, and media personalities. Membership in this media elite does not derive from the boards of the corporations dominant in the industry. A serious study of media elites must combine analysis of their corporate and ideological roles. The same problem arises in Porter's study of the social backgrounds – rather than their professions, ideological roles, institutional bases, and roles in education and social service – of members of the Royal Society of Canada and of Catholic and Anglican bishops. Because serious analysis of these issues is less a matter of extending Porter's work than covering a different range of inquiry, ideological elites are not included in this essay.

Two Concepts of 'Elites' in Sociology

While the term 'elite' is used quite loosely in sociology, a fundamental distinction concerns whether power *in entire societies* is understood in terms of elites. In the tradition of Pareto and Mosca, elite *theory* begins with the idea that, of necessity, a distinct and organized 'elite' rules society. How this elite is recruited and changes, the 'circulation' of elites, becomes the critical parameter distinguishing between societies and eras; for fuller discussions see Bottomore (1993) and Burton and Higley (1987). Elite theory is a broad perspective on complex societies – an alternative to Marxist, Weberian, technological, and other theoretical perspectives. Indeed, Pareto and Mosca were explicitly anti-Marxist.[2]

Unlike class theory, elite theory is not based on a particular understanding of the *social structure* in a specific place and time. In contemporary sociology, elite theorists direct their attention to policy conflicts, which they understand in terms of interest groups represented by competing elites. Recent work in this tradition includes G. William Domhoff's *The Power Elite and the State: How Policy Is Made in America* (1990), and John Higley, Desley Deacon and Don Smart's *Elites in Australia* (1979). The fullest Canadian formulation is Robert Presthus's now dated *Elite Accommodation in Canadian Politics* (1973). The conception of

Canadian politics in terms of brokerage implies the importance of elites and their interrelations.

One can also study elites without accepting the central tenet of elite theory, that society is ruled by a distinct and organized, but *not* predominantly class-based, social group. What can be termed *elite studies* includes theory and empirical studies that deal with elite groups in the context of theoretical traditions other than elite *theory*. Elite studies may be restricted to particular sectors of society, such as business, politics, or cultural communities, to 'demographic' or ethnic groups, or to geographic areas. These differ from elite theory in not claiming that the characteristics of elites explain broader patterns of inequality or state policies. Nor is the recruitment and circulation of elites privileged over structured social inequality. In the broader context of a class theory of capitalist society, for example, the particular characteristics of national elites might explain the political choices made by business and labour, their relationship to political parties, and the relative success of those parties. Two British examples of this approach are John Scott's *Who Rules Britain?* (1991) and Philip Stanworth and Anthony Giddens's edited *Elites and Power in British Society* (1974).

Of course, elite studies are *not* generally understood as an appropriate complement to class theory, and they are commonly criticized for the 'instrumentalist logic of focusing on the decision-making capacity of elites and on the direct ties between the state and capital' (Albo and Jenson 1989: 192). Instrumentalism, in this context, is the derivation of the interests of classes (particularly the capitalist class) and institutions (particularly the state) from the characteristics of the individuals who direct them, rather than from consideration of the economic and social structure of society. In contrast, Marxists emphasize the economic relations embodied in the class structure and explain social inequality and the form of rule in terms of the characteristics of these 'structures,' the 'logic' of capital, and the 'character' of the capitalist state. Regulation theory combines these into a more integrated conception of the related economic and social features of entire eras (e.g., see Jenson 1989; Jessop 1993). In avoiding the problem of reducing the character of society to the characteristics of individual elites, class theorists run the opposite risk of disembodying society. Leaning too heavily on the logic and evolution of 'structures,' it is difficult to think of people making their society or history; this is the now-familiar structure-agency problem; for example, see Sztompka (1994).

There is a natural, although not perfect, alignment between researchers' theoretical views of elites and the empirical evidence used to support them. Elite *theorists* tend to focus on overt political conflicts, for example municipal planning decisions, whose outcomes have some degree of uncertainty. They identify prominent actors in the such conflicts and determine what interests they represent and whether there is a closed circle of participants. This naturally feeds into pluralist conceptions of power and the dynamics of brokerage politics. Elite *studies*, on the other hand, usually begin with a consideration of the structural bases of class or organizational power, then focus on the characteristics and relationships among their leaders. The idea is not to assume the importance of economic and social structure, but to situate political argument and action in a material context. Many empirical studies have shown that, in terms of class background, gender, ethnic, and racial make-up, and careers, elites are *not* very representative of their own sectoral bases and that they are radically different from the whole population (see Eulau and Czudnowski 1976; Czudnowski 1982; Clarke and Czudnowski 1987). Because elites from different sectors are very unequal in power (compare corporate and labour elites, for example), central questions about power in society often fail to reach public debate. The *anti*-democratic conclusion is that elites are unaccountable and insensitive to the needs of the broader community.

The value of elite studies lies in the potential to connect politics and social change to the social organization of classes, class fractions, state organizations, professional groups, political parties, and social groups. For example, the Marxist argument that the capitalist class is the ruling class cannot mean, literally, that the entire capitalist class – *all* the owners of the means of production – rules. But it must also mean more than the general, unfalsifiable argument that the social order embodies unequal class relations and institutionalizes and protects private property and capital. Understanding whether and how a capitalist class rules requires empirical knowledge about the social organization of capital, the state, political parties, and interest groups. This is why it is worth examining the social backgrounds, careers, and interpersonal networks of elites and the organizations that they control.

Elites in *The Vertical Mosaic*

Porter understood power in Canadian society in terms of functionally defined elites in the economic, labour, political, bureaucratic, and ideological realms: 'People in power roles belong to an elite. Thus in each of these interrelated systems of power there is an elite' (1965: 207). The powers of these elites, however, are sharply circumscribed: 'It could be said that in the 'western' system the values of capitalism, particularly those of private property and profit-making, unify the elites ... Although elite groups present arguments for changes which will improve their relative positions, they never make demands for changes in the foundations of the economic order, that is, for public ownership as a substitute for corporate and private ownership of the society's productive instruments' (p. 212).

Later on, explaining the presence of the corporate elite on the boards of universities, Porter remarked: 'The explanation does not lie in an intrinsic link between the two [corporations and universities], but lies rather in the structural characteristics of a society based on corporate capitalism. The corporate elite are the society's leading citizens and as such "govern" more things than universities' (p. 301). Despite its circumspect language, this is no different from the Marxist argument that the pervasive power of corporate capital in developed capitalist societies allows it to dominate social institutions without the need for rules to formally structure its power in universities and other major institutions.[3] Porter thus granted a structural pre-eminence to corporate elites. Contrast Presthus (1973: 354ff), who dealt with three elite groups in his study of Canadian politics: legislators, bureaucrats, and 'interest group directors.' His definition of interest groups is minimalist: they are simply organizations with 'a telephone, a director, major income from non-public sources, and status as a non-profit organization' (1973: 355). So, Presthus lumped together, as interest groups with the same status, business organizations (primarily industry associations), labour unions, welfare organizations, and professional associations.[4]

In *The Vertical Mosaic*, corporate elites receive the first and most extensive treatment. In this sense, Porter was closer to radicals like Gustavus Myers (1914) and Ferdinand Lundberg (1940) and to Marxists such as Libbie and Frank Park (1962) than to conventional elite theorists. Likewise, in the deep concern with inequality that animates *The Vertical Mosaic*, Porter had more in common with the class theorists he explicitly dismissed[5] than with elite theorists. In view of the relative weakness of organized labour in Canada, it is also significant that Porter proceeded from the economic elite to the labour elite. So he analytically privileged capital and labour, again more in keeping with class than elite theory.

Perhaps not too heavy an emphasis should be placed on theory in what Porter himself saw as an empirical study. Recalling his theoretical

orientations in writing *The Vertical Mosaic,* some years later, Porter
described an eclectic mélange:

> I decided, by adding some Mosca and Weber, to elaborate Aron's Pareto-Marx
> synthesis into a scheme for the study of power in Canada. I accepted the 'anti-
> democratic' view of the minority rule school. Moreover, what they had said was
> consistent with much of what was being written about authoritarianism by writ-
> ers like Fromm and other social psychologists. The democratic personality was
> not yet the basic personality of modern industrial society and, until it was, obe-
> dience, submissiveness, and apathy would continue to characterize the posture
> toward power and authority of people within large-scale social systems. I don't
> think that at any time I graced this scheme, or framework, with the word
> 'theory,' because I was not concerned to develop theory, to derive interrelated
> propositions, or test hypotheses. I was analyzing important aspects of a large
> scale social system. (1987: 18)

A deep ambivalence shapes Porter's approach to power. He accepted a
functionalist division of labour among elites and the implication that
these elites, except for politicians to some extent, are largely outside the
reach of public will. Porter's concerns about democracy, however, surely
cannot have been that labour leaders are elected by union members
rather than the public, that politicians compete for office, or that bureaucrats represent an educated minority who have scaled the organizational
ladder. The problem for democracy is that the enormous power of corporate elites derives from their private ownership and control of capital. In
observing that all the elites are constrained by the power of capital and
are unable to voice alternatives to capitalism, Porter acknowledged the
structured inequality among elites in the face of *capitalist* hegemony. In
the many anecdotes sprinkled through the chapter on elites, Porter
showed how this hegemony gently wraps the discourse and personal
relations among elites. Where others have pointed to the (usually polite
and bureaucratic) struggles over unemployment insurance, pensions,
health insurance, and other programs that marked the development of
the welfare state, and to the strikes that marked the establishment of
trade unions, Porter described the exercise of power in discussions and
personal relations among the powerful elites. It is telling that the hege-
monically framed discourse among elites that Porter understood as the
substance of *bourgeois* power includes the state elites, but not labour.

Though the politeness and reasonableness of the higher circles may have appealed to Porter, his research showed how unequal the access to these circles is. He regarded the closed social network of elites and their discourse that excludes fundamental questions of class power as properties of the (capitalist) system, rather than the conscious exercise of power by elites. The disappearance of issues (the 'silences') is what hegemony is all about.

Porter observed this state of affairs less with approval than resignation, hanging his hopes on the uncontroversial and reformist notions of increasing access to education and more equal opportunity. While this reflects Porter's political views, like all ideological positions it also corresponds to life experience. For Porter's generation, higher education was still uncommon, and it provided a route of rapid upward mobility for some working-class men, particularly former servicemen and second generation immigrants from the Jewish and perhaps some other ethnic groups. Educational reform and expansion was also the 'class' – more correctly the guild or professional – interest of academic elites, especially at a time of dramatic expansion of universities. In retrospect, Porter's optimism about the improving effects of education also reflects the time that Hobsbawm (1994) characterized as the *golden years*, an unusual and hopeful period between the end of the Second World War and the *crisis decades* of the 1970s, 1980s, and 1990s. It is worth remembering that the Canadian welfare state, while only explicitly being dismantled from the mid-1980s, had reached its apex by 1971 (see the chapters by Julia O'Connor and Pat Armstrong in this volume).

As the collection of reviews of *The Vertical Mosaic* edited by James Heap (1974) revealed, there were arguments over just what Porter meant. He was denounced for rejecting his earlier radicalism *and* congratulated for exposing the deep inequalities of Canadian society. This criticism and praise reflects the genuine ambivalence and ambiguity in Porter's work. Radical, though not Marxist or even social democratic, criticism can be read into *The Vertical Mosaic*. Perhaps the personal and intellectual qualities that gave Porter such insight into the subtle exercise of class power, and his own peripheral membership in the hegemonic circles he described, are not the qualities of a forceful critic of capitalism; for a thoughtful and fuller discussion of Porter's politics, see Helmes-Hayes (1990).

There has been no second *Vertical Mosaic*. Perhaps this is because of the breadth of Porter's original project, which would only be increased by the much richer empirical data now available to describe the Canadian class structure, education, and occupational mobility. Maybe the increased specialization in our discipline has also damped the ambition of sociologists. Perhaps it is more sensible to ask why there has been no effort to replicate the elite studies in *The Vertical Mosaic* as a whole. One important reason, I think, is that *elite theory*, even in the more radical form given to it by Porter, has *never* been a focus of sustained scholarship in Canada. Even the sociologists whose work was directly inspired by *The Vertical Mosaic* did not share Porter's enthusiasm for elite theory. And, after its publication, Porter directed his attention away from elites and towards the large-scale studies of education and stratification in order to address questions about class that he raised in the first half of *The Vertical Mosaic*. I will return to this question in the Conclusion below.

The following discussion of research on elites since the publication of *The Vertical Mosaic* begins with the economic elite. Rather than focusing on individual works or scholars, the discussion is structured around the analytic issues addressed by Porter and raised subsequently. Each section begins with a précis of what I understand to be Porter's approach. While I will summarize the findings of the newer research, my primary concern is with the general direction this work has taken and the emerging theoretical and substantive issues it has addressed.

The Economic Elite

Porter understood the Canadian economic elite in terms of three interrelated phenomena. He began by considering the structural basis of the business elite that is found in the concentration of economic power in the largest corporations. This provided the basis for identifying the individuals who controlled the dominant corporations. Having identified the economic elite, Porter examined their social backgrounds, ethnicity and nationality, and careers, drawing attention both to the inequitable processes of recruitment and to the implications of the resulting sociocultural milieu of the business elite. Finally, information about individuals in the corporate elite was used to draw conclusions about the relations between corporations and the characteristics of more important corporations. Partly because this agenda reflects Porter's particular concerns, only Wallace Clement's explicit replication of Porter's study addresses all three issues. Porter did not explicitly study the ideology of corporate elites, and this additional topic is treated separately.

The Structure of Corporate Capital and the Economic Elite

Corporate Capital

Since Porter conceived of the economic elite in terms of their control over the 'dominant' Canadian corporations, his first task was to identify those corporations. This was more than a stepping stone to the elite, however. Porter recognized corporate concentration as a central aspect of the structure of developed capitalism. While there has been a longstanding academic interest in economic concentration, Porter was prescient in recognizing the importance of the nationality of owner-ship of the largest corporations and their distribution across industries five years before the publication of Kari Levitt's influential *Silent Surrender* (1970).

It is significant that Porter identified the 'dominant' Canadian corpo-rations in terms of market shares *within* industries rather than the size of corporations (though, practically, the two are related). Most of the 'dom-inant' firms were identified from a 1948 listing of manufacturing estab-lishments with 500 or more employees, from which were deleted firms that did not also have a dominant position in their industries[6] and firms Porter thought were 'too small' (see Porter's Appendix II for details). To the initial list were added ten firms with assets of more than $10 million but fewer than 500 employees, and the largest firms in the main non-manufacturing industries of private power generation, telephones and retail trade. By these criteria, there were 170 'dominant' non-financial corporations in 1950.

Because he intended to replicate this research and look at change over time in *The Canadian Corporate Elite* (1975) and to make comparisons between Canada and the United States in a later work, *Continental Cor-porate Power* (1977a),[7] Wallace Clement also devoted significant effort to identifying dominant corporations, though he used size rather than market power as the criterion. One hundred thirteen dominant corpora-tions met Clement's criteria of having 'assets of greater than $250 mil-lion and income of over $50 million' (1975: 128). He added: 'These guidelines remained flexible so that within particular functionally-defined sectors, such as banking and insurance, when the largest corpo-rations accounted for 80 per cent of more of all sales and assets within that sector, only these were selected' (1975: 128). The decline in the num-ber of dominant corporations from Porter's to Clement's study reflects only differences in their methodology *not* an increase in corporate con-centration. While Clement identified one-third fewer dominant corporations than Porter, the number of directors *increased* from 1,304 to 1,454, because the size of boards increased.[8]

Reflecting a growing concern with the impact of foreign ownership, Clement divided the corporate elite into 'indigenous' and 'comprador' elites (1975: 117), on the basis of whether the firms with which they were associated were Canadian- or foreign-controlled. The comprador elite was made up of the directors and executives of 'dominant foreign controlled branch plants.' These two elites were defined in terms of *positions* on corporate boards of directors, rather than individuals and Clement (1975: 150ff) reported his findings in this way; so a director of two corporations could actually be a member of both elites.[9]

Rather than identifying dominant corporations on the basis of their market position or absolute size, for their longitudinal study of interlocking directorates, Carroll, Fox, and Ornstein (1982; see also Carroll 1986) adopted the simpler strategy of selecting the largest 100 Canadian corporations as ranked by assets, at five-year intervals between 1946 and 1976. For each year, their intention was to include the 70 largest industrial firms, the 20 largest financial firms, and the 10 largest merchandising firms. Because their assets are put to different uses, there is an element of arbitrariness in any combination of financial, industrial, and merchandising corporations. The changing industrial structure and concentration within industries also required various ad hoc modifications to Carroll, Fox, and Ornstein's scheme. For example, the large property development corporations emerged only in the later years of their study, and there were only three merchandisers large enough to include in the 1946 sample (see Carroll 1986: Chapter 4 for details). Interestingly, Carroll (1986: 65) reported that the proportion of all industrial assets in Canada held by the largest 70 industrial firms (around 50 per cent) changed very little between 1946 and 1976.

Thanks to reports required by the Corporations and Labour Unions Returns Act (CALURA) designed to monitor foreign ownership, vastly improved corporate rankings are now provided annually by Statistics Canada. Thus Carroll (1986: 163) examined corporate concentration and control between 1975 and 1982, Edward Grabb (1990) examined changes in corporate concentration between 1975 and 1985, and Ornstein (1988a: 191) examined concentration in 1983 – all directly from the CALURA reports. Much improved rankings of corporations by the *Financial Post*, The *Globe and Mail*, and *Canadian Business* provide additional information on corporate ownership and many other characteristics. With these data, the problem of identifying the dominant firms for a study of the corporate elite in Canada can be solved by reversing the steps used in the earlier studies: one can select a larger-than-necessary number of firms; *then* eliminate insignificant ones on the basis of analysis of their financial characteristics or the absence of directorate interlocks with larger firms.

From Corporations to the Economic Elite
Porter moved from economic institutions to individuals by assuming that the directors of the dominant corporations constituted a 'corporate elite.' Directors of two or more dominant corporations, the 'interlocking directorate,' form a network of relationships between corporations. The strength of the link between each pair of corporations increases with the number of common directors, the presence of directors who are executives of one of the firms, and the number of 'indirect' links through the boards of other corporations. Porter analysed this network to examine the extent of relationships between firms, the links between industries, the number and composition of 'cliques' of corporations, and the positions of individual corporations.[10]

Porter was mainly interested in the characteristics of the individual directors in the corporate elite, reflecting his theoretical view that the major institutional interests in modern society are represented by the high-level officials in formal organizations. This particular definition of a positional elite can be distinguished from the following alternative elites: the upper class 'establishment' of people from a social layer of traditional wealth; the 'elite' that would be discovered by directly examining the business and social relationships of the corporate executives who actively manage large corporations; and the capitalist class proper ('big bourgeoisie' or 'monopoly capital'), which Marxists identify as the owners of corporations.

Rather than treating them as interchangeable members of an elite, in *The Economy of Canada: A Study of Ownership and Control* (1978) and *Canadian Capitalism: A Study of Power in the Canadian Business Establishment* (1981), Niosi differentiated corporate directors according to their particular roles in the management of large corporations. Aside from the explicitly Marxist orientation of Niosi's work (neither Porter nor Clement had an entry in the index for 'capitalist' or for 'capitalist class'), what distinguishes Niosi is a robust concept of the capitalist class, defined in terms of the *ownership* of large corporations. Using data from the Ontario and Quebec Securities Commissions on the controlling shareholders of major corporations, Niosi (1978) first identified directors belonging to the capitalist class proper by virtue of their having substantial ownership of corporations. The *non*-controlling directors were then divided into four groups according to their function: legal advisers, financial advisers, career managers, and the owners and managers of other companies. These non-controlling directors, Niosi showed, do not have significant ownership in the large corporations.

In *Canadian Capitalism*, Niosi examined divisions within Canadian capitalism, distinguishing the 'Canadian bourgeoisie,' the 'new French-Canadian bourgeoisie,' state-owned enterprises, and the subsidiaries of foreign-owned companies (home of the 'comprador elite'). While his understanding of the historical emergence of the capitalist class differs only in emphasis from the nationalist interpretations of Levitt (1970) and Naylor (1972), by the early 1970s Niosi saw evidence of new, regionally based and ethnic capitalist class fractions, the repatriation of formerly foreign-owned enterprises, and the growing power of state enterprises. This is a sharp contrast to Clement's characterization of Canadian capital as he saw it in 1975: 'Canada in the 1960s witnessed a great transformation in its economic power structure. Primarily using the multinational corporation, U.S. economic elites have penetrated the Canadian power structure and created a distorted elite formation' (1975: 117).

In pointing to the emergence of French-Canadian and Jewish fractions of capital, Niosi circumscribed their autonomy and placed a political interpretation on his analysis:

The francophone bourgeoisie is, in fact, only the French Canadian section of the Canadian capitalist class. Its markets, its investments, its ambitions are all Canada-wide. While it has helped build up the Québec government apparatus and depends on it for support, it is a not at all interested in the separation of Québec. On the other hand, the programme and practice of the PQ government encourages the petty bourgeoisie, with its institutional base in the co-operative movement, in its dreams of being able to defend itself against the incursions of large-scale capital. The petty bourgeoisie and public-sector workers who live 'by the word' are the main producers and transmitters of pro-independence ideology in Québec today. (1981: 68)

After examining the affiliations of their directors and executives, Niosi argued that state capital in the large crown corporations is controlled by the indigenous, private sector bourgeoisie. He also pointed to a decline in the comprador bourgeoisie, as crown corporations and regional elements of Canadian capital flourished in the 1970s.

Class and Ethnic Origins

Porter was very concerned with the extent of unequal opportunity reflected in the recruitment of elites in Canadian society.[11] Of course, the 'circulation of elites' is a long-standing interest of elite theorists, who were liberal in their political views only to the extent of believing that elites should maintain their ability to govern effectively by recruiting the most able members of subordinate groups.[12] Porter also took the evidence about the common social backgrounds of elites to indicate the extent to which they shared a common culture, experiences, and outlook.

The Class Background of the Corporate Elite

Porter (1965: 291ff) found that 50 per cent of the Canadian-resident economic elite had what he defined as 'upper class' backgrounds and another 32 per cent had middle-class backgrounds, leaving 18 per cent potentially from working-class backgrounds. More than twenty years later, Clement (1975: 194) found that 59 per cent of the corporate elite were from upper-class backgrounds, 35 per cent from the middle class, and only 6 per cent, potentially, from the working class.[13] The identification of corporate elites from a 'working class' background by Porter and Clement is qualified because it is based on the *absence* of contrary bibliographic evidence showing that an individual was middle or upper class, rather than any specific confirmatory information. There can be no doubt about the very high degree of recruitment of corporate elites from extremely privileged backgrounds, though the change in the definition of the dominant corporations and the questionable use of having a university education as a criterion of middle-class background leave some doubt about Clement's conclusion that recruitment became more exclusive over time. It is unfortunate that our knowledge of the class origins of the Canadian corporate elite is limited to two studies, the most recent of which describes the corporate elite of twenty-five years ago.

In characterizing the capitalist class in terms of the *directors* of corporations, rather than their top level managers (or both), the corporate elites identified by Porter and Clement are likely weighted towards the inheritors of corporate wealth, especially for the corporations that are not widely held or in which there is a controlling individual or family. This would explain why the Canadian-resident directors of foreign-controlled corporations and *inside* directors are less likely to be from the upper class. In any event, in a future study of the social backgrounds of corporate elites, it would be interesting to differentiate them according to Niosi's criteria: comparing 'inside directors,' who are executives, to 'outside directors,' board members with substantial stock to non-owning directors, and differentiating non-controlling directors according to their function on the board.

As interpreted by Clement and the left-nationalist political economists of the mid-1970s, the Canadian corporate elite pictured in Porter's and Clement's studies was conservative and ingrown, lacking the courage to recruit from outside a narrow and privileged stratum, and with neither the interest nor ability to differentiate its interests from American capital. These plutocratic heirs of the nineteenth-century 'mercantile' elite that built the railways and owned the banks had little interest in industry and were responsible for Canada's semi-dependent status in the world economy.

The traditional [economic] elite has chosen to centre itself in transportation, utilities, finance and the mass media. In so doing it has stifled the development of indigenous social forces in most manufacturing and resource activities – the sectors which are actually engaged in the creation of surplus in a capitalist society ... The kind of bourgeoisie which emerges from this political economy is a conservative mercantile and financial type which inevitably is dependent up on the dynamic, creative *productive* industrial bourgeoisies of the metropolis, first British, then American. (Clement 1975: 355)

For Clement, the character of the corporate elites has a broad and powerful impact on society: 'The existence of a powerful Canadian commercial elite controlled by the upper class and of a predominantly foreign elite in production means that Canada remains a "low mobility" society' (1975: 357).[14]

More recent information about the social background of Canadian economic elites is both fragmentary and from such different samples that nothing at all can be said about change after 1972 (the date to which Clement referred). A study concerned mainly with the political ideology of corporate elites, conducted by Ornstein and Stevenson (n.d.) provides some information on the chief executives of the largest Canadian corporations in 1981. Based on 222 interviews, the distribution of their fathers' occupations was as follows: 37 per cent professional and managerial occupations, 25 per cent skilled non-manual occupations, 7 per cent skilled manual occupations, 7 per cent less skilled non-manual occupations and 8 per cent less skilled manual and farm occupations, and 16 per cent farmers. Thirty-nine per cent of the chief executives' fathers owned businesses; and of these owners, 18 per cent had no employees, 42 per cent had one to nine employees 19 per cent had 10 to 99 employees, and 19 per cent had 100 or more employees. While they come from privileged backgrounds relative to the population, as a group the chief executives of Canadian corporations in 1981 did not have the extremely privileged backgrounds of the corporate elites defined by Porter and Clement.

With the elevation of successful business executives to role models in the 1980s, a number of business journalists have made small-scale studies of business executives, including Diane Francis's (1986) profile of 31 families ('dynasties'!) and James Fleming's (1991) survey of and bibliographic research on the directors of the twenty largest (non-financial) corporations, ranked by assets and the five 'big banks,' for 1989. This work is too unsystematic to tell us much about the changing social backgrounds of corporate elites.[15]

Ethnic Origins of the Corporate Elite
There is evidence of a decline in the proportion of corporate elites of British origin and a corresponding increase in the proportion of the corporate elite from French and 'other' origins. Porter found that 92.3 per cent of the corporate elite were from British, 6.7 per cent from French, and only 1.0 per cent from 'other' backgrounds. Clement found that the British representation had fallen to 86.2 per cent and that French and 'other' representation had risen to 8.4 and 5.4 per cent, respectively. The ethnic composition of corporate chief executives in 1981, Ornstein and Stevenson (1984) found, was 65 per cent British, 9 per cent French, and 26 per cent of other groups. Hunter, in a similar analysis of the ethnic backgrounds of the 184 Canadian families with wealth of $20 million or more in 1975, indicated that 55 per cent were English, 7 per cent were French, and 38 per cent had other origins (1986: 157). Ogmundson and McLauglin (1992) found that 69.7 per cent of the directors of the twenty largest industrial corporations (ranked by assets) in 1985 were British, 15.2 per cent were French, and 15.1 per cent from 'other' ethnic groups.

While more is known about the ethnic backgrounds of the corporate elite than about their class backgrounds, these comparisons are still seriously compromised by differences in the samples. More important, the focus on the representation of the charter groups takes no account of the dramatic transformation in the conceptualization of ethnicity and race since Porter's time. The 'other' ethnic group is not *a* group, and its rise could as easily reflect the emergence of a small number of new 'charter' groups (Jews or Chinese, for example) as a broader diversification of the social backgrounds of elites. Nakhaie (1997) argued that any decline in the proportion of British elites should be measured against their decreasing share in the population, so that unadjusted comparisons tend to exaggerate the decline in British dominance. This criticism makes sense if the concern is mobility into elites, but not if the concern is to understand their cultural background.

Relations between Corporations

While intercorporate *ownership* results in observable, direct links between corporations, more numerous and complex relations result from shared membership on corporate boards of directors.[16] Porter used the distribution of the numbers of directorships of individuals as an indicator of the overall concentration of power. He was less interested in the resulting network of relationships between corporations, though his ability to examine the network was certainly restricted by the lack of computerized files.

In addition to the distribution of the number of directorships held by individuals in the corporate elite, Clement computed the number of interlocking directorates of each firm and examined the strength of the relations between major industrial sectors (finance, manufacturing, resources, trade, and utilities). Having more interlocks were corporations in finance rather than industry, Canadian-controlled rather than foreign-controlled corporations, and widely held rather than family-controlled corporations.

Clement's analysis was based on 'direct' interlocks, that is, the links formed by individuals with positions on two or more boards. Because they are prohibited from sharing directors, analysis of direct interlocks would show that the five banks were competing centres. What connects the boards of the 'competing' banks, of course, are very large numbers of 'indirect' ties which are formed when directors of two different banks sit on the board of a third corporation. Many such indirect links provide linkages between the banks, and between many other pairs of corporations with no direct connections. This is where the development of network theory and methods and increasingly powerful computing, from the mid-1960s onward, allowed researchers to ask entirely new questions about the relationships between the largest corporations and their directors. It became possible to quantify the positions of corporations in the network and to identify groups (termed 'cliques') of heavily interlocked corporations. The positions of corporations in the network could also be related to their size, nationality and type of ownership, industry, and so on. Dominant corporations could be identified by examining the network directly.

The capitalist class revealed by the quantitative studies of directorates was much more robust, centralized, integrated, and Canadian than previous studies suggested. Looking at the network of interlocks in 1973, Ornstein (1976) showed that the largest Canadian-controlled financial *and industrial* firms had the largest boards and the most interlocks. When Carroll, Fox, and Ornstein (1982) developed 'maps' of the network, using a statistical technique called 'smallest space analysis,' they found that the large, Canadian financial *and industrial* corporations were at its centre. Instead of there being 'cliques' of corporations, suggestive of the banking–industrial groups in Sweden, Germany, and some other European countries, directorate interlocks tied the corporations into a single dense network. Corporations were largely differentiated in terms of their 'centrality,' with the more important corporations in the centre and less important corporations on the periphery of the network.

In order to understand whether the Canadian capitalist class was distinctive, perhaps bearing the mark of truncated economic development, Ornstein (1989) compared the network of Canadian interlocks to the networks of nine developed capitalist nations. Using a variety of quantitative measures, he showed that the Canadian network was quite unexceptional. These conclusions are buttressed by Carroll's detailed examination of groups of corporations linked by multiple common directors. He concluded that 'not only are institutional relations among indigenous firms stronger than those linking Canadian to foreign interests, but they also seem to be more directly related to the accumulation process itself' (1986: 172).

Corporate Ideology

As William Domhoff insisted, corporate elites *act*; even if they are *structurally* dominant, they must struggle for *political* dominance. While some of the political success of capital in the past decade may be attributed to the efforts of the Business Council on National Issues, the Fraser Institute, and the Canadian Federation of Independent Business, that these organizations are needed is telling evidence that the political domination of capital is not automatic. Domhoff remarked:

But is the privileged position of business an all-important idea? I think not. Given the tensions and uncertainties of a dynamic and volatile capitalist economic system, and the possibilities for social changes in a democratic state system where elected legislatures can greatly influence the functioning of administrative agencies and businesses themselves, it is just a fairy tale to think that it does not take continuous efforts on the part of the corporate community to dominate the state structure. No American capitalists ever have been so serene and confident as to rely on underlying 'structural imperatives' to insure that people in decision-making positions will do what needs to be done for the sake of capitalism. (1990: 194)

Researchers are all too aware of the limits of empirical studies of the economics of large corporations. For example, on the basis of the patterns of directorate interlocks, Carroll suspected that Canadian banks and financial institutions have become increasingly important sources of financing to Canadian industry, but there is little public information on such arrangements. No such problem faces the researcher with an interest in the political ideology of corporate capital. Quite the opposite, a wealth of information is available from business interest groups and the business press, whose political success has precisely to do with their ability to communicate. Furthermore, given the views they express publicly, it is hard to imagine they have a more extreme 'secret agenda.'

Despite its importance, lamentably little effort has been devoted to understanding the political agenda, or maybe agendas, of Canadian corporations. With the exception of David Langille's very fine 1987 article on the Business Council on National Issues, there is no major study of the political activity of business interest groups. Despite stronger disclosure regulations, which provide important information on the links between corporations and political parties at the federal, provincial, and municipal levels, there appears to have been no serious study of corporate donations.

An alternative to positional and document-based studies, though much more difficult and expensive, is to conduct a survey of corporate elites. Surveys can provide much more detailed information about individuals' political views than can be gleaned from corporate publications designed to represent their public face. Ornstein and Stevenson (1984; see also Ornstein 1985a 1985b 1986) have presented a complex picture of corporate ideology. While far to the right of the state and other elites covered in the study, their 1981 interviews revealed a relatively pragmatic and liberal corporate elite, especially compared with the views of present-day corporate culture,[17] not to mention some provincial governments. They also found that, while corporations are commonly seen as adopting an entirely pragmatic orientation to the two major conservative parties, elite supporters of the Liberal Party are significantly more liberal (Ornstein and Stevenson 1984). This finding is consistent with a remark of Niosi (1981: 35), speaking of the ascendance of new corporate elites:

> Nevertheless, new industries created new paths to fortune, and the Canadian capitalist class, at one time exclusive Anglo-Saxon and Protestant, has had to adapt to the arrival of Jewish and French Canadian newcomers. These nouveaux riches have, however, not been well received by the older members of the bourgeoisie, and they have fought their exclusion from the circles of the social elite through their position of influence in the party of the non-WASPs – the Liberal Party of Canada.

Reading Stevie Cameron's (1994) devastating study of the social circle around Brian Mulroney, one is struck by the absence of Jews (not to mention Ontario Anglo-Protestants), a striking confirmation of Niosi's observation.

The Labour Elite

John Porter is the only sociologist to have undertaken a systematic study of the labour elite in Canada. The humbler backgrounds of labour elites prevented him from using the same bibliographic sources used to determine the social backgrounds of the corporate and state elites. So Porter conducted a survey of the labour elites by mail. The labour elite described by Porter is dramatically less privileged than *all the other* elites: 68 per cent had not graduated from high school, 24 per cent were high school graduates, and only 8 per cent were university graduates (1965: 341), compared with 58, 52,[18] and 79 per cent of the corporate, political, and bureaucratic elites, respectively (1965: 282, 388, 433). Unfortunately, given the lack of later, comparable research, Porter's description of the labour elite in 1957 is of mainly historical interest. He described the bygone era of industrially based postwar capitalism, in which the public sector was quite small and unorganized, a quarter of the labour elite were born in England, and almost all were men.[19]

Considering the establishment of labour studies programs in a number of universities, it is interesting to speculate on why no more recent study of labour elites has been conducted.[20] Perhaps the academic researchers most interested in the organization of work and the labour movement are fearful that a close examination of the leadership of trade unions will somehow play into the hands of business.

The Political Elite

In the political elite, Porter included federal cabinet ministers, provincial premiers, justices of the Supreme Court, presidents of the Exchequer Court, and provincial chief justices over the period 1940–60. Though 16 per cent of the political elite were from families with at least one elite predecessor, as a group they came from much less privileged backgrounds than the corporate elites. Both the legal and political sides of this elite – obviously the judges, but also the cabinet members and provincial premiers – were dominated by French and English lawyers from middle- or upper-middle class backgrounds. Porter found that routes into the political elite are much less institutionalized than the channels to the other elites. Political elites tend not to be professional politicians in the way that economic elites have managerial careers. Porter's statistical portrait is accompanied by a rich description and commentary on Canadian federal politicians.

By the time Dennis Olsen conducted his replication of the studies of the political and bureaucratic elites much had changed. Comparing the political elites of the 1961–73 period with Porter's of 1940–60, Olsen (1980) found only a minor diversification of the ethnic origins of the elites, but a marked reduction in the representation of lawyers, in the federal cabinet. There were more teachers and academics, more businessmen, and a few journalists and broadcasters in the political elite. As measured by fathers' occupations, however, there was virtually no change in their class origins. Olsen was quite instrumentalist in his assessment of the class origins of the political elite:

The Canadian state recruits primarily from the middle class, a middle class that was quite small, perhaps 15 to 20 per cent of the population, in the time of the current elite's fathers. So the elite are the sons of the middle class, but they are also middle class by virtue of their own occupations before entering politics ... This middle class is not really a class for itself in a national sense, that is, one that aspires to be a ruling class and produces a national program and ideology to that end. There is no real attempt on its part to build a lasting alliance with the larger Canadian working class. This is the reason there are so few members of the elite with working-class backgrounds. It is a middle class that is content to leave the small upper class dominant in society, while elite members themselves *individually* aspire to move up the ladder. (1980: 30)

Porter made almost exactly the same point (though it is oddly placed in small print in a methodological appendix):

The reason why political leaders in Canada may appear to serve the corporate elite is not because the former are the agents of the latter, but rather because they are predominantly middle class in origin ... The middle class characteristics of the politicians of both major parties easily leads to a community of interest between politicians and corporate power. It is the middle class for whom the prospects of upward social mobility are greatest, so that a preservation of the *status quo* becomes a desirable political goal. (1965: 607)

Ogmundson and McLauglin's (1992) study of the ethnicity of political elites gives evidence of a significant increase in the number of political elites who are neither English nor French in the federal and provincial cabinets and among Members of Parliament. While the use of surnames to measure ethnicity is a significant weakness of this work, it seems unlikely that more detailed studies would show a different trend.

Why has so much more scholarly attention been devoted to economic than political elites; why should sociologists find economic elites more interesting than political elites; and why have political scientists shown so little interest in political elites? It does not seem reasonable to argue that political elites are inherently less interesting than corporate elites. Indeed, because of the more rapid turnover of political elites, one might think there was more to be gained from new studies of political elites. Surely, Mulroney, Rae, Klein, Harris, and Manning are much more *unlike* their predecessors than the current crop of bank presidents is from theirs!

A methodological issue also deserves attention. Porter's theoretical orientation, which led him to define the various elites as office-holders, makes much less sense for political elites than for the others. By Porter's definition, advisers to political leaders are not members of the elite because 'behind the scenes men do not occupy power roles in the political system' (1965: 606). While the influence of bureaucrats *is* tightly tied to the *positions* they hold, it makes more sense to conceptualize the political elite as a set of *individuals*, who *may* hold elective office, but who could also be former office-holders, officials of the political parties, paid advisers of government officials, or devoted amateurs. The characteristics of this more broadly defined political elite could be quite different from the positional elite described in Porter's study.

Another extension of Porter's perspective would be to consider the provincial and municipal elites, which offers interesting possibilities for comparative research. For example, one could ask whether the links between business elites and the different provincial parties reflect their distinctive economies or whether there are common patterns of business–government relations. Canadian political scientists have devoted a great deal of effort to understanding the extent and nature of local political cultures, but this is usually conceived in terms of voting patterns and the resulting party alignments, rather than political elites. In the smaller worlds of provincial politics, class and regional interests may be more strongly represented than federally. For example, the cabinet of the recently elected Conservative government of Ontario prominently features proprietors of small businesses from outside the major metropolitan centre of the province, and from industries that are most likely to employ minimum wage labour, oppose unions and government regulation of wage-setting and promotion practices (in the form of pay and employment equity, for example), and resent taxes.

Similar questions can be asked about municipal elites, though again sociologists and political scientists have shown little interest. The involvement of individuals with links to the construction and development industry is potentially critical in the politics of local government. Since municipal politics are rarely organized along party lines, analysis of patterns of voting in municipal councils is much more interesting than in the federal and provincial legislatures, which are governed by party discipline. Again, studies that compare locations and time periods would be the most interesting.

Finally, a comparative study of ethnic community elites would provide a valuable addition to Porter's national perspective and could offer insights into the way that communities are attached to the political process and into the stratification within ethnic communities. In Ontario, one need only think of the historical attachments of the Polish and conservative Ukrainian communities to the Progressive Conservative party, of the radical Ukrainians, Finns, and Jews to the Communist party, of most Italian-Canadians and upwardly mobile elements of the Jewish community to the Liberal party, and of the left-wing Italians to the NDP. Traditional studies of ethnic communities usually do not address these issues, while more recent ethnographic studies tend to focus on everyday experience, not within-community stratification.

English-Canadian social scientists' remarkable lack of interest in political elites must reflect the dominant theoretical currents in Canadian
social science. While the state has been a major focus of research interest,
especially within political economy, the structuralist perspective has led
away from studying elites. Political economists find themselves oddly
aligned with traditional institutionalists in ignoring elites.[21]

The Bureaucratic Elite

After a brief, rather functionalist, summary of Weber's views, much of
Porter's chapter on the bureaucratic elite, entitled 'The Federal Bureaucracy,' is an account of the influence of high-level civil servants during
the government of Mackenzie King (which, even at the time it was published, referred to a past era). Again Porter provided a small-scale
empirical study of the social background of the bureaucratic elite, in
which he included federal civil servants from the level of 'director'
upwards and executives of crown corporations, in 1953. There is also
some commentary on the turnover of this elite in the Diefenbaker and
Pearson administrations. In his account of the bureaucratic elite Porter
seemed to glimpse a bygone era of civility and elite liberalism, and he
was much more sympathetic to the bureaucrats than to the other elites.

Particularly considering the time at which Porter examined them
(1953, twelve years before *The Vertical Mosaic* actually appeared), the
federal bureaucratic elite was extraordinarily well educated, with nearly
half having some post-graduate education. Former university faculty
were very well represented in the bureaucratic elite of that time and
Porter noted that 'Because the orientation of the bureaucracy to intellectual values, intellectual accomplishment gives prestige. A medal from a
learned society, an important article, a brief on some important economic, social or scientific question enhances the individual's reputation
within the system' (1965: 435).

The federal bureaucrats were also decidedly middle and upper class
in origin: 9 per cent came from elite families and another 9 per cent came
from upper-class but not elite families; and 69 per cent could be
assigned to the middle class because they went to private schools or had
fathers in middle-class occupations; leaving 13 per cent from origins
below the middle class. Porter was happy that fears the Liberal elite
would change when Diefenbaker was elected proved to be unfounded.

Repeating Porter's study in 1973, Olsen (1980: 79) found that the number of federal bureaucrats with upper-class backgrounds (adding the

elite and upper class categories mentioned above), had fallen from 18 to
10 per cent. Furthermore, the representation of elites of British origin fell
from 84 to 65 per cent, while the representation of the French and 'other'
groups rose from 13 and 3 per cent to 24 and 11 per cent, respectively.
Also, the proportion of university-educated bureaucrats with university
training in the social sciences grew from 24 to 48 per cent between 1953
and 1973. Of course, Olsen's view of these findings was quite different
from Porter's. Olsen described 'the kind of alliance that the Canadian
state, or at least the bureaucracy – its more permanent arm – has put
together': 'It is an unequal alliance for both classes and ethnic categories
that would harbour its own tensions and contradictions. The British-
Canadian middle class has the greatest representation ... There are equal
numbers of upper-class British and French Canadians, so that at this level
there seems to be a straightforward sharing of power ... The working class
is underrepresented' (1980: 80). Ogmundson and McLaughlin (1992: 231)
reported a similar growth in the ethnic diversity of the provincial bureaucratic elites: 7, 14, and 22 per cent of *provincial* deputy ministers were neither British nor French in 1965, 1975, and 1985, respectively.

Campbell and Szablowski (1979) describe the social origins of the high-
level bureaucrats in the 'central agencies' – the Prime Minister's Office,
the Privy Council Office, the Federal–Provincial Relations Office, the
Department of Finance, and the Treasury Board Secretariat – as follows:

The Canadian bureaucratic elite represents the general populace better than the
senior levels of public service in almost any other advanced liberal democracy.
Moreover, perhaps because our central agencies include several 'high fliers'
who represent the new breed of the bureaucratic establishment, their backgrounds reflect very dramatically how the ranks of senior officials in Canada
have become more open to previously underrepresented groups, especially
Catholics, non-charter ethnics, and Jews. Indeed, our finding that 44 per cent of
their fathers never graduated from high school highlights how our respondents
have experienced rapid upward mobility. These officials benefited more from
educational achievement than from anything else. In fact, of all characteristics,
earning a graduate degree delineates our respondents' backgrounds most
sharply from those of senior officials previously studied in Ottawa. Further, our
central agents need not have received their education at an elite prep school or
university to begin graduate work. Most of our respondents went to public high
schools and received their BAs at non-elite universities. (1979: 121)

Whatever the demographic changes in this elite, there is a striking

continuity between Porter's description of the culture of the bureaucratic elite between the 1930s and the immediate postwar period and
Campbell and Szablowski's picture of the elite in the central agencies in
1976. In his more recent study of deputy ministers in 1989, Fleming
found that 'higher education was clearly a means of climbing the ladder
from humble origins to the pinnacle of bureaucratic power. The majority of deputy ministers were born into modest, middle class homes,
judging from the occupations of their fathers, and therefore had no kinship ties or family connections to help them land jobs ... Their work
experience doesn't tend to extend much beyond government. Most deputy ministers [14 out of a total of 27] went straight into the civil service
after university; 22 had spent most of their career [sic] in the civil service' (1991: 77). While the evidence is somewhat scattered, there appears
to have been a democratization of this elite.

Considering the organizational basis of the bureaucratic elite, it is
interesting that elite theorists have done little to conceptualize the
bureaucratic elite in organizational terms. The bureaucratic elite has
been conceptualized mainly as a hierarchy, rather than in terms of vertical divisions. So, in deciding how to select an elite to compare with Porter's (who studied a much smaller government), the key problem for
Olsen was what *levels* of bureaucrats should be included in his study.
The result was to gloss over a central question about the unity of the
bureaucratic elite. Marxists speak of class conflict being 'inscribed' in
the state, of the (necessary or potential) contradiction between fostering
accumulation and legitimation, and of the 'unequal structure of representation.' An obvious question is whether the bureaucratic elite itself is
unified, and an interesting means of testing this would be to examine
the extent of movement *between* the different ministries. With no more
than a series of government telephone books for a data source, it would
be possible to trace the mobility of bureaucrats over time.

Relationships between the Elites

It is significant that the concluding chapter of *The Vertical Mosaic* is
devoted to 'Relations between Elites.' For elite theorists, the relationships between elites are the substance of politics: elites act for their constituencies, in the process consolidating their powers atop their separate
domains; and the relationships among the economic, labour, political,
and other elites describe the fundamental nature of power in Canadian
society. Porter recognized this explicitly at the beginning of the chapter,

in which he argued that thinking of power in Canadian society in terms of an 'establishment' or a 'power elite' suggests a degree of unity that is not found in the actual relations between elites. Porter's account emphasized elite consensus: 'Nothing brings elites together so much as mutual respect which flows from sharing in the confraternity of power' (1965: 532). He also viewed this consensus in functionalist terms, as a kind of systemic resource used to achieve system goals. While a functional division of labour among elites may actually breed conflict over some kinds of issues, the shared framework and goals allow for their resolution and may even strengthen their bonds.

Porter went on to describe the variety of arrangements that link the elites, illustrating them with many examples 'collected from newspapers, magazines, biographies and historical accounts' (1965: 523). The elites are linked informally, by kinship and friendships (often formed at elite schools), and by what Porter termed 'formal co-ordinating mechanisms,' including commissions, boards, and councils. The *conflicts* between elites that Porter described in detail all involve readily apparent commercial interests, for example, rivalries over the establishment of the CNR, public hydroelectric power in British Columbia, and the trans-Canada natural gas pipeline. The economic, political, and bureaucratic elites rule in a partnership cemented by structural ties, personal acquaintance, and common ideology. Because the elites correspond to the functional needs of a complex society, their coordination reflects a division of labour. Contention over fundamental issues, even between capital and labour, simply cannot figure prominently in a model that divides social functions vertically, with elites commanding the different sectors. Disrupting this consensus, but only occasionally, are conflicts between corporations and the state, or between rival corporations, which involve simple economic self-interest. Interestingly, the more systemic conflicts between capital and the state that punctuated the development of the Canadian welfare state, over unemployment insurance and medical care, for example, are absent from Porter's account.

While elite theorists are concerned with the overall level of elite integration, class theorists' main concern is the relationship between capital and the state. Clement argued (1975: 346) that the interpenetration of the capitalist and political elites increased dramatically in the twenty years since Porter's study: 'In terms of main career patterns it was shown that while only 1.8 per cent or 14 members of the economic elite had their main careers in the political, bureaucratic or military elite; by 1972, this had increased to 5.8 per cent.' Describing the Trudeau cabinets, Clement

(1977b: 231) cited a minister's husband in the corporate elite, one with a son in this position, and another whose brother was director of a number of large corporations. In addition to the links formed by common social backgrounds, careers crossing between elites and membership in advisory bodies, Clement also pointed to the role of political party financing in corporate efforts to influence the political elite. This stress on the strong relations between capital and the state was commonly taken as confirmation of an instrumentalist interpretation of corporate–state relations. Citing Clement, Leo Panitch argued, 'Whatever the merits of Poulantzas' contention that the most efficient state is that with the least direct ties to the dominant class, it is a rather academic point as applied to Canada' (1977: 11).

One obvious question is whether the anecdotal evidence about relations between the corporate and state elites reflects a broad pattern. One can think of the relations between capital and the state in terms of a network of connecting institutions, with individuals whose careers span both types of institutions serving as links between them. While not different in principle from the network of *intercorporate* directorships, many of the links between corporations and the state do not involve simultaneous membership in two or more organizations. For example, members of the cabinet may have been or may become corporate executives, but they cannot be executives while they are in office. Also, there are difficult questions about the numerical base from which to make estimates: a tiny proportion of *all* elected officials have been executives of large corporations, but the proportion is much larger if one considers, for example, federal cabinet ministers. The links between corporations and the state must also be distinguished according to their direction in time. Clement (1975: 182) reported that 18 former members of the bureaucratic elite and 17 former members of the political elite *joined* the corporate elite (defined for 1972); and these 35 constitute a total of 4.5 per cent of the corporate elite. Olsen (1980: 27) reported that while 26 out of 96 federal cabinet ministers in office between 1961 and 1973 *came from* business backgrounds, only 3 of the cabinet ministers had *previously* been part of the Canadian corporate elite. It is much more common for retiring political and bureaucratic elites to join the corporate elite than for the large corporations to serve as a recruiting ground for state elites. This makes sense for corporations, which can attract former politicians with dramatically increased pay and gain valuable insiders' knowledge in return.

Fox and Ornstein (1986; see also Ornstein, 1988b) used the longitudinal database they developed with Carroll to examine the connections between the largest Canadian corporations and a variety of state institutions between 1946 and 1976. Counting a connection made by *any* member of two organizations as a link between the organizations, they found a very dense network of connections between corporations and the state, though corporations are more much strongly connected to each other than to state organizations. They summarized some of their results as follows:

All of the categories of private [i.e., corporate] organizations are tied to substantial numbers of state organizations ... Particularly large densities are observed for the financial firms ... [which have] very large boards and numerous interlocks with other corporations ... The extent to which specific state sectors are tied to private organizations is much more uneven ... The universities and hospitals maintain many and dense ties with capitalist institutions. In general the federal government is much more strongly linked to big capital than are the provincial governments. Ties between crown corporations and the private sector are especially numerous, while the ties linking the federal cabinet and the Senate to the private sector are particularly dense ... The federal and provincial cabinets are much more strongly linked to capital than are the corresponding bureaucracies ... The implication is that pressure from business is more likely to flow from the cabinet to the bureaucracy, rather than the reverse. (1986: 490–2)

At the individual level, of course, the ties between elites are less dense, but still very substantial. About one-fifth of all members of federal cabinets, the Senate, judges in the two highest courts, and hospital and university board members had a corporate position; compared with 7.3 per cent of federal bureaucrats, 4.7 per cent of provincial cabinet members, and 3.1 per cent of provincial bureaucrats. About two-thirds of the time service in the state organizations *preceded* the corporate positions (Fox and Ornstein 1986: 497). The strong links between the corporate and political elites largely take the form of corporations recruiting former political and bureaucratic elites.

The empirical research on the relationship between elites does not do justice to the theoretical importance attached to relations between corporations and the state in many different theoretical approaches. While Porter saw this relationship as quite unproblematic, he understood the importance of the issue and the need for empirical studies. There are many case studies, particularly of corporate–state relations and studies of particular industries, but not the broader scale studies that are needed.

Conclusion: Porter's Unfulfilled Legacy

Despite the celebrated status of *The Vertical Mosaic*, except for studies of corporate elites that were largely conducted from the perspective of class rather than elite theory, English-Canadian social science has done little to perpetuate Porter's legacy of elite studies. With the exception of Clement's now somewhat dated replication, there has been no serious study of the social background of corporate elites, and the studies of directorates are scattered in time and not very systematic, except for the 1946–76 longitudinal study by Carroll, Fox, and Ornstein (1982).

Of the hundreds of papers delivered at the 1995 annual meeting of the Canadian Association of Sociology and Anthropology, only one dealt with elites, and it was concerned with corporate elites. As the review above indicates, the paucity of recent research on elites certainly cannot be taken as indication that there is already a wealth of existing data or that the important research questions are resolved. The major studies of corporate elites reviewed above are now quite dated. For example, they do not take account of the consolidation of the 'four pillars' in finance, or the effects of the 1980s boom and bust. Studies of state elites have yet to tackle the Mulroney era, or even Trudeau's.

This state of affairs has less to do with the limited interest in elite theory among English-Canadian sociologists than with what seems like a general decline in systematic empirical research on social structure and social inequality in Canada. Research on inequality has taken other interesting directions, particularly towards the study of exploitation and subjective accounts. The difficulty is not that the field of enquiry has been broadened, but that some of the central questions about inequality raised by John Porter now receive scant attention. Sociological analysis of the economy has largely been abandoned to economists, while analysis of public policy is mainly in the hands of political scientists. Both disciplines, but especially economics, have weaker critical traditions than sociology, and the result is more market oriented and less critical studies of the economy and more pluralist and less critical studies of politics.

It can be comforting to see oneself as the victim of broad value shifts and changing tastes, but English-Canadian sociologists with a commitment to the *critical* quantitative analysis of Canadian social structure have also failed to develop viable traditions and institutions. The active researchers are small in number and scattered among universities; they have difficulty attracting graduate students; and there is no distinctive outlet for their work (in the way *Studies in Political Economy*, for example, functions for political economy).

Sociologists interested in class and power have largely favoured blurring the lines among the social science disciplines over the past two decades, and they have happily entered the terrains of history, economics, and political science, not to mention literature. This has been something of a one-way street, however. While there has been significant interest in things sociological, in history, for example, the more heavily institutionalized disciplines have not been subject to the same centripetal forces. In principle, there is no reason why 'sociological' studies of inequality and power should not be carried out in the context of, say, political economy. But, as a close look at the journal *Studies in Political Economy* shows, in practice, sociological concerns tend to be subordinated to interests from economics and political science.

New studies of Canadian elites are overdue. Not only would they address critical questions about the exercise of political and economic power in Canada, but an understanding of elites must be an important element of any description of social inequality in Canada. For studies of corporate elites at least, time and technology are on our side. Both ownership and directorate information is now becoming available in machine-readable form, and, while the quality is far from sufficient to think of fully automated studies, it will be possible to avoid data entry almost entirely. With this data it will be possible to track corporate concentration over time, look at changing patterns of intercorporate ownership, and study the network, over time. A new replication of the Porter and Clement studies would be worthwhile, especially if it were possible to obtain their earlier data and convert it to machine-readable form for comparisons and to take account of Niosi's (1978: Chapter 4) convincing arguments for examining the real control of corporate stock and for differentiating the roles of directors.

Notes

1 I thank David Northrup, Gordon Darroch, David Langille, and Penni Stewart for comments on this chapter and Bob Drummond and Greg Albo for helpful advice. Richard Helmes-Hayes provided valuable and detailed advice, and I must also thank him for the invitation to write this essay. I thank Anne Oram for proofreading and Anita Valencia for processing this document.
2 For a nice review of the development of elite theory and its political context, see Cox, Furlong, and Page (1985), especially Chapter 4.

3 I thank Gordon Darroch for drawing this point to my attention.

4 Porter's view should be situated historically, though. The mid- to late-1950s, about which he speaks, marked the high tide of industrial unionism in Canada and predated the massive growth of the state, and state institutions like universities, in the 1960s.

5 I put little weight on Porter's explicit remarks about Marxism (1965: 18ff). Writing before the renewal of Marxist thinking of the late 1960s, Porter rejected a crude rendition of Marxist theory. Porter was, perhaps purposely, ambiguous, but many of his important assumptions are readily recast in Marxist terms. For example, what he described as elite consensus of the 'values' of capitalism is little different from the idea of hegemony.

6 Porter also omitted the printing and publishing industry 'because the power of these firms does not lie so much in their use of economic resources as their ability to influence opinion' (1965: 572). This seeming eccentricity reflects Porter's theoretical view of the institutional bases of the different elites.

7 It is not clear how Clement defined the dominant U.S. corporations. In the main text (p. 141) he referred the reader to Appendix V. A footnote in that appendix (p. 315) indicated: 'For an elaboration of the method used to determine dominant corporations, see Clement, *Canadian Corporate Elite*, pp. 369–99. The same procedures were used to determine Canada's 113 dominant corporations.' Applying the financial limits used to define the dominant Canadian corporations to the United States, however, would have resulted in a much larger number of dominant U.S. corporations than Clement actually obtained.

8 In concluding that there has been 'an overall expansion in the number of elite positions of about nine per cent since 1951 but a contraction by almost a third in the number of dominant corporations' (1975: 150–1), Clement made the consequences of arbitrary changes in methodology into research findings.

9 To understand the role of individuals with directorships in both Canadian- and foreign-controlled corporations, who are members of the 'indigenous' and 'comprador' elites, requires information on their primary affiliation, if any, and where they live. Clement actually defined the comprador elite as 'the senior management and directors of dominant foreign controlled branch plants' (1975: 117), but restricted his empirical analysis to the directors of these corporations.

10 The significance of interlocking directorships is the subject of considerable debate: interlocks between corporations may signify direct, instrumental relations between firms or relations among an elite corps of individuals. For a discussion of this point and empirical analysis based on the Carroll, Fox, and Ornstein longitudinal data set, see Ornstein (1984).

11 Because elites on the national stage are so small in number, the patterns of elite recruitment are not accessible from the sample surveys of the population. For this reason there is a strong methodological argument for supplementing standard mobility surveys with samples of elites.

12 Bottomore (1993: Chapter 3) provided a very nice summary and assessment of classical views of the 'circulation of elites.'

13 Ogmundson (1990 1992 1993) mounted a somewhat enlightening, but ill-tempered, attack on Porter's and Clement's background data and interpretation. For a reply, see Clement (1990).

14 Though there is a large body of comparative literature on occupational mobility, Clement made no reference to it. In Ganzeboom, Luijkx, and Treiman's (1989) analysis of 149 intergenerational class mobility tables from 35 countries, Canada and Quebec do not stand out.

15 Fleming's study has a reasonable sample, but the large amount of missing data raises serious questions about the potential bias in his findings.

16 In fact there are two networks, which are the 'duals' of one another: one linking corporations, formed by individual directors with two or more directorships; and one linking individuals, formed by corporate boards (all of which have more than two members).

17 In my observation, there was a dramatic rightward lurch in the editorials of Canadian business-oriented newspapers, such as the *Globe and Mail*, in the late 1970s.

18 For the corporate and political elites, Porter gave the percentage with 'university education,' which suggests that not all such people obtained degrees.

19 Porter did not indicate how many of his 275 leaders of English-Canadian unions were women, though the number must have been very small (but not zero).

20 Ogmundson and McLaughlin (1992) have made a minor addition, providing information on the ethnicity of labour elites, defined as 'presidents of national unions or Canadian vice-presidents of international unions,' in 1965, 1975, and 1985. The data are very sparse, referring to only 29, 24, and 17 observations in the three years, and relating only to ethnicity, which was determined on the basis of surnames. Especially for women included in the hierarchy, this provides error-prone data.

21 For this point I thank Greg Albo.

References

Albo, Gregory, and Jane Jenson. (1989). 'A Contested Concept: The Relative Autonomy of the State.' Pp. 180–211 in Wallace Clement and Glen Williams (eds.), *The New Canadian Political Economy*. Kingston and Montreal: McGill–Queen's University Press.

Bottomore, Tom. (1993). *Elites and Society* (2nd ed.). London: Routledge.

Burton, Michael G., and John Higley. (1987). 'Invitation to Elite Theory: The Basic Contentions Reconsidered.' Pp. 219–38 in G. William Domhoff and Thomas R. Dye (eds.), *Power Elites and Organizations*. Newbury Park: Sage.

Cameron, Stevie. (1994). *On the Take: Crime, Corruption and Greed in the Mulroney Years*. Toronto: Macfarlane.

Campbell, Colin, and George J. Szablowski. (1979). *The Superbureaucrats: Structure and Behaviour in Central Agencies*. Toronto: Macmillan.

Carroll, William K. (1986). *Corporate Power and Canadian Capitalism*. Vancouver: University of British Columbia Press.

Carroll, William K., John Fox, and Michael Ornstein. (1982). 'The Network of Directorate Interlocks among the Largest Canadian Firms.' *Canadian Review of Sociology and Anthropology* 19(1): 44–69.

Clarke, Harold D., and Moshe M. Czudnowski (eds.). (1987). *Political Elites in Anglo-American Democracies: Changes in Stable Regimes*. DeKalb, Ill: Northern Illinois University Press.

Clement, Wallace. (1975). *The Canadian Corporate Elite: An Analysis of Economic Power*. Toronto: McClelland and Stewart.

– (1977a). *Continental Corporate Power*. Toronto: McClelland and Stewart.

– (1977b). 'The Corporate Elite, the Capitalist Class, and the Canadian State.' Pp. 225–48 in Leo Panitch (ed.), *The Canadian State: Political Economy and Political Power*. Toronto: University of Toronto Press.

– (1990). 'A Critical Response to "Perspectives on the Class and Ethnic Origins of Canada Elites."' *Canadian Journal of Sociology* 15(2): 179–85.

Cox, Andrew, Paul Furlong, and Edward Page. (1985). *Power in Capitalist Society: Theory, Explanations and Cases*. New York: St Martin's.

Czudnowski, Moshe M. (ed.). (1982). *Does Who Governs Matter?* DeKalb, Ill: Northern Illinois University Press.

Domhoff, G. William. (1990). *The Power Elite and the State: How Policy Is Made in America*. New York: Aldine de Gruyter.

Eulau, Heinz, and Moshe M. Czudnowski (eds.). (1976). *Elite Recruitment in Democratic Polities: Comparative Studies Across Nations*. New York: Sage.

Fleming, James. (1991). *Circles of Power: The Most Influential People in Canada*. Toronto: Doubleday.

Fox, John, and Michael Ornstein. (1986). 'The Canadian State and Corporate Elites in the Post-War Period.' *Canadian Review of Sociology and Anthropology* 23(4): 481–506.

Francis, Diane. (1986). *Controlling Interest*. Toronto: Macmillan.

Ganzeboom, Harry B.G., Rund Luijkx, and Donald J. Treiman. (1989). 'Intergenerational Class Mobility in Comparative Perspective.' *Research in Social Strati-fication and Mobility* 8: 3–84.

Grabb, Edward G. (1990). 'Who Owns Canada? Concentration of Ownership in the Distribution of Economic Assets 1975–1985.' *Journal of Canadian Studies* 25(2): 72–91.

Heap, James. (1974). *Everybody's Canada:* The Vertical Mosaic *Reviewed and Re-Evaluated.* Toronto: Burns and MacEachern.

Helmes-Hayes, Richard. (1990). '"Hobhouse Twice Removed": John Porter and the LSE years.' *Canadian Review of Sociology and Anthropology* 27(3): 357–89.

Higley, John, Desley Deacon, and Don Smart. (1979). *Elites in Australia.* London: Routledge and Kegan Paul.

Hobsbawn, Eric. (1994). *The Age of Extremes: A History of the World, 1914–1991.* New York: Pantheon.

Hunter, Alfred. (1986) *Class Tells: On Social Inequality in Canada.* Toronto: Butterworths.

Jenson, Jane. (1989) '"Different" but Not "Exceptional": Canada's Permeable Fordism.' *Canadian Review of Sociology and Anthropology* 26(1): 69–94.

Jessop, Bob. (1993). 'The Schumpeterian Workfare State.' *Studies in Political Economy* 40 (Spring): 7–39.

Langille, David. (1987). 'The Business Council on National Issues.' *Studies in Political Economy* 24: 41–85.

Levitt, Kari. (1970). *Silent Surrender: The Multinational Corporation in Canada.* Toronto: Macmillan.

Lundberg, Ferdinand. (1940). *America's 60 Families.* New York: Halcyon.

Myers, Gustavus. (1914). *A History of Canadian Wealth.* Chicago: Charles H. Kerr. (Republished 1972, Toronto: James Lewis and Samuel).

Nakhaie, M. Reza. (1997). 'Vertical Mosaic among Elites: The New Imagery Revisited.' *Canadian Review of Sociology and Anthropology* 34(1): 1–24.

Naylor, R. Tom. (1972). 'The Rise and Fall of the Third Commercial Empire of the St Lawrence.' Pp. 1–41 in Gary Teeple (ed.), *Capitalism and the National Question in Canada.* Toronto: University of Toronto Press.

Niosi, Jorge. (1978). *The Economy of Canada: A Study of Ownership and Control.* Montreal: Black Rose.

– (1981). *Canadian Capitalism: A Study of Power in the Canadian Business Establishment.* Toronto: Lorimer.

Ogmundson, Rick. (1990). 'Perspectives on the Class and Ethnic Origins of Canadian Elites: A Methodological Critique of the Porter/Clement/Olson tradition.' *Canadian Journal of Sociology* 15(2): 165–77.

– (1992). 'Commentary and Debate.' *Canadian Journal of Sociology* 17(3): 313–25.

– (1993). 'At the Top of the Mosaic: Doubts about the Data.' *American Review of Canadian Studies* (Autumn): 373–86.

Ogmundson, Rick, and J. McLaughlin. (1992). 'Trends in the Ethnic Origins of Canadian Elites: The Decline of the BRITS?' *Canadian Review of Sociology and Anthropology* 29(2): 227–42.

Olsen, Dennis. (1980). *The State Elite*. Toronto: McClelland and Stewart.

Ornstein, Michael. (1976). 'The Boards and Executives of the Largest Canadian Corporations: Size, Composition and Interlocks.' *Canadian Journal of Sociology* 1(4): 411–36.

– (1984). 'Interlocking Directorates in Canada: Intercorporate or Class Alliance?' *Administrative Science Quarterly* 29: 210–31.

– (1985a). 'The Political Ideology of the "Inner Group" of Canadian Capital.' *Journal of Political and Military Sociology* 13: 219–237.

– (1985b). 'Canadian Capital and the Canadian state: Ideology in an Era of Crisis.' Pp. 129–66 in Robert Brym (ed.), *The Structure of the Canadian Capitalist Class*. Toronto: Garamond.

– (1986). 'The Political Ideology of the Canadian Capitalist Class.' *Canadian Review of Sociology and Anthropology* 23(2): 182–209.

– (1988a). 'Social Class and Economic Inequality.' Pp. 185–221 in James Curtis and Lorne Tepperman (eds.), *Understanding Canadian Society*. Toronto: McGraw-Hill Ryerson.

– (1988b). 'Corporate Involvement in Canadian Hospital and University Boards.' *Canadian Review of Sociology and Anthropology* 25(3): 365–88.

– (1989). 'The Social Organization of the Canadian Capitalist Class in Comparative Perspective.' *Canadian Review of Sociology and Anthropology* 26(1): 151–77.

Ornstein, Michael, and H. Michael Stevenson. (1984). 'Ideology and Public Policy in Canada,' *British Journal of Political Science* 14: 313–34.

– (n.d.). *In the Bosom of the State: Ideology and Politics in Canada*. Unpublished ms.

Panitch, Leo (ed.). (1977). *The Canadian State: Political Economy and Political Power*. Toronto: University of Toronto Press.

Park, Libbie, and Frank Park. (1962). *Anatomy of Big Business*. Toronto: Progress Books (Republished 1973, Toronto: James Lewis and Samuel).

Porter, John. (1965). *The Vertical Mosaic: An Analysis of Social Class and Power in Canada*. Toronto: University of Toronto Press.

– (1987). *The Measure of Canadian Society: Education, Equality and Opportunity*. Ottawa: Carleton University Press.

Presthus, Robert. (1973). *Elite Accommodation in Canadian Politics*. Toronto: Macmillan.

Scott, John. (1991). *Who Rules Britain?* Cambridge: Polity Press.

Stanworth, Philip, and Anthony Giddens (eds.). (1974). *Elites and Power in British Society*. Cambridge: Cambridge University Press.

Sztompka, Piotr. (1994). *Agency and Structure: Reorienting Social Theory*. Yverdon, Switzerland: Gordon and Breach.

Social Justice, Social Citizenship, and the Welfare State, 1965–1995: Canada in Comparative Context[1]

JULIA S. O'CONNOR

In 1965, when John Porter's *The Vertical Mosaic* was first published, it was a 'given' of liberal thinking that a strong welfare state was a key to the development and maintenance of 'the good society.' From the early 1940s and the issuing of the Marsh Report (1975[1943]), and especially during the 1960s, the Canadian welfare state had expanded rapidly. Indeed, it was perhaps in the 1960s more than any other period when a form of unalloyed reconstructive optimism gripped the builders of the Canadian welfare state. Certainly, there was not much sense that it would decline in influence or – as now – be compelled to justify itself. Moreover, while there was some scholarly attention being paid to the philosophy and practice of the welfare state, it was much less a focus of negative, critical attention than it now is. In this regard, Porter's interest in the state and its ameliorative potential was typical. Throughout his career, and certainly in *The Vertical Mosaic*, Porter demonstrated a deep concern about the quality of life in Canadian society – about the degree to which it might reasonably be claimed that Canada was a 'democracy' where 'social justice' prevailed. Indeed, a part of his motivation for writing the book was to document the existence of some deep and fundamental inequalities in Canadian society – a deceptively hidebound class structure and a system of plural elite rule that called into question Canada's view of itself as a democratic and classless (or at least middle class) society. In such a society, Porter argued, the role of the welfare state was crucial, for it was a vehicle of rational and humane social planning and policy intervention. Indeed, in Porter's view, a broadly conceived welfare state, properly run, could do much to make Canada a more just and democratic society by reducing inequality of both opportunity and condition.

This chapter considers the degree to which the Canadian welfare state has been used to solve or ameliorate problems of social inequality over the past three decades and the extent to which it has been successful in this objective. Central to the analysis are concepts that were pivotal to John Porter's analysis of Canadian society, including social inequality, but most importantly the concepts of social justice and citizenship which he discussed in his later work, together with his emphasis on comparative analysis. I link some of his key insights on these issues to recent debates on welfare state analysis, in particular those focusing on citizenship and the analysis of welfare state regimes.

In analysing the Canadian welfare state over the 1960–95 period two sets of questions are addressed, one comparative and the other historical. First, where does Canada stand relative to welfare states in other liberal democracies at broadly similar levels of economic development? Specifically, how does Canada fare relative to other Organization for Economic Cooperation and Development (OECD) countries – not only in terms of social expenditure, but in terms of the scope and quality of social citizenship rights? Has its position changed over the period 1960 to the early 1990s?[2] Second, what have been the major developments in the Canadian welfare state over this period in terms of the enhancement of citizenship rights, the lessening of social inequality, and the achievement of social justice? In particular, to what extent has the welfare state had an impact on distributional inequalities in Canadian society?

The format of the chapter is as follows. In the next section I outline briefly some arguments made by John Porter on equality, social justice, and social citizenship. This is followed by a brief outline of the key arguments of T.H. Marshall on citizenship and of fundamental issues relevant to welfare state regimes and citizenship. With this background in place, and informed by the gender critique of citizenship and welfare state regimes, I identify four dimensions on which the Canadian welfare state can be situated comparatively and historically. This evaluation is presented in the third section, which focuses on the Canadian welfare state from 1960 to the early 1990s, using the four dimensions to assess its position and identify its key characteristics. The next section discusses the growth and retrenchment of the Canadian welfare state over the 1960–95 period. It demonstrates that while the period 1960–73 was one of growth and development, the era since 1973 has been one of retrenchment and maintenance. In the concluding section, I present an analysis of the Canadian welfare state as a mechanism for the amelioration of social inequality.

John Porter on Equality, Social Justice, and Social Citizenship

In his early work John Porter held out considerable hope for the achievement of a just society, that is, a society characterized by a considerable degree of equality achieved through the educational system and the vehicle of equality of opportunity (Porter 1987 [1968]: 65–87). His studies of the links between class and education undermined this faith, and by the mid-1970s he was strongly questioning the role of education, based on the principle of equality of opportunity, as a mechanism for the achievement of equality (Porter 1987 [1979]: 241–80). Porter recognized that while an analytical distinction could be made between equality of opportunity and equality of condition 'in the real world the distinction is a questionable one because inequality of condition can nullify the effects of whatever might be introduced to implement equality of opportunity' (Porter 1987 [1979]: 245). His recognition of the failure of the educational system to achieve a reduction of the barriers to elite positions led him to focus on the basic structure of inequality and the need for a shift in strategy from educational institutions to 'plans for equality of condition to reduce the undeserved advantages that are transmitted through the family' (Porter 1987 [1979]: 260). Equality of condition was to be achieved by instruments other than education, such as the 'abolition of unjustified levels of inheritance, progressive taxation, reduction of differential wage structures, and the elimination of occupational monopolies' (Porter 1987 [1979]: 250).

Despite Porter's recognition that the educational system on its own could not create social justice or erase social inequality, he nonetheless argued that, within limits, modern industrial societies 'are of a type with their own capacity to achieve social welfare, to implement citizenship and achieve equality and justice in the here and now' (Porter 1975, as quoted in Clement 1980: 111). In advocating a macrosociology that is capable of both explanation and evaluation, Porter drew on both L.T. Hobhouse and T.H. Marshall. He traced the roots of his commitment to an empirical, dynamic, and evaluative macrosociology to his education at the London School of Economics and in particular the work of L.T. Hobhouse via Morris Ginsberg and others at LSE in the late 1940s.[3] Hobhouse (1911; 1964 [1911]) is famous not only as a political theorist but as the holder of the first chair of sociology at a British university. To Hobhouse 'the relationship between social values and social science was close. He was firmly convinced of the need for an empirical social science and believed one could be developed which was closely linked to ethical principles, or at least address itself to ethical problems' (Porter 1987: 12). Porter was greatly influenced by Hobhouse's view of social development, namely, 'that a community develops as it grows in scale, efficiency, freedom, and mutuality: efficiency toward an end, freedom and scope for thought, mutuality in a service toward an end in which each participates. Social development corresponds in its concrete entirety to the requirements of rational ethics ... Good is the principle of organic harmony in things' (Porter 1970: 151; citing Hobhouse 1924: 88, 93).

Hobhouse was a major contributor to the tradition of social liberalism. Central to this social liberalism was an emphasis on the role of the state in promoting both the individual and social good through the creation of 'organic harmony.' Porter's commitment in his early work to equality of opportunity and the role of education in achieving social justice is consistent with this perspective.

Porter argued that 'the *guiding judgemental principle* ... for an evaluative sociology derives from the concept of citizenship as it has been developed by T.H. Marshall' (Porter 1987 [1979]: 3; emphasis added). He argued that social indicators could be developed to measure the distribution of legal, political and social rights, which are the three dimensions of citizenship discussed by Marshall (1964). Porter linked the concepts of social justice and social development to citizenship rights in asking how social justice could be translated into legal, political, and social rights. In this exploration, and in particular in trying to identify the distributive principles that might be applied in the achievement of a just society, Porter drew on the work of the philosopher, John Rawls. In *A Theory of Justice* (1971) Rawls's objective was to establish those social, economic, and political principles that would define a just society, which is one in which the institutions 'satisfy certain principles that people would have agreed to as basic terms of co-operation, had they been given the opportunity to decide' (King and Waldron 1988: 440). To realize his objective, Rawls conducted a 'thought experiment,' that is, he imagined what kind of society people would choose if they could reconstruct it from the ground up. He posited a hypothetical 'original position' in which individuals had to choose the principles that would constitute the contractual basis of a just social order. Rawls argued that, being ignorant of their specific social identities and positions, they would choose two principles:

First principle
Each person is to have an equal right to the most extensive total system of equal basic liberties compatible with a similar liberty for all.

Second principle
Social and economic inequalities are to be arranged so that they are both (a) to the greatest benefit of the least advantaged ... and (b) attached to positions and offices open to all under conditions of fair equality of opportunity. (Rawls 1971: 302)

These principles mean that justice demands 'maximum equal liberty' and a distribution of economic benefits which makes the least favoured person as well-off as possible, that is, the minimum benefit to the least advantaged in society is maximized. Despite criticism from both left and right – on the one hand, that it is too limited and essentially liberal and individualistic in its implications, and, on the other, that it goes too far and provides a justification for extensive state involvement in redistribution – Rawls's approach is widely recognized as a defence of redistribution based on citizenship rights (Pierson 1991: 198). For Porter it provided a justification for his version of egalitarianism (Porter 1987 [1979]: 250).

Although Porter's work did not directly address the debates of his era about the welfare state, he defined education as part of the welfare state broadly conceived and identified several major issues that are central to many contemporary analyses of welfare states.[4] In establishing the achievement of a just society as the objective and in identifying citizenship rights as the guiding judgmental principle for evaluating the degree to which the just society had been achieved he was foreshadowing the concerns of much recent welfare state analysis, especially comparative analysis. I now outline some of the key arguments in this analysis and identify several dimensions, or 'social indicators' in Porter's terminology, on which welfare states can be evaluated in terms of their achievement of a just society.

Welfare State Regimes and Citizenship

Citizenship rights, in particular social citizenship rights, are central to welfare states. The development of welfare states can be seen as a process of the transition from access to services and benefits entirely on the basis of class position and associated resources to access to certain categories of services and benefits (e.g., health care in Canada), on the basis of citizenship. Most contemporary discussions of citizenship take as their source the essay 'On Citizenship and Social Class,' presented by T.H. Marshall in 1949 (Marshall 1964: 65–122). On the basis of British history, Marshall divided the development of citizenship into three stages: civil, political, and social. Civil citizenship, relating to liberty of the person and property rights, is dated from the eighteenth century with the development of the judicial system and legal rights. Political citizenship, relating primarily to the right to vote and to organize, for example, in trade unions, is dated from the nineteenth century. Social citizenship, which relates to rights to economic welfare and security, is dated from the twentieth century with the extension of the educational system and the development of the welfare state. None of these rights evolved naturally; all were achieved through prolonged collective struggle. In the case of social rights this collective struggle was possible because of the existence of civil and political rights. Marshall's analysis and periodization relates to the British situation, and it is problematic even when applied there because it assumes a universal category of citizens, all of whom equally benefit from achieved citizenship rights. However, historical evidence indicates that this assumption is untenable. The timing of political citizenship rights, most noteworthy the right to vote, was later for women than for men, and the ability to exercise citizenship rights is influenced by class position (Barbalet 1988), by gender, and in some countries, by race. A tiered system of social rights has been identified in several countries and is particularly marked in some welfare states, such as the United States and Canada (Nelson 1984; Fraser 1989). This is linked to labour market status and is comprised, at one extreme, of a predominantly female stratum of welfare or social assistance clients who are generally outside the labour market and are granted benefits and services on the basis of demonstrated need, generally household need, and, at the other extreme, a predominantly male stratum with individual rights to benefits and services based on social insurance contributions related to paid work.[5]

There is now an extensive critique of the liberal conception of citizenship, and in particular of Marshall's conception, by feminist political theorists and welfare state analysts. The common thread running through these critiques is that the assumption of an undifferentiated citizen, as now conceived, is in fact based on the full-time male worker who is perceived to be without caring responsibilities. This is problematic when gender is incorporated into the analysis. A solution to this problem depends on a recognition that the apparent gender neutrality of the dominant discourse on citizenship veils a profoundly gendered concept (O'Connor 1996: 48–77). Yet, despite its limitations, Marshall's analysis provides major insights into citizenship and provides the background for the conception of citizenship embodied in much of the welfare state literature, in particular, the comparative analysis literature centring on *welfare state regimes*.

As outlined by Gøsta Esping-Andersen, in his 1990 book, *The Three Worlds of Welfare Capitalism*, welfare state regimes refer to clusters of more or less distinct welfare states differentiated from one another by the principles of stratification and the bases of social rights on which social policy is built. These principles result in qualitatively different arrangements among the state, the market, and the family. They are reflected in the character of programs (targeted or universal), the conditions of eligibility for, and the quality of, benefits and services and 'the extent to which employment and working life are encompassed in the state's extension of citizen rights' (Esping-Andersen 1990: 20). Marshall's conception of social citizenship is taken as 'the core idea of the welfare state' and of the welfare regime concept. Esping-Andersen identifies three closely linked dimensions to the concept of social citizenship: (1) The granting of social rights and the extent to which these are decommodifying, that is, the extent to which individuals are protected from reliance on the labour market for survival. (2) The social stratification dimension, which centres on the continuum between class and citizenship as a basis for access to services necessary for survival. (3) The relations among the state, the market, and the family in the provision of services, for example, caring services to dependent people; this is a recognition that welfare states cannot be understood exclusively in terms of the rights they grant. Based on these dimensions, Esping-Andersen has identified *three worlds of welfare capitalism or welfare state regimes*: the social democratic, exemplified by Sweden and Norway; the conservative-corporatist or status-based as exemplified by Germany, France, and Italy; and the liberal, exemplified by the United States, Canada, Australia, and, to a lesser extent, the United Kingdom. The social democratic regime is characterized by universalism in social rights, a strong role for the state, and the integration of social and economic policy, which is reflected in a commitment to full employment. In contrast, in the liberal regime state intervention is clearly subordinate to the market, and there is a strong emphasis on income- and/or means-testing for access to benefits. Where universalism is applied it is universalism with a focus on equal opportunity. The conservative welfare state regime is characterized by the linkage of rights to class and status through a variety of social insurance schemes and the emphasis on the maintenance of the traditional family. The latter is reflected in the public provision of social services only when the family's ability to cope is exhausted.

While the welfare regime concept as outlined by Esping-Andersen has inspired considerable innovative work on the comparative analysis of welfare states, it has also been the subject of some criticism, for example, in relation to the categorization of particular countries (Castles and Mitchell 1992; Leibfried 1993; Olsen 1994). The most well-developed critique of typologies of welfare state regimes, especially the Esping-Andersen version, has been made by scholars interested in a gender-sensitive analysis of welfare states. All three of the dimensions identified by Esping-Andersen have been the subject of criticism on the grounds that the gender angle has not been considered. Yet, with the incorporation of a gender-sensitive focus, which recognizes the profoundly gendered nature of citizenship, and the addition of a dimension relating to services facilitating access to the labour market, they capture the essential elements of welfare state variation. Gender-sensitive analysis is based on the recognition that gender and class are produced within the same ongoing practices. 'Looking at them from one angle we see class, from another we see gender, neither is complete without the other' (Acker 1989: 239). Gender-sensitive welfare state analysis is built on the recognition of the *interaction* of gender and class and is linked to a more general critique of the dominant conception of citizenship which underpins welfare state research.

John Porter's analysis of Canadian society was not gender-sensitive. This is not surprising given the era in which he wrote. In 1965, when the *The Vertical Mosaic* was published, critical attention to the implications of gender differences in labour force participation and conditions, such as pay and employment inequity, and of barriers to access to the labour market for those with caring responsibilities were non-issues for the vast majority of social scientists. Gender-sensitive analysis of welfare state benefits and services and the institutional structure of welfare states was not evident in the social science literature until the late 1970s (Wilson 1977; Andrew 1984).

The Canadian Welfare State from the 1960s to the 1990s

In this section I consider the Canadian welfare state within the context of OECD countries. This is not a systematic comparative analysis. The objective is to identify key characteristics of the Canadian welfare state and in the process to locate it relative to other OECD countries and to identify stability or change in that location over the past thirty years. This analysis is presented under the four dimensions identified in the previous section.

Under the heading of 'de-commodification' I present Canadian expenditure data (a) relative to the OECD averages, (b) relative to the three other liberal welfare state regimes – the United States, Australia, and the United Kingdom, (c) relative to the former West Germany (FRG) as an exemplar of conservative welfare state regimes, and (d) relative to Sweden as an exemplar of social democratic regimes. This selection of countries combines a 'most similar' and 'most different' approach to comparative analysis. On the basis of the welfare regime categorization developed by Esping-Andersen, one would expect broad similarities between Canada and the other liberal welfare states and some key differences between Canada and both Sweden and Germany. However, expenditure captures only one aspect of welfare state regimes, that is, *the potential* for de-commodification. Whether or not de-commodification results depends on the range and quality of social rights and the criteria for access to benefits and services. This relates to the welfare state as a mechanism of stratification and is the subject of the second part of this section. Recognizing that before de-commodification becomes an issue it is necessary to be a participant in the labour market, I discuss provision of services that facilitate labour market participation in the third part of this section. This is followed by a discussion of the relationship between state, market, and family in the provision of social services.

Social Expenditure and the Potential for De-commodification

De-commodification, or protection from total dependence on the labour market for survival, is central to the welfare state project and associated historical struggles. Commodification of labour refers to the situation where the individual's ability to sell her or his labour is the sole determinant of her or his access to resources. De-commodification, by contrast, reflects a level of insulation from total dependence on the labour market for survival: the entitlements reflected in social security payments and public services, which to varying degrees in different countries and at different times in individual countries are independent of class position, facilitate resistance to the pressures of the market. The concern is not with pure de-commodification – this is not possible under capitalism. The concern is with degrees of protection. Differences in expenditures across welfare states give an indication of the potential for this protection.

The best summary measure of social expenditure is what the OECD identifies as 'public expenditure on social protection' (Table 1). This includes three categories of expenditure: (i) old age and survivor

TABLE 1
Public expenditure on social protection as percentage of GDP[1]

	1960[2]	1970[2]	1980	1990	Percentage Change		
					1960–70[3]	1970–80[3]	1980–90
Canada	9.12	11.80	14.37	18.79	29.4	21.8	30.8
United States	7.26	10.38	14.10	14.58	43.0	35.8	2.7
Australia	7.39	7.37	10.98	12.96	-0.3	49.0	18.0
United Kingdom	10.21	13.20	21.30	24.03	29.3	61.4	12.8
Germany	18.10	19.53	25.40	22.94	7.9	30.0	-9.7
Sweden	10.83	16.76	32.42	33.13	54.7	93.4	2.5
OECD averages	10.11	14.02	20.14	20.98	38.7	43.7	5.3
N	16	17	21	21			
Canada's rank	9	13	16	17			

[1] Expenditure on Social Protection includes (1) old age and survivor benefits, (2) disability pensions and services, employment promotion benefits, unemployment compensation, family allowances, indigenous persons benefits, housing benefits, other miscellaneous benefits and services and administration costs, (3) health expenditures.

[2] Historical Series. Figures based on the historical series and the new series are available for 1980. The most significant differences between them is evident for Sweden, the United Kingdom, and Australia. Using the historical series the expenditure for Sweden and the U.K. are considerably lower – 25.94% and 16.42% respectively. The Australian expenditure at 12.79% is higher using the historical series. For all other countries there is only a minuscule difference between the two series.

[3] % change 1960–70 and 1970–80 calculated on Historical Series figures.

Source: OECD 1994 New Orientations for Social Policy, Tables 1a and 1b.

TABLE 2
Social protection excluding health expenditure as a percentage of GDP

| | 1960[1] | 1970[1] | 1980 | 1990 | Percentage Change | | |
					1960–70[2]	1970–80[2]	1980–90
Canada	6.74	6.72	8.86	11.94	-0.3	31.8	34.8
United States	5.97	7.54	10.22	8.36	12.1	35.5	-8.4
Australia	5.04	4.15	6.40	7.37	-14.8	54.2	15.2
United Kingdom	6.88	9.29	16.13	17.15	34.8	73.6	6.3
Germany	14.93	15.44	19.08	17.51	2.2	23.6	-8.2
Sweden	7.43	10.59	23.70	26.25	42.5	123.8	10.8
OECD Averages	7.66	10.12	14.88	15.90	32.7	47.0	6.0
N	16	19	21	21			
Canada's rank	9	13	19	17			

[1] Historical Series. See note 2, Table 1.
[2] See Note 3, Table 1.

Source: OECD 1994. *New Orientations for Social Policy.*

benefits; (ii) disability pensions and services, employment promotion benefits, unemployment compensation, family allowances, indigenous persons benefits, housing benefits, other miscellaneous benefits and services, and administration costs; and (iii) health expenditures. Consistent with practice in most welfare state analysis it does not include educational expenditure. I consider reasons for this below.

Looking at the total social expenditure we find that Canadian expenditure as a percentage of gross domestic product (GDP) is consistently below the OECD average: In 1960 it ranked 9th out of 16 OECD countries and in 1990 it ranked 17th out of 21 countries. The countries that consistently devoted lower percentages of GDP to social protection were Japan and two other liberal welfare states – the United States and Australia. Interestingly, Finland and Norway, which are now high expenditure countries, had lower expenditure on social protection than Canada in 1960. When we exclude health expenditure Canada's rank does not change in any year except 1980 (Table 2). While the other two elements of its social expenditure (see (i) and (ii) in previous paragraph) increased at a considerably lower rate than its health expenditure over the entire 1960 to 1990 period – 77 per cent relative to 194 per cent – the most marked increase in health expenditure was in the 1960–70 period and the most marked increase in other expenditure on social protection was in the 1970s (see last two columns in Tables 2 and 3). Despite an increase above the OECD average in the 1980s, Canada's *non-health social expenditure* is still low by OECD standards: Of 24 OECD countries, only the United States, Australia, Japan, and Portugal had lower expenditure in 1990. The relatively high increase during the 1980s was disproportionately in expenditure on the aged (40 per cent increase compared with 32 per cent in the non-aged component). These increases were largely a response to an increase in demand reflected in the increase in the population aged 65 and over, from 7.6 per cent in 1960 to 9.7 per cent in 1980 and 11.5 per cent in 1990 (OECD 1992a: 6) and an increase in unemployment; this was 9.2 per cent in the 1980–90 period compared with 7.2 per cent in the 1974–9 period, 5.4 in the 1968–73 period, and 4.8 in the 1960–7 period (OECD 1992b: Table 2.15).

In contrast, Canada's *health expenditure* is high by OECD standards, and its health system is a major factor differentiating it from the United States but not from the two other liberal welfare states – Australia and the United Kingdom – both of which have national health systems. The 1960s increase in social protection expenditure relates exclusively to health expenditure, which increased from 2.3 per cent to almost 5 per

TABLE 3
Health expenditure in six OECD countries as a percentage of GDP

	1960	1970	1980	1990	Percentage Change		
					1960–70	1970–80	1980–90
A. Public expenditures							
Canada	2.33	4.96	5.51	6.85	113.4	11.1	24.3
United States	1.29	2.74	3.88	5.88	114.5	41.6	51.5
Australia	2.35	3.22	4.58	5.59	20.4	42.2	22.1
United Kingdom	3.33	3.91	5.17	5.18	17.9	32.2	0.2
Germany	3.17	4.09	6.32	5.96	35.0	54.5	–5.7
Sweden	3.40	6.17	8.72	6.88	81.3	41.3	–21.1
OECD averages	2.45	3.90	5.36	5.63	59.2	37.4	5.4
N	27	22	24	24			
Canada's Rank	13	2	12	4			
B. Total expenditures							
Canada	5.47	7.07	7.38	9.48	29.3	4.4	28.6
United States	5.27	7.35	9.24	12.35	39.5	25.7	33.7
Australia	4.94	5.67	7.29	8.22	35.0	28.6	12.8
United Kingdom	3.91	4.50	5.77	6.20	15.1	28.2	7.5
Germany	4.80	5.88	8.42	8.32	22.5	43.2	–1.2
Sweden	4.68	7.17	9.42	8.62	53.2	31.4	–8.5
OECD averages	3.90	5.34	6.98	7.60	36.9	30.7	8.9
N	21	22	24	24			
Canada's rank	1	3	8	2			

Source: OECD 1994, *New Orientations for Social Policy*, Table 2.

cent of GDP (Table 3). This increase of 113 per cent was well above the OECD average (59 per cent based on 22 countries).

The Canadian increase can be explained by the extension of hospital insurance to all provinces and territories and by the introduction of medical care insurance (Taylor 1978). Canada's public expenditure on health increased modestly throughout the 1970s (7 per cent compared with an OECD average of 37 per cent) but relatively strongly through-out the 1980s (24 per cent relative to the OECD average of 5 per cent). By 1990 Canadian public expenditure on health as a share of GDP was well above the OECD average, and ranked fourth after Norway, Iceland, and Sweden, while its total expenditure was second only to the United States (Table 3). It is noteworthy that private health expenditure in Can-ada rose throughout the 1980s after a consistent decline from 1960 to 1980. The increase in total health expenditure throughout the 1980s is linked, not to an increase in entitlement, but to patterns of medical prac-tice and inflation in medical costs.[6]

Expenditure on Education
I noted above that, especially early in his career, Porter saw state-funded education as a means of breaking down class-based barriers to equality of opportunity. Thus, the following discussion of public expenditure on education is especially salient to the purpose of this chapter. Educa-tional expenditure is usually not included in discussions of social expen-diture and welfare effort. The rationale for exclusion relates to its focus on equality of opportunity and its skewed distributional consequences, which are reflected in the disproportionate use of the upper levels of education by children from higher social class backgrounds. Flora and Heidenheimer pointed out that, in its emphasis on merit, 'equality of opportunity inherently legitimizes inequality, mainly in the form of income and status differences' (1981: 25). Castles (1978: 61–4) provided a somewhat different interpretation of public educational expenditure, arguing that, despite its meritocratic character, equality of educational opportunity does provide to working-class children the right of access to a mobility route that is absent without such equality. The extent to which this right can be exercised is related to the degree of income ine-quality and the scope and effectiveness of programs directed to address-ing this inequality. A further difference between educational and social security expenditure is the postulated link between educational expen-diture and the growth of productivity and consequently economic growth (Wilkinson 1986: 544–6). Each of these would lead to different

pressures for the increase of educational expenditure or the maintenance of high levels of such expenditure than are associated with other types of social expenditure.

Despite its difference from the elements of the public expenditure on social protection package, there is considerable evidence of the importance of participation in education as *a facilitator of enhanced labour market status* and, thus, as a protection against poverty. This is illustrated by the differences in poverty and unemployment rates between those with university education and those who leave school at the secondary level or below in Canada. For example, in 1991, 20 per cent of those with 0–8 years education were in poverty as measured by the Statistics Canada definition compared with 6 per cent of families headed by someone with a university degree (Ross et al. 1994: 59). Looking at the number of people unemployed by level of educational attainment per 100 persons in the population aged 25–64 in 1991, there was a consistent decrease as level of education increased from grade school or less (14.1) to university (5.1), and this same pattern is evident across OECD countries (OECD 1993: 188). There is no doubt that the higher than average school dropout rates of poor children in Canada is a significant contributor to the perpetuation of social inequality. For these reasons, I include a brief analysis of educational expenditure here and educational participation later.

Like its health expenditure, Canada's expenditure on education is high by OECD standards (Table 4). Public expenditure on education increased from 4.6 per cent in 1960 to 8.1 per cent in 1970. Public expenditure for education grew in all OECD countries during the 1960s and early 1970s (O'Connor 1989). This can be accounted for, in part, by common trends, specifically, growth in enrolment, lengthening of the compulsory attendance period, and an increase in the quality of education provided (OECD 1985: 41–2). Canada differs from other OECD countries in the size of the increase in enrolments – the increase of 4 per cent in the student body as a percentage of the total population in Canada from the early 1960s to the early 1970s was twice the average increase in OECD countries (OECD 1976: 10).

As with several other OECD countries, Canada's public expenditure on education has decreased slightly as a percentage of GDP since 1970 and was 6.7 per cent in 1991. This decline is not surprising in view of the decrease in enrolments at the elementary and secondary levels since 1970. Despite the decrease, Canada's public expenditure on education is among the highest in the OECD – in 1991 its total expenditure was the

TABLE 4
Expenditure on education as percentage of GDP

	1965	1970	1975	1980	1986	1991
A. *Public expenditure on education as a percentage of GDP*						
Canada	5.3	8.1	7.1	6.8	6.7	6.7
United States	5.3	6.5	5.4	4.8	4.8	5.5
Australia	3.5	3.5	5.9	5.4	5.3	5.5
United Kingdom	5.1	5.2	–	–	5.0	5.3
Germany	3.0	3.7	5.4	5.0	4.3	4.0
Sweden	5.9	7.7	6.6	9.0	7.3	6.5
OECD average						5.4
Canada's rank						3
B. *Private expenditure on education as percentage of GDP*						
Canada			0.6	0.5	0.6	0.7
United States			1.4	1.4	1.7	1.5
Australia			–	–	0.4	0.3
United Kingdom			–	–	–	–
Germany			0.1	0.1	0.2	–
Sweden			–	–	–	–
OECD average						0.9

Sources: OECD 1984 *Educational Trends in the 1970s* for 1965 and 1970; OECD 1993 *Education at a Glance* for 1975 to 1991 figures.

highest in the OECD, and its public expenditure was exceeded only by Norway (6.8 per cent) and then only marginally. Canada is more like European countries than the United States in its public/private split in educational expenditure. In Canada just over 90 per cent of educational expenditure was borne by the public sector in the early 1990s, compared with 79 per cent in the United States. In most European countries the public sector is responsible for about 95 per cent of educational expenditure (OECD 1976, 1993).

As John Porter recognized by the 1970s, the important point about education from a public policy perspective is that on its own an equal opportunity focus, as reflected in equal access to primary and secondary levels of education, is inadequate as a mechanism to overcome inequality of condition. When post-secondary education is taken into account, the class distribution is even more skewed (Porter 1987 [1979]). The context within which the educational system operates is crucial to its success or failure as a mechanism for lessening social inequality. I return to this issue in the final section.

In summary, Canada's social expenditure is consistently below the OECD average in the 1960–90 period, and this is especially evident when health expenditure is excluded. In contrast, its expenditure on health and education has been consistently above the OECD average since 1970. The level of educational expenditure is not surprising; the equal opportunity focus of universal access to primary and secondary education fits within a liberal welfare state framework. I consider these issues further in the final section. As previously stated, expenditure is a blunt measure of welfare state success: it indicates the potential for de-commodification. Whether or not protection from dependence on the labour market is realized, and for whom, depends on the criteria for access to benefits.

The Quality of Social Rights and the Welfare State as a Mechanism of Stratification

Recognition that the welfare state is a mechanism of social stratification, that it is 'an active force in the ordering of social relations' (Esping-Andersen 1990: 23), revolves around the criteria for access to, and duration of, benefits. These criteria are means and/or income testing, social insurance contributions, and citizenship. All welfare states make use of the three criteria of eligibility, but the dominance of one criterion or another differentiates among welfare states and reflects differences in the role of the welfare state as a mechanism of social stratification. In the social democratic welfare state the citizenship criterion is dominant, as is reflected in the strong emphasis on universality of access to services and benefits. The liberal welfare state is characterized by a strong emphasis on income- and/or means-tested programs, and, while there may be an emphasis on equality, it is focused on equality of opportunity. The conservative welfare state regime is characterized by a variety of social insurance schemes linked to class and status. Each of these is reflected in a particular form of stratification. For example, means testing promotes social dualisms, that is, the division of society into a category of citizens with rights to services and a category whose access to benefits and services is conditional on the demonstration of need – as in the case of welfare in Canada and the United States. A variety of social insurance programs, as in conservative welfare regimes, is likely to consolidate divisions along class and status lines. While in theory access on the basis of citizenship is the most egalitarian and least stratifying, it may also promote dualism if the universal access is to a low level of benefit or services. In this instance the more affluent are likely to purchase private supplementary insurance (Esping-Andersen 1990: 24). Not only does this promote dualism, but it is also likely to weaken support for universal services.

A key element of Canada's designation as a liberal welfare state regime is the emphasis on means and/or income testing as a criterion for eligibility for services. In the mid-1980s Canada, at 17.9 per cent, ranked third after the United Kingdom (24.4 per cent) and the United States (19.3 per cent) in its expenditure on income and/or means-tested programs as a percentage of total public social expenditure, compared with an average of 5.9 per cent for 17 OECD countries. The corresponding figure for Sweden was 1.1 per cent and for Germany 4.9 per cent (ILO 1992: Table 7). It is important to recognize that the users of these programs are not equally distributed across all demographic groups. In particular, there is considerable cross-national evidence of the gender-stratifying impact of benefit criteria which are generally linked to labour market and family status (O'Connor 1993; Orloff 1993). There is considerable evidence that, irrespective of welfare state regime, women constitute the vast majority of recipients of social assistance and make claims on the basis of need, usually family need, rather than as individuals with employment- and/or citizenship-related entitlements. The dependants of social insurance beneficiaries, who are mostly women and children, have an indirect right to services, the continuity of which is dependent on their link to an insured labour force participant. While women's representation in the direct social insurance rights category is increasing with the increase in female participation in the labour force, their concentration in lower level jobs in all countries, and in part-time work in several, is associated with lower level benefits and, consequently, greater exposure to economic dependence. A good illustration is women's lower access to employment-related pensions.

One of the major changes in the Canadian welfare state over the past decade has been the ending of social citizenship entitlement in social protection as illustrated by the Old Age Security (OAS) clawback and the abolition of family allowances. The clawback on OAS is consistent with the relatively high dependence on private pensions in Canada relative to other OECD countries. In 1980 Canada, at 38 per cent, ranked highest among 18 OECD countries in private pensions as a percentage of total pensions; the average was 13 per cent (Esping-Andersen 1990:

70–1). Up-to-date comparable figures are not available but it is clear that heavy reliance on private pensions continues in Canada. This is likely to be increased in 2001 when the Old Age Security system is abolished and incorporated with the Guaranteed Income System, that is the fully income-tested pension element, into a new income-tested Seniors Benefit.[7]

The result of the changes to family allowances and Old Age Security is that the only social citizenship entitlements in the Canadian welfare state are health care and first- and second-level education.

Another change over the past two decades has been a lessening of the quality of social insurance entitlements – here I am referring to the tightening of eligibility criteria for, and the shortening of the period covered by, unemployment insurance, which started in the early 1970s. This is associated with additional pressure on income-tested programs. This has been accompanied by a change in the nature of income testing with an increase in levels of surveillance in some provinces. These trends reinforce the liberal character of the Canadian welfare state. Despite this the Canadian welfare state does have a dual character, the other side of which is reflected in access to health services as a citizenship right.

Services Facilitating Labour Force Participation and Improving Its Quality

While benefits and services that insulate individuals from total dependence on the labour market for survival are a central protection for both men and women in the labour force, it is important to recognize that before de-commodification becomes an issue it is necessary to be a participant in the labour market. The primary concern for many women is not de-commodification but commodification as reflected in labour market participation. But not all members of society have equal access to the labour market, nor do they enter it on the same terms. Recognition of this implies a need to incorporate the relationship between unpaid and paid work into welfare state analysis. This means that analysis of de-commodification must be accompanied by analysis of services that facilitate participation in the labour market; services such as child care and parental leave, flexibility in working time, and also measures directed towards improving the quality of employment – measures such as pay equity and employment equity. The key question being considered here is whether or not the institutional structure facilitates the equal participation of women and men in the labour market.

Since the 1960s all OECD countries have been characterized to some extent by a shift away from the household with a male breadwinner towards a structure based on dual breadwinners or single breadwinners with caring responsibilities. In some countries, including Canada, this shift has been significant (O'Connor et al. in press). For example, female labour force participation in Canada is high by OECD standards. It increased from 34 per cent in 1960 to 68 per cent in 1990, when women's share of the labour force had reached 45 per cent (ibid.). These figures continue to be lower than those for the social democratic welfare states, where female labour force participation ranges from 71 to 81 per cent, but Canada and the United States immediately follow this cluster. In considering services that facilitate labour market participation, it is particularly noteworthy that in Canada the participation of women with preschool children had reached 57 per cent in 1991 compared with 42 per cent in 1981. Comparing Canada and the United States with the other countries that have high rates of female labour force participation, for example, Sweden, we discover that the key differentiating factor is the level of labour market supports. While in Canada and the United States there is now a dual breadwinner family structure, a dual bread-winner social policy framework has not been developed. I use this term not only to identify a social policy framework that would recognize the phenomenon of dual breadwinning but the more general phenomenon of workers with caring responsibilities.[8] While in this section I concentrate on child care and parental leave, I recognize that these services reflect only one element of the services necessary to facilitate workers with caring responsibilites.

Canada is close to the 'maximum private responsibility' end of the public-private continuum of child care provision (O'Connor et al. in press). Most of the children of employed parents are in informal care arrangements, which includes care by friends, neighbours, relatives and, for a minority, nanny care – the last-mentioned is tax deductible and is used primarily by high-income couples. It is estimated that in 1990 only 12 per cent of children were in licensed child care arrangements, mostly licensed day care or licensed home care. Twenty-one per cent of those children in day care are subsidized to some extent with subsidization restricted to low-income families (Crompton 1991). Most public funding of child care is given in the form of subsidies to low-income families. 'As a result, publicly funded child care has come to be seen as a welfare service and not a program to which all children should have access' (National Council of Welfare 1988: 7–8). Yet, most families who qualify for subsidized care do not get it because of the absence of licensed spaces. On a national basis only 15 per cent of those eligible for a full or partial subsidy in 1987 received assistance (ibid.: 11).

It is noteworthy that proposals from the federal government relating to provision of child care spaces consistently fall far short of need as identified by analysts, for example, the National Child Care Study (Lero et al. 1989) and the Canadian Day Care Advocacy Association (O'Connor 1998). The approach to public child care in Canada is typified by the statement made by the Minister of Health and Welfare, when announcing in April 1992 the abandonment of the strategy to create new child care places which had been announced in 1987. He justified this action on the grounds that 'there are other priorities that must come first. These include addressing the problems faced by children at risk – child physical and sexual abuse, poor nutrition and health, low income' (Canada 1992). The fragile status of public child care is clearly reflected in its high rank on the list of discretionary services that provincial and municipal governments consider expendable in the budget cutbacks of the early 1990s. This does not bode well for the child care proposals outlined by the federal Liberal government in its 1993 election platform and in subsequent policy statements. These include a commitment 'to expanding existing child care in Canada by 50,000 new quality child care spaces in each year that followed a year of 3 per cent economic growth, up to a total of 150,000 new spaces' (Liberal Party of Canada 1993: 40).[9] Since it is proposed to continue equal funding with the provinces, with each level assuming 40 per cent of the costs, and income-determined parental fees making up the remaining 20 per cent, the success of the plan is dependent on provincial cooperation. Moreover, even if such commitments were honoured, they would still leave the majority of parents dependent on informal arrangements. It is noteworthy, however, that child care is recognized in these proposals as an economic issue, facilitating women's participation in the labour force, in particular women in low-income dual-parent families and single mothers.

While Canada compares well with other liberal welfare states in terms of maternity and parental leave and benefits, it compares unfavourably with the social democratic welfare states where leave provisions and replacement ratios are considerably better. It compares unfavourably with France in terms of child care and Germany in terms of parental leave. It is noteworthy that Germany's generous maternity and parental leave provisions are a substitute rather than a complement for adequate child care provision and reflect the country's heavy reliance on the family as a provider of services.

In summary, the comparatively high full-time participation of women in the labour force in Canada is achieved through dependence by the majority of those with caring responsibilities on market and/or family or other personal informal arrangements rather than through citizenship rights to services such as child care or other care services. While Canada is better than the other liberal welfare states in terms of the social right to paid maternity and parental leave, and better than all but Australia in relation to child care, social policy relating to labour market support services in Canada fits a liberal framework in which state intervention is clearly subordinate to the market. I consider issues related to the improvement in the quality of labour force participation – specifically, pay equity and employment equity in the final section.

The Division of Responsibility between State, Market, and Family

While the first two dimensions of welfare states discussed above have to do with *the redistributive role of the state*, services facilitating participation in the labour market and the division of responsibility between state, market, and family concern *the provision of services* and *the regulatory role of the state*. In comparing countries on the division of responsibility between state, market, and family the key question is: To what extent does the state actively get involved in the achievement of justice in market distribution?

The key identifying characteristic of liberal welfare states is the primacy of the market. The state intervenes when the market fails. In contrast, in social democratic welfare states there is heavy reliance on the state for the provision of services, and the state has traditionally adopted a relatively strong role in relation to the achievement and maintenance of full employment. Restructuring of the welfare state is to a significant extent a restructuring around the division of responsibility among state, market, and family in relation to caregiving. This is to a significant extent a restructuring around gender. This restructuring is reflected in the emphasis on community care of dependent people without the provision of public services to make this a reality. This disproportionately affects women in two ways. The jobs that are being cut in residential services are for the most part jobs performed by women, often highly skilled jobs such as nursing and social work. While some of these will be replaced by jobs in community-based units, those jobs will generally require less skill and be lower paid. In addition, one of the assumptions underlying proposals for community care is that there is a caring community that can be tapped to take over, to some extent, services previously provided in residential centres. This assumption may have been appropriate when there was a large percentage of women outside the labour force, but it is questionable in the changed context of increased full-time participation in the labour force by women in the absence of gender-neutral distribution of unpaid caring work (O'Connor 1996: 19–25).

The state/market/family division has much broader implications, however. The state/market relationship has implications for the regulatory role of the state, for example, in relation to minimum wage legislation, employment standards legislation, industrial relations legislation, pay equity and employment equity legislation, and environmental legislation. The politically contested nature of the state/market/family division of responsibility is clearly reflected both in the U.S. Republican Party 'Contract with America' in the 1994 Congressional election, much of which concerned commitments to lessen the regulatory role of the state, and the Ontario Progressive Conservative government action on labour legislation and employment equity, immediately they gained office in 1995.

Historically, the most significant difference among welfare states has been the role of the state in relation to employment. In particular, there is variation in the extent to which employment is regarded as a citizenship right and in the extent to which the state is prepared to act to guarantee such a right. Despite rising levels of unemployment in several OECD countries throughout the 1980s, and in most by the early 1990s, there are differences across countries in the reaction to the problem, in particular in the commitment by governments to alleviate it.

Cross-national analyses of unemployment between 1960 and 1990 consistently indicate that high unemployment is a political and strategic choice, not an economic inevitability (Martin 1986; Schmidt 1984; Scharpf 1984; Therborn 1986). This is not to deny that the location of a country in the international economic order and/or high levels of foreign ownership constrain the policy options and outlook for *the achievement* of economic and welfare goals. In a study of 16 OECD countries over the 1974–84 period, Therborn (1986) demonstrated that not all the countries with low unemployment were favoured economically. What distinguishes countries with full employment and high unemployment countries is not the openness of their economies, though this is a constraint, but the extent to which full employment policies were consistently pursued and institutionalized (Therborn 1986: 23).[10]

There has never been a commitment to full employment in Canada, despite the public policy documents since the post–Second World War period that have affirmed the desirability of a high and stable level of employment. In general, reducing the level of inflation has been pursued at the expense of high unemployment. This policy has been explicit in the statements of federal finance ministers and the governor of the Bank of Canada throughout the late 1980s and early 1990s. It is noteworthy that the definition of the 'full employment' unemployment rate has been adjusted upwards each decade since the 1950s (Muszynski 1985). This reflects an acceptance of the consistent rise in Canada's average annual unemployment rate: it was 5 per cent in the 1960–73 period, 7.2 per cent in the 1974–9 period, 9.3 per cent in the 1980–9 period, and 10.2 per cent in the 1990–3 period (OECD 1995: Table 2.15). In other words, what is politically acceptable has been adjusted to match the prevailing rate of unemployment.

Changes in employment and training policies during the 1980s reflect a more active approach to problems in the labour market, but with an emphasis on efficiency rather than equity. Specifically, the focus shifted to meeting skill shortages and upgrading of skills. This was funded through the Unemployment Insurance Fund, the money being made available through more stringent conditions of access to unemployment insurance and a reduction in the duration of benefits. This is a supply-side strategy with the focus on job readiness skills and based on the assumption that the market will create the jobs (Yates 1995).

In conclusion, with the exception of its health care system, the Canadian welfare state fits clearly within the framework of a liberal welfare regime on all four dimensions. This mix of 'two worlds' of social policy (Tuohy 1993) can be explained by the political configuration of Canada within the context of its particular variant of federalism and its exceptional level of dependence on the United States as its major trading partner (O'Connor 1989). I return to the redistributive implications of the characteristics of the Canadian welfare state in the final section, where I discuss the Welfare State as a Mechanism for the Amelioration of Inequality. First, I outline key developments in the growth and retrenchment of the Canadian welfare state over the past thirty years.

1960–95: Growth and Retrenchment of the Canadian Welfare State

As in other OECD countries, the 1960–95 period can be divided into two periods in terms of the fortunes of the welfare state in Canada: 1960–73 was a period of growth; 1974 to the present has been a period of intensifying levels of retrenchment.

Growth and Development: 1960–73

In some countries the 1960–73 period is now described as the 'golden age' of development of the welfare state and of the lessening of inequality (Persson 1990). In Canada also we see the 1960s as a relatively golden era in terms of the welfare state. Yet the picture for Canada is mixed. On the one hand this was the era which saw a relative flurry of legislative activity at the federal government level: the Canada Pension Plan in 1964, the Canada Assistance Plan, the Guaranteed Income Supplement (GIS) for low-income people over 65, and Medicare in 1966. Likewise, the Unemployment Insurance Act of 1971 expanded coverage, increased the earnings replacement rate to a maximum of 75 per cent of insurable earnings, reduced eligibility criteria, and introduced maternity leave. In 1973 a new Family Allowance Act increased benefits by almost a third. Finally, the 1960s was characterized by a massive expansion in public expenditure on education and health (Tables 3 and 4). Yet this was also the era of the rediscovery of poverty (Guest 1985: 167), documented in several reports including the *Fifth Annual Review* of the Economic Council of Canada (1968); *Social Policies for Canada, Part 1*, produced by the Canadian Welfare Council (1969); *Poverty in Canada* (the Croll Report 1971), produced by the Senate Committee on Poverty (1971); *The Real Poverty Report*, by four dissident members of Senator Croll's staff (I. Adams et al. 1971); and the *Report of the Royal Commission on the Status of Women in Canada* (1970).

These reports not only indicated a high level of poverty amidst affluence but also the overrepresentation of native Canadians, French Canadians, and women among the poor. The Senate Report is especially significant for its identification of close to two million 'working poor.' These concerns were reflected in the establishment of the Social Security Review 1973–6. This review was initiated by the issuing of the *Working Paper on Social Security in Canada* (often identified as the Orange Paper) which outlined the 'broad directions of policy which would, in the view of the Federal government, lead to a more effective and better coordinated system of social security for Canadians' (Canada, Minister for National Health and Welfare 1973: 2). The scope of the review was extensive, being based on five strategies: community employment, social insurance, income support and supplementation, social and employment services, and a federal-provincial strategy relating to jurisdiction for social security. However, the main objective of the review was 'to come to grips with one of the most intractable problems in the social security system – the risk to income adequacy created by low or intermittent earnings' (Guest 1985: 186–7).

It is important to recognize that the proposals for change in income support emerging from the Social Security Review maintained the residualist character of the Canadian welfare state. That is, there was a continued emphasis on 'designing programmes for the poor and re-emphasizing the *cause* of need' (Guest 1985: 192) and a renewed commitment to the 'less eligibility' principle established in the 1834 modification of the British Poor Law. Even in the case of insurance programs, such as the Canada Pension Plan, the market dimension and residualist character were reflected in the assumption that private pensions would be a necessary supplement to the public pension benefit. At a more fundamental level, the primacy of the market was reflected in the White Paper's rejection of the option of full employment as a 'simplistic assumption' which should be borne in mind in constructing the social security system (Canada, Minister for National Health and Welfare 1973: 6). Further, it was asserted that higher rates of unemployment were inevitable because of the unpredictable size of the increase in the labour force. The role of the state as a guarantor of full employment was not considered. This contrasts with the view expressed in the Marsh and Beveridge reports that the state should play a vigorous role in the creation of employment (Marsh 1975 [1943], Part II; Beveridge 1944: 36).

Although the tripling of family allowance payments and a commitment to increase them in line with the consumer price index under the new 1973 Family Allowance Act can be associated with the Social Security Review, as can the improvement in old age security payments and the maximum pension under the Canada and Quebec Pension Plans, the primary objective was not fulfilled. Specifically, the proposal in the White Paper for a needs-based guaranteed annual income for the unemployable and an income supplement for the working poor was not implemented. This was the result not only of provincial objections but also of the worsening economic situation, which was exacerbated by the oil crisis of 1973 and was reflected in rising levels of unemployment and rising inflation. Thus, the Social Security Review, although less revolutionary in its objectives than was claimed by its proponents, was to a significant extent the victim of timing. Indeed, by 1976–7, rather than expanding programs, the government was cutting expenditure. It froze the indexing of family allowances for one year and had already started to cut back on the unemployment insurance system embodied in the 1971 act. In 1978 significant reductions were made in the family allowance benefit, which had been increased in 1973, with the objective of funding the Refundable Child Tax Credit introduced that year. This was directed to benefit low- and moderate-income families with children. However, the funding mechanism reflects the beginning of a process of selectivity, since the tax credit declines with income to a maximum cut-off (Moscovitz 1986: 83–4). The selectivity was reinforced in subsequent years by the privileging of the tax credit relative to the family allowance benefit and child tax deductions. The refundable tax credit also reflects the first use of the taxation system to redistribute income towards children in an explicitly progressive way.

Retrenchment: Mid-1970s to 1990s

We are conscious in the mid-1990s of the erosion of social programs through the action of federal and provincial governments. Yet, as indicated above, the roots of this erosion were set in the 1970s. In a review of Canadian social transfer programs Keith Banting (1987b) identified a pattern of erosion or stagnation of benefit levels and increased emphasis on income-tested access to benefits from the late 1970s to mid-1980s. The pattern varied by program with pensions being the most favoured and unemployment insurance and the Canada Assistance Plan being the least favoured. This pattern continued throughout the rest of the 1980s and has intensified in the early 1990s.

The 1989 budget introduced a clawback on old age security and family allowances of 15 cents on each dollar of individual or family income in excess of $50,000 in the 1989 tax year. Since this threshold was only partially indexed for inflation (to the amount of inflation over 3 per cent), it is estimated that by the end of the decade the clawback will apply to incomes equal to $37,400 in 1990 dollars (Ross 1991: 14). The effect of this change was to impose a targeted tax on old age security and family allowances and to end the universality of these programs. This follows a pattern established in 1985 when child benefits were partially de-indexed for inflation. Unless inflation was zero this meant an effective decrease in benefits of up to 3 per cent annually, since payments were increased only by the amount of inflation over 3 per cent.

The 1992 budget went further in this direction with the elimination of universal family allowances. With effect from January 1993 these were replaced by programs designed to target those with lower incomes, with further targeting of the working poor. As already pointed out, the process of selectivity had begun in 1978 with the introduction of the refundable child tax credit and was continued by increasing expenditure on the tax credit element to a relatively greater extent than that on family allowances. The privileging of income-tested programs is also evident in pensions with the more favourable treatment throughout the 1980s and early 1990s of the income-tested supplements – the Guaranteed Income Supplement and the Spouse's Allowance – relative to the universal, but now subject to clawback, Old Age Security payment. This process was concluded in the 1996 budget with the commitment to replace the existing OAS/GIS benefits by an income-tested Seniors Benefit in 2001.

The 1990 federal budget put a limit of 5 per cent on the Canada Assistance Plan (CAP) payments to British Columbia, Ontario, and Alberta. This was extended for a further three years in the 1991 budget. In 1989 welfare payments for a couple with two children were equivalent to 61 per cent of the poverty line in Ontario, 53 per cent in British Columbia, and 58 per cent in Alberta (National Council of Welfare 1990: Table 3). In addition to these low levels before the cutbacks, need is increasing rapidly because of restrictions in access to, and on the duration of, unemployment insurance and the exhaustion of benefits due to high levels of long-term unemployment.[11] Whereas the original CAP formula was based on a 50–50 share of the costs by the federal and provincial governments, the cutbacks and increased need resulted in a situation where the federal share was down to 28 per cent in Ontario and 36 per cent in British Columbia by 1992–3. Alberta was not seriously affected because the federal cutbacks were in tune with the political commitment of the provincial government, which cut welfare programs substantially (National Council of Welfare 1995b: 7). For example, welfare payments to a couple with two children were reduced by 16 per cent over the 1986–94 period.

These cutbacks to the Canada Assistance Plan and unemployment insurance were part of a broader pattern that also included cutbacks in social housing expenditure and the freezing of Established Program Financing (EPF) transfers from the federal government to the provinces for health and post-secondary education. The EPF mechanism, which was agreed in 1977, consisted of an unconditional tax-points element and a cash element dependent on conformity to national standards.[12] Increases were to be linked to increases in GNP and population.

In 1986 the annual increase in federal transfers under EPF were restricted to the increase in the Gross National Product less two percentage points; in 1989 this was changed to the increase in GNP less 3 percentage points with effect from 1990–1. In the 1991 budget this was extended for a further three years through 1994–5. This process continued in the 1995 Liberal budget and is reflected in the decision to change the process of funding established programs and to reduce the amount of transfers to the provinces from 1996–7. The new system, identified as the Canada Health and Social Transfer (CHST), takes the form of a block grant to the provinces to cover health, post-secondary education, and welfare. In other words, the Canada Assistance Plan and the old EPF system have been abolished, and the resources they entailed are reduced and amalgamated. There is considerable concern among social policy advocates that this will produce negative consequences for beneficiaries of the Canada Assistance Plan. The new system gives greater discretion to provincial governments to shift spending priorities. Since the constituencies who support health and post-secondary education services are considerably bigger and have more political resources, they are likely to be more successful at defending their interests than are supporters of the former CAP-funded programs.

So far I have concentrated on the federal level. However, the provision of social programs is largely a provincial matter. Consequently, the restrictions on the increase in Established Program Financing and in the Canada Assistance Plan throughout the 1980s were played out at the provincial level and reflected in decisions about health, post-secondary education, and welfare taken by provincial governments. While disputes about conformity to the principles of the Canada Health Act have usually been resolved by the provinces agreeing to conform, at least in principle, there has been a gradual erosion in quality of health care, reflected in longer waiting lists, the delisting of some services, and pressure for increased privatization. The impact of the freezing of EPF transfers is also reflected in reduced funding of post-secondary educational institutions, especially during the 1990s, with the consequence of higher fees and higher borrowing requirements for students. While there are legitimate concerns about the equity implications of the private gains from post-secondary education and the skewed socioeconomic background of those who participate, higher tuition fees and an emphasis on borrowing disproportionately exclude people from lower socioeconomic backgrounds.

An examination of welfare benefits across provinces indicates that some provinces had started to reduce the real level of welfare benefits by the mid-1980s, and there was evidence of a more general pattern of increased restrictions on eligibility and increased monitoring of clients by that stage (National Council of Welfare 1987). This intensified throughout the rest of the 1980s and early 1990s. Over the 1986 to 1994 period the real value of welfare benefits for a couple with two children declined in six provinces.[13] It is noteworthy that the 'couple with two children' category of welfare beneficiary fared better in most provinces than single employable people and single parents with one child. Benefits increased in British Columbia (8 per cent), Manitoba (10 per cent), New Brunswick (2 per cent) and Ontario (31 per cent), although in all of these provinces there were increased restrictions and monitoring. Despite the relatively large increase in Ontario over the 1986–94 period, welfare benefits for a couple with two children in 1994 were equivalent to only 72 per cent of the poverty line and 34 per cent of estimated average income. The corresponding figures relating to benefits as a percentage of the poverty line were worse in all other provinces, and only two provinces were marginally better than Ontario in the benefit-to-average-income ratio (National Council of Welfare 1995c: Tables 3, 4, and 5). The Ontario rates were cut by 22 per cent by the Progressive Conservative government in August 1995.

While welfare payments and subsidized child care are the most obvious and visible targets for provincial governments, it is important to recognize that the CAP covered a wide range of programs, including casework, counselling, assessment, and referral services to abused or neglected children; preventive services for children in their own homes; community development services; rehabilitation services, including life-skills training; job referral and placement services for the chronically unemployed; and special help and services to aid independent living for elderly people and those with physical and mental disabilities. It gave support to more than 6,000 provincially approved social service agencies, such as Children's Aid Societies, family service agencies, and day care centres. The CAP also provided money for more than 7,000 homes for special care, such as homes for the aged, shelters for battered women and their children, residences for people with disabilities, and rehabilitation centres for people with alcohol and drug addictions. In addition, it covered certain non-medicare health care costs and child welfare services such as the maintenance of children in foster homes (National Council of Welfare 1995b: 5–6).

I have pointed out in previous sections that women are more likely to be dependent on means-tested income services than men because of their family situations. It is obvious from the above list that children and dependent adults were the major users of CAP-funded services. Consequently, the cutbacks are likely to have a disproportionate impact on them and their primary carers, most likely women. The consequences of EPF cutbacks are also borne disproportionately by women because of their relatively high levels of employment in the public sector. Privatization of services means the loss of relatively well-paid and often unionized jobs in the public sector for generally lower paid, insecure jobs in the private sector. Similarly, cuts in daycare provision and junior kindergarten have a disproportionate impact on women, because of their reliance on these service to facilitate their participation in the labour force.

The restructuring of the benefit package and the associated reconfiguring of the balance between income testing, social insurance, and citizenship access, point to two important issues associated with welfare effort. First, the relative privilege of some programs in terms of public perception and electoral attractiveness ensures less likelihood of cutbacks; second, there is a tension between the redistributive and solidarity objectives of the welfare state. There is considerable evidence that health care enjoys a privileged status in terms of public support in Canada, and this is reflected in the lesser cutbacks in this area relative to the Canada Assistance Plan and unemployment insurance. Likewise, surveys of public opinion in various countries have demonstrated that pensions are more likely to be seen as deserved and legitimate rewards than are other social security benefits (Coughlin 1980; Tomasson 1984). Consequently, it is easier to mobilize support for pension programs than for programs such as family allowances or unemployment insurance. The broad range of support for pensions was evident in the composition of the opposition to the proposed de-indexing of the universal aspect of the Canadian pension program in the 1985 budget (O'Connor 1987).[14] However, a partial de-indexing was implemented in 1989 without widespread protest, and the 1996 budget proposal to replace the Old Age Security Benefit by an income-tested system in 2001 was not greeted by strong protests. It is noteworthy that selectivity in family allowances was raised by the Liberal government in 1982 but dropped because of its political unpopularity (Moscovitz 1986: 83–4). This objective was effected later in the decade through the clawback and partial de-indexing without widespread protest. This illustrates the success of the ideological battle waged by the federal Conservative and Liberal governments and business interests. Support for cutbacks was generated by focusing on a purported link between the cost of social programs and the federal deficit. A similar ideological battle is under way in the mid-1990s relating to the issue of the provision of private health services, the restructuring of the Canada Pension Plan, and the funding of post-secondary education.

The tension between redistribution and solidarity is evident in regard to both pensions and family benefits. Universal programs foster solidarity, but benefits are not targeted to those most in need. Targeting can make a contribution to redistribution. For example, increased targeting of low-income groups through the pension system has lessened poverty among elderly people (National Council of Welfare 1988: 1). Similarly, the targeting of low-income families through the changes in the family benefits package has had positive redistributive effects. However, the increase in redistribution associated with targeting is achieved at the expense of the universality that ensures a political constituency for the defence of programs in the long term. The objective of increased redistribution could be achieved on a more cost-effective basis through a progressive income tax and the maintenance of universality. While many factors contribute to the lessening of support for expenditure for social programs, it is noteworthy that this lessening of support has coincided with the lessening of universality.

The trickle-down effect of federal cutbacks – first to provinces, then to municipalities – is reflected not only in cuts to welfare payments, but in longer waiting lists for certain health care procedures, reduced funding to health and post-secondary education, an increase in user fees (which are regressive), a restructuring of the provision of services (reflected in privatization of provision), and cutbacks in discretionary services such as day care and junior kindergarten, which have never been established as citizenship rights in Canada. Yet, when we look at the framework of social policy in the 1990s relative to the 1960s, what we see mostly is not the abandonment of programs but a fundamental erosion in the quality of several programs through incremental change. It is *the quality of social citizenship rights* that is being eroded in areas like health care and education.

How can this general pattern of cutbacks be explained? Social programs have been increasingly under attack as the federal deficit has increased. In addition, although the process of retrenchment was initiated before they came into office, the ideology and agenda of the federal Conservative government, in power between 1984 and 1993, was directly linked to the intensification of the process. This intensification was particularly evident during the second mandate (1988–93). This ideology is premised on the primacy of the market and a reduced role for government, but it is usually framed around a discourse of deficit and debt. It is consistent with the opposition by business groups to government action that would set limits on private market activity. For example, there has been pressure from business groups, especially during the two sets of free trade negotiations, to move towards the harmonization with the United States of at least some Canadian social programs, especially unemployment insurance. In addition, these groups pressed for the targeting of other programs, such as pensions and family allowances, to those perceived to be most in need. This process is now clearly on track. The Liberal government elected in 1993 has not altered the course, but has affirmed a commitment to 'save the social safety net' through restructuring social programs and has made the deficit and debt more central to its justification for reduced funding to the provinces. The provincial governments have also been reacting to the competing pressure of increased need associated with long-term unemployment, the intensification in inequality, and debt and deficit constraints. While the direction taken is similar across provinces, the mechanisms chosen to cope, and in particular, the intensity of the measures, have varied with the ideological complexion of government. The most neo-conservative approach, that is, one focusing on the size of government as the problem, has been adopted by the Social Credit government in British Columbia in the early 1980s and the Conservative governments under Ralph Klein in Alberta and Mike Harris in Ontario in the 1990s.

The Welfare State and the Amelioration of Social Inequality in Canada

Based on the four dimensions of the welfare state considered in this chapter and the pattern of development and retrenchment of programs over the past three decades, what conclusions can we reach about the Canadian welfare state in the 1960 to 1990 period? I concluded earlier that, with the exception of the health care system, the Canadian welfare state bears all the hallmarks of a liberal welfare state. This is most sharply illustrated by the relatively high emphasis on income-testing, the low and decreasing access to services and benefits on the basis of citizenship, the increased restrictions in the insurance-based benefits such as unemployment insurance and pensions, the increased reliance, and restrictions, on income-tested programs, and the relatively strong emphasis on the market as a mechanism for the provision of services and governing access. It is also illustrated by the reluctance of the state to set limits on market activity through its regulatory role, for example, in relation to the maintenance of the minimum wage at least equal to the poverty line. The liberal character of the Canadian welfare state is also clearly reflected in the reliance on the market to meet labour supply. Yet, the welfare state in Canada as elsewhere remains, despite its limitations in terms of scope and quality, 'the most broadly based institution for promoting social justice' (Goodin and Dryzek 1987: 37). This is clearly illustrated when we examine redistribution as reflected in social transfer payments, such as pensions, unemployment insurance, and welfare, that is, those programs that protect individuals from total dependence on the market. Later I look at health, education, and public sector employment.

Social protection is one element of the redistributive framework – taxation is the other. A lessening of inequality through the taxation system is dependent on progressive taxation. Several recently published studies of the Canadian tax system up to 1988 demonstrated that its one progressive element is the federal income tax system (Ruggeri, Van Wart, and Howard 1994; Vermaeten, Gillespie, and Vermaeten 1994; Vermaeten and Gillespie 1995). 'All other taxes combined have an inverted U shape, indicating that they redistribute income from the middle class to both low- and high-income households' (Ruggeri, Van Wart, and Howard 1994: 418). Canada is one of the few countries in the OECD that has neither an annual net wealth tax nor a wealth transfer tax. The federal and provincial governments abolished all inheritance and gift taxes in the late 1960s and early 1970s (Banting 1991). Wealth taxes do not produce large revenues in any country due to the combination of high thresholds and exemptions. These characteristics reflect problems about the definition of assets, but also the ability of wealth holders to resist taxation.

Despite the relatively low social transfer expenditure in Canada by OECD standards, it is important to recognize that social transfers do mitigate inequality and are considerably more effective than the taxation system in mitigating the inequality associated with the primary distribution of income. This difference is consistently evident throughout the 1980s and into the 1990s. A comparison of Gini coefficients, which are summary measures of the degree of inequality in the distribution of income, indicates that in 1981 the reduction in inequality due to social transfer payments was almost two and a half times as large as the reduction due to direct taxes (Vaillancourt 1985: 11). Gini coefficients for the three categories of income necessary to make these calculations – that is, for market income, transfer income, and disposable income – are not available for later years, but the relative impact of transfers and taxes is clearly evident in a comparison of the shares of income going to the extremes of the distribution. Taking the shares of market income, that is, income from earnings and investment, we find that the top quintile of families had almost fifteen times the share of the bottom quintile in 1991. After the addition of transfer payments such as unemployment insurance, pensions, and social assistance, the difference in shares was reduced to just over six times. After federal and provincial income taxes, the difference was further reduced, but families in the highest quintile still received five times the share of those in the bottom quintile (Table 5). It is noteworthy that the disparity in shares of national income at each stage is more unequal in 1991 than in 1981 and the difference is especially marked at the market income stage: an almost fifteen times difference in 1991 relative to an eight times difference in 1981. The post-transfer difference was 6.3 in 1991 compared with 5.3 in 1981, and the post-transfer and tax difference was 5 in 1991 relative to 4.5 in 1981.

These patterns indicate that over this decade the role of social transfers in modifying the impact of inequality in the primary distribution of incomes became more important both in absolute terms and relative to taxation. In 1981 social transfers were almost four times as effective as direct taxes in reducing inequality. In 1991 they were six times as effective (Table 5). Apart from people over the age of 65, among whom the Guaranteed Income Supplement effected a decrease in inequality, the increased effectiveness of social transfers reflects not so much an improvement in the level of particular social transfer payments, such as unemployment insurance payments and welfare benefits, but an increase in need as reflected in high levels of unemployment and increases in the number of people who could be classified as the working poor.[15] The increase in the working poor reflects a decline in the real value of the minimum wage over the past couple of decades. When we compare the value of the minimum wage as a percentage of the poverty line in 1992 relative to 1976 we find an across-the-board decline in both the federal and provincial rates. In 1976 the value of the minimum wage across provinces ranged from 96 to 118 per cent of the poverty line, with a median of 105. In 1992 the range was 55 to 83 per cent, with a median of 76 (National Council of Welfare 1993: 69–70).

The increasing polarization in market incomes is not confined to the extremes of the income distribution framework. Indeed, the pattern that is evident for Canada is that the bottom three quintiles in terms of income distribution received a lower share of market income in 1991 than in 1981 – 32.5 per cent compared with 37 per cent. While the top two quintiles received a higher share, the increase was particularly marked for the highest quintile (Table 5). When we look at the decile distribution of market income among families with never-married children under 18 over a longer period – 1973–91 – we find even stronger

TABLE 5

Quintile shares of different definitions of family income, all families with children under 18 years of age

Income/year	Percentage share		Percentage change
	1981	1991	1981–91
Market income			
Lowest	4.8	2.9	−1.9
Second	13.4	11.4	−2.0
Middle	18.8	18.2	−0.6
Fourth	24.6	25.1	0.5
Highest	38.4	42.4	4.0
Highest: lowest	8.0	14.6	
Transfer income			
Lowest	6.9	6.2	−0.7
Second	13.9	12.7	−0.6
Middle	18.6	18.0	−0.6
Fourth	23.9	23.9	0.0
Highest	36.7	39.2	2.5
Highest: lowest	5.3	6.3	
Disposable income			
Lowest	7.8	7.3	−0.5
Second	14.5	13.9	−0.6
Middle	18.8	18.5	−0.3
Fourth	23.6	23.7	0.1
Highest	35.3	36.6	1.3
Highest: lowest	4.5	5.0	

'Market Income' refers to income from earnings and investments. 'Transfer Income' refers to market income plus government transfers such as Unemployment Insurance, social assistance and so on. 'Disposable Income' refers to transfer income after federal and provincial income taxes have been paid.

Source: Ross et al. 1994. Tabulations by the authors based on Statistics Canada's Survey of Consumer Finances microdata tapes

evidence of increasing polarization in market incomes. The highest 10 per cent increased its share by just under 14 per cent over the period, while the shares of the lowest and second deciles decreased by 47 per cent and 39 per cent respectively (Table 6a). It is noteworthy that the share of market income earned by the lowest three deciles has declined consistently throughout this period. Even more striking is that they also lost, although to a considerably lesser extent, when total incomes, that is, market income plus transfer payments, are considered (Table 6b). Furthermore, since the early 1970s, it was only during the 1973–9 period that the top decile's share of both market and total income declined even slightly (1 per cent). At all other periods its share of national income has been increasing.

In summary, a review of income distribution from 1981 to 1991 indicates increasing inequality as reflected in the shares of the bottom three quintiles relative to the top two, irrespective of the stage in the process: market, post-transfer, or post–direct tax income. A similar trend is evident over the 1973 to 1991 period using decile distributions of market and post-transfer income. The lowest six deciles lose, and the highest four deciles gain. Social transfers are considerably more effective than direct taxes in modifying income inequality; but even when both are taken into account families in the highest quintile receive five times the share of national income of those in the lowest quintile. Despite this, it is noteworthy that social transfers were able to lessen the impact of sharply increasing inequality in market income associated with increasing long-term unemployment and an increasing working poor population in the 1981–91 period. This success must be put in the context of increasing poverty rates since 1989 for groups other than those over the age of 65. Poverty rates for children under 18 increased from 14.9 per cent in 1980 to 19.6 per cent in 1984 and fell to 14.5 per cent in 1989, but they have increased consistently to 20.8 per cent in 1993. A broadly similar pattern is evident for families and unattached individuals with consistent increases since 1989 (National Council of Welfare 1995a: Tables 3 and 5).

When we focus on direct provision of services the two programs with widest impact are health and education. These are the two areas in which Canada's expenditure compares favourably with other OECD countries. In the case of health care there is still universal access, although there are indications that the quality of the social right to health services may be declining because of lengthening waiting lists and the delisting of certain procedures. This is associated with calls for recognition of private medical services and the associated danger of a lessening of support for universal services.

In considering the amelioration of inequality, it is important to recognize that access to health services cannot be equated with health status. There is considerable evidence of the persistence of socioeconomic

TABLE 6a
Distribution of market income among economic families with children under 18, by deciles, 1973–91[1]

	Share of market income (%)				Change in share (%)		
Decile	1973	1979	1987	1991	1973–9	1973–87	1973–91
1	1.35	0.97	0.77	0.72	−28.15	−43.00	−46.54
2	4.18	3.90	3.27	2.56	−6.70	−21.50	−38.87
3	6.06	5.99	5.40	4.65	−1.15	−10.90	−23.34
4	7.46	7.51	7.12	6.52	0.67	−4.60	−12.54
5	8.65	8.77	8.59	8.27	1.39	0.60	−4.39
6	9.91	10.08	9.92	9.79	1.72	0.00	−1.20
7	11.28	11.43	11.41	11.57	1.33	1.10	2.59
8	12.87	13.09	13.12	13.54	1.71	1.09	5.20
9	15.29	15.54	15.74	16.25	1.64	3.00	6.27
10	22.95	22.73	24.65	26.13	−1.00	7.40	13.86

[1] Market income refers to earnings from wages, salaries, and self-employment plus returns on investment.

Source: Yalnizyan (1994), based on Statistics Canada, Household Surveys Division, Survey of Consumer Finances, unpublished data.

TABLE 6b.
Distribution of total income among economic families with children under 18, by deciles, 1973–91[1]

	Share of market income (%)				Change in share (%)		
Decile	1973	1979	1987	1991	1973–9	1973–87	1973–91
1	2.33	2.04	2.19	2.10	−12.45	−5.00	−9.33
2	4.74	4.50	4.25	4.00	−5.26	−10.30	−15.15
3	6.30	6.24	5.93	5.70	−0.95	−5.90	−9.88
4	7.52	7.60	7.32	7.10	1.06	−2.66	−6.29
5	8.64	8.76	8.54	8.30	1.39	−1.16	−3.46
6	9.78	9.93	9.74	9.60	1.53	−0.41	−1.44
7	11.06	11.22	11.08	11.10	1.45	0.18	0.57
8	12.63	12.77	12.67	12.80	1.11	0.32	1.23
9	14.88	15.06	15.02	15.20	1.21	0.94	2.19
10	22.12	21.89	23.26	24.00	−1.04	5.15	8.70

[1] Total income refers to market income plus transfer payments (UI, social assistance, CPP, etc.) and retirement income.

Source: Yalnizyan (1994), based on Statistics Canada, Household Surveys Division, Survey of Consumer Finances, unpublished data.

differences in health status in Canada despite equalization of access (Manga 1993). This is consistent with the extensive historical and cross-national evidence on the relationship between economic inequalities and health status (Hay 1994). Several factors contribute to these inequalities, for example, inequalities in income and housing, poor working conditions, environmental pollution, and unemployment (Brenner 1980; Sclar 1980; Bolaria and Bolaria 1994). With the exception of inequality in income none of these is directly addressed by the introduction of a social citizenship right to health services, and the effects of income inequality are not eradicated (Manga and Weller 1980; see Bolaria and Bolaria 1994 regarding immigration and race). While the introduction of medicare reflected a concern with payment for medical services rather than a focus on the structural causation of disease, it is noteworthy that examinations of the escalating costs of health care and of health status are increasingly framed within the context of the need for prevention and some recognition of the links between socioeconomic inequalities and health status. As pointed out by Walters, Lenton, and McKeary (1995), however, this is not reflected in funding priorities.

It was noted above that education is not usually included in evaluation of social expenditure because of its focus on equality of opportunity. The limitations of equality of opportunity as a mechanism for the achievement of equality were pointed out by John Porter in the 1970s, and these criticisms are still valid. However, educational participation is an indicator of the level of inequality in society, and differences in participation reinforce existing levels of inequality. There is extensive evidence from Canada and elsewhere – including evidence gathered by Porter and his colleagues – that ascribed characteristics, such as family background, gender, ethnicity, and race, affect educational opportunities and achievement as reflected in such factors as drop-out rates, leaving without a diploma, and university attendance (Gilbert and Orok 1994; Porter, Porter, and Blishen 1982; Oakes 1985). The impact of parents' education on children's education is evident at all levels of education, but it is most strongly reflected in post-secondary participation rates (Richer 1988; Guppy and Arai 1993). For example, data from the 1986 General Social Survey indicate that educational attainment increases consistently with both mother's and father's levels of education. Post-secondary attendance for 25- to 44-year-olds increased from 38 per cent, through 54 per cent to 81 per cent for women as mother's education increased from Grade 8 or less through high school to post-secondary – a difference of 43 per cent between the end-points. For men the difference between the end-points was 23 per cent. The difference between the endpoints when father's education is the focus is 38 per cent for both men and women. A comparison of these findings with those for an older cohort – 45- to 64-year-olds – indicates that while parents' education was still highly significant in the 1980s, its impact was slightly lessened relative to two or three decades earlier (Guppy and Arai 1993: 221–3). An interesting finding is the stronger association between mother's and daughter's education than between mother's and son's education. There is no significant difference for father's education for the younger cohort.

Since direct measures of the impact of social class on educational attainment are rarely available, father's occupation is often used as a proxy for social class. Again, when we look at the mid-1980s, we find a clear association between father's occupation and post-secondary attendance for men and women. For example, 76 per cent of women and 79 per cent of men aged 25 to 44 whose fathers were in the high-level management and professional occupational groups attended post-secondary institutions, compared with 42 per cent of women and 50 per cent of men whose fathers were in blue-collar occupations. The same pattern is evident for the cohort aged 45 to 64, but the occupational differences are greater. Comparing the two cohorts, we find that while educational levels have increased overall and while the range of educational attainment across occupational groups has declined over time for both sexes, it is greater for men than for women (Guppy and Arai 1993: 223).

Traditionally, there were significant sex differences in post-secondary educational participation. This has now been reversed and is reflected in the fact that in 1991 women earned 56 per cent of the bachelors' and first professional degrees. However, women are still concentrated in traditional areas of study, such as health, education, and the social sciences and have very low representation in engineering and the physical sciences (Thompson et al. 1993: 10, 12). Not surprisingly, these women have come disproportionately from higher socioeconomic backgrounds. This has had the consequence of broadening the social class differences in post-secondary attendance (Guppy and Arai 1993). It is noteworthy that while the surge in degree attainment by women at the bachelor's level is also evident at the master's and doctoral levels, its size decreases with level: women earned 47 per cent of masters' degrees and 32 per cent of doctorates in 1991 (Statistics Canada 1993: 150). It is also noteworthy that the greater educational achievement of women is not reflected in female-male pay differentials. One of the best illustrations of this is an analysis by Wannell (1990), which indicated that in 1987 women with identical educational background, age, and similar labour force experience compared with men earned $7,000 less (cited by Guppy and Arai 1993).

Despite the persistence of gender-based earning differentials and gender-based occupational segregation it is noteworthy that, if one accepts participation in the labour force as the key to independence, the welfare state has contributed to the lessening of gender inequalities. It has absorbed a significant part of women's increasing participation in the labour force over the 1960 to 1990 period and, in its regulatory role, has contributed, at least to some extent, to an improvement in the quality of women's employment through pay and employment equity legislation (O'Connor 1998). While employment equity has had little impact on the overall gender segregation of the labour force, it has had an impact at the upper end of the occupational distribution.[16] Similarly, pay equity has not had a major generalized impact on female-male pay differentials, but it has had some effect, especially in the public sector.[16] For example, the ratio of female-to-male earnings for full-time workers was 72 per cent in 1993, but the female-male relativity is far higher for government sector workers than for those in the private sector: 79.8 per cent compared with 67.9 per cent in 1992, and the rate of increase in the female-male relativities between 1990 and 1992 was 7.4 per cent for government workers and 4.5 per cent for private sector workers (Table 7). This reverses the 1980s pattern when women working in the private sector were making relatively greater progress, although starting from a much lower base. The figures for the early 1990s may reflect the impact of pay equity policies in the public service. The visibility of procedures relating to remuneration which characterizes the public sector may facilitate the enforcement of pay equity. In addition, unionization is considerably higher in the public sector, and unionized workers are in a stronger position to exercise their rights.

While the welfare state contributed to the integration of women into the labour force, particularly from the mid-1960s to the mid-1980s, their concentration in the public sector has left them vulnerable in the 1990s. The cutbacks in public sector employment in general, and welfare state employment in particular, will have a disproportionate impact on women. It will affect some through job losses and these women as well as others through cutbacks in the caring services that facilitate participation in the labour force.

Despite the persistence of substantial levels of inequality in Canadian society, the welfare state has contributed significantly to the ameliora-

Table 7
Ratio of female to male earnings for full-time workers,
Canada 1980–92 (selected years)

Year	Sector		Total full-time workforce
	Private	Government	
1980	60.6	73.8	64.2
1987	62.5	73.0	65.9
1990	65.0	74.3	67.9
1992	67.9	79.8	71.8

Source: Statistics Canada, Household Surveys Division,
Survey of Consumer Finances, unpublished data.

tion of inequality in market incomes. Furthermore, while there has been a sharp increase in this inequality over the past two decades, the social transfer system has maintained relative stability in the final distribution of income. This success has to be put in the context of persistent high levels of inequality in the final distribution of income, cutbacks to services (especially non-mandated services once funded through the Canada Assistance Plan), and the dilution of the quality of social citizenship rights not only to social insurance programs such as unemployment insurance, but also to health care. It also has to be put in the context of the persisting difference in health status among socioeconomic, racial, and ethnic groups, and the persisting socioeconomic differences in school drop-out rates and in post-secondary educational participation.

Conclusion

In conclusion, then, we can say with certainty that the welfare state in Canada contributes significantly to the amelioration of market and associated inequities and that this contributes to the achievement of social justice. However, these inequities are increasing over time, and, in the absence of a political commitment to address this increase, Canada is moving further away from the achievement of a just society, if one is to define that as a society characterized by a considerable degree of equality of condition or even of opportunity. This is exacerbated by the changing context within which the welfare state is operating in the 1990s relative to the 1960s. Canadian governments of all hues are preoccupied with the *fiscal deficit*, and this is a legitimate concern. However, if it is not considered within the context of what is being identified as the *social deficit* (Osberg 1992: 230) and the *democratic deficit* (Myles 1996), we

222   Julia S. O'Connor

are likely to end up with fiscal respectability, but within the context of
not only increased social inequality but also increased levels of social
exclusion and decreased political legitimacy. We may here usefully
remind ourselves of John Porter's remarks about social development
that I cited earlier. It is precisely the social deficit and the democratic
deficit to which Porter referred when he talked about the principles of
freedom and mutuality. Inequality constrains the freedom of the disadvantaged and prevents the development of mutuality. The socially
included make the decisions about what ends are to be sought through
public policy and what means will be used to achieve them. If the fate of
the Canadian welfare state over the past two decades is any indication,
then we are a long way from realizing the social equality and democratic participation to which John Porter aspired.

Notes

1 I wish to acknowledge Rick Helmes-Hayes for his advice on sources and his
  insightful comments in relation to John Porter. The comments of participants
  at the colloquium where the original paper was presented contributed to the
  revision.
2 Canada was one of the twenty founding member countries of the Organization for Economic Cooperation and Development (OECD) which came into
  being in 1961. By 1973 four other countries had joined and its membership of
  24 – the Western European countries, the United States, Canada, Australia,
  New Zealand, and Japan, Turkey, and Iceland – was constant up to 1994
  when Mexico was admitted; in 1996 the Czech Republic and Hungary were
  admitted. The aims of the OECD are 'to achieve the highest sustainable economic growth and employment and a rising standard of living in Member
  countries, while maintanting financial stabililty,' to contribute to sound economic expansion in member and non-member countries and to contribute to
  the expansion of non-discriminatory multilateral trade (OECD 1985: 2). The
  organization carries out its work through several committees – the Economic
  Policy Committee, the Committee for Scientific Research, the Trade Committee, and the Development Assistance Committee – and a secretariat based in
  Paris. It publishes regular statistical bulletins, covering the main economic
  and some social and educational statistics of member countries, reviews of
  the economic prospects of member countries, and special studies on a wide
  range of subjects, for example, *The Future of Social Protection* (1988) and
  Women and Structural Change (1994).

3 The linkages between Hobhouse and Porter are traced and analysed by Richard Helmes-Hayes in a paper on Porter's LSE years (Helmes-Hayes 1990).

4 The dominant welfare state perspective in North America in the 1960s and 1970s was based on the logic of industrialism view of social change and posited a convergence towards a common welfare state model. Harold Wilensky's 1975 study of sixty countries is a classic statement of this perspective: Industrialization is associated both with economic growth and the emergence of new needs, such as the needs of a dependent population over the age of 65. Welfare policy and expenditure are a response to these needs and are facilitated by additional resources associated with economic growth (Wilensky 1975). The polar opposite of this perspective is the Marxist structuralist position which stresses the structural constraints that preselect the issues to which the state in capitalist society is capable of responding and that set the upper limits on what can be done by the state in terms of welfare effort. This type of explanation draws on the early works of Poulantzas (1972 1973), in which the capitalist state is interpreted as relatively autonomous from the capitalist class but as acting as a factor of cohesion for that class.

5 Two other categories of welfare state beneficiaries are those whose access and eligibility are dependent on the social insurance contributions of family members in the labour force, that is, those with indirect rights to benefits and services, and those people with occupational benefits who are in receipt of tax subsidies for their contributions to these benefit funds (O'Connor 1996: 62–3). The distinction being emphasized in the text is that between rights and needs as the basis for access to benefits and services.

6 Medical cost inflation refers to the increase in prices of medical services which is often greater than the inflation in general prices.

7 There is a third tier to the Canadian pension system, that is, the employment-related Canada and Quebec pensions systems. The Canada Pension Plan is now under review and some groups, for example, the Reform party and the Fraser Institute, a neo-conservative policy analysis body, are arguing for privatization on the lines of a model adopted in Chile in the 1980s, where individuals would be totally dependent on registered retirement savings plans. The most striking feature of the Chilean plan is its regressive nature, for example, in 1987 the commission payable for administration represented an 18 per cent reduction in the deposit of an insured individual in the 10,000 pesos per month bracket, but only 0.9 per cent reduction for someone with ten times that income (Mesa-Lago 1994: 123–4, as cited by Huber 1996: 21).

8 Canada has not ratified ILO Convention 156 on Workers with Family Responsibilities (ILO 1993).

9 In a news release issued in December 1995, it was stated that $720 million

would be spent over three to five years starting in the fiscal year 1995–96. This consists of a First Nations/Innuit child care initiative ($72 million over three years, with ongoing funding of $36 million per year after the three-year period), a partnership offer with the provinces and territories (up to $630 million over three to five years, with an unspecified amount of ongoing funding after this developmental period), and a research and development program ($18 million).

10 'An institutionalized commitment to full employment involves: a/ an explicit commitment to maintaining/achieving full employment; b/ the existence and use of countercyclical mechanisms and policies; c/ the existence and use of specific mechanisms to adjust supply and demand in the labour market to the goal of full employment; d/ a conscious decision not to use high unemployment as a means to secure other policy objectives' (Therborn 1986: 23).

11 A series of changes to the unemployment insurance system introduced since 1976 have resulted not only in a cutback in benefits but also an increase in eligibility conditions and a lessening in the duration of benefits.

12 Because of the de-indexing of the income tax system in 1985 the cash component of the EPF system was gradually dwindling relative to the tax points component, and as a consequence the ability of the federal government to impose sanctions for non-conformity to national standards would eventually be ended.

13 These provinces are Newfoundland (–5 per cent), Prince Edward Island (–3 per cent), Nova Scotia (–1 per cent), Quebec (–1 per cent), Saskatchewan (–8 per cent), and Alberta (–16 per cent).

14 In addition to pensioner organizations the participants included the New Democratic party, the Liberal party, the CLC and several labour unions, women's rights groups, the Canadian Council on Social Development, the National Council of Welfare, and the National Anti-Poverty Organization. With the exception of the Liberal party these groups could be identified as the public pension lobby. It is noteworthy that in addition to these groups, opposition came from the private pension lobby, including the Business Council on National Issues, the Canadian Chamber of Commerce, and the Canadian Organization of Small Business. In contrast to the public pension lobby these groups were not opposed to de-indexing per se; what they opposed was the erosion of 'support for the elderly poor' (Thomas d'Aquino, President of the BCNI).

15 Picot and Myles (1995) illustrated the importance of social transfers in mitigating the impact on child poverty rates of the decline in the market incomes of adults under the age of 35 in Canada since the 1970s.

16 A comparison of major occupational distributions for the early 1980s and early 1990s indicates that gender segregation has declined but at a slow rate and then only at the upper end of the occupational distribution. In fact, women's representation in clerical, sales, and service occupations increased slightly over the decade (O'Connor et al. in press). There may be contradictory influences at work here as is evident from an analysis of the Swedish situation where the high levels of employment in the public sector have contributed to very high levels of occupational segregation.

17 It is noteworthy that the most inclusive and proactive legislation, that is, the Ontario legislation, was not fully implemented until 1994 and may have a more substantial effect, especially on the private sector, as it works its way through the system.

References

Acker, Joan. (1989). 'The Problem with Patriarchy.' *Sociology* 23(2): 25–40.

Adams, Ian, William Cameron, Brian Hill, and Peter Penz. (1971). *The Real Poverty Report*. Edmonton: M.G. Hurtig.

Andrew, Caroline. (1984). 'Women and the Welfare State.' *Canadian Journal of Political Science* 17(4): 667–83.

Atkinson, Anthony, Lee Rainwater, and Timothy Smeeding. (1995). *Income Distribution in OECD Countries*. Paris: Organization for Economic Development.

Banting, Keith G. (1987a). *The Welfare State and Canadian Federalism* (2nd ed.). Kingston and Montreal: McGill-Queen's University Press.

– (1987b). 'The Welfare State and Inequality in the 1980s.' *Canadian Review of Sociology and Anthropology* 24(3): 311–38.

– (1991). 'The Politics of Wealth Taxes.' *Canadian Public Policy* 17(3): 351–67.

Banting, Keith G., Charles Beach, and Gordon Betcherman. (1994). 'Polarization and Social Policy Reform: Evidence and Issues.' Pp. 1–20 in Keith G. Banting and Charles Beach (eds.), *Labour Market Polarization and Social Policy Reform*. Kingston: School of Policy Studies, Queen's University.

Barbalet, Jack M. (1988). *Citizenship Rights, Struggles and Class Inequality*. Minneapolis: University of Minnesota Press.

Beveridge, William H. (1944). *Full Employment in a Free Society*. London: Allen and Unwin.

Bolaria, B. Singh, and Rosemary Bolaria (eds.). (1994). *Racial Minorities, Medicine and Health*. Halifax: Fernwood.

Brenner, M. Harvey. (1980). 'Industrialization and Economic Growth: Estimates of Their Effects on the Health of Populations.' Pp.65–116 in M. Harvey Bren-

226 Julia S. O'Connor

ner, Anne Money, and Thomas J. Nagy (eds.), *Assessing the Contributions of the Social Sciences to Health*. Boulder: Westview Press.

Canada. (1970). *Report of the Royal Commission on the Status of Women in Canada*. Ottawa: Information Canada.

– (1971). Report of the Special Senate Committee (1971): *Poverty in Canada*. Ottawa: Information Canada.

– (1994). *Improving Social Security in Canada*. Ottawa: Minister of Supply and Services.

Canada, Minister of National Health and Welfare. (1973). *Working Paper on Social Security in Canada*. Ottawa: Minister of Supply and Services.

Canadian Welfare Council. (1969). *Social Policies for Canada, Part I*. Ottawa: Canadian Welfare Council.

Castles, Francis G. (1978). *The Social Democratic Image of Society*. London: Routledge and Kegan Paul.

Castles, Francis G., and Daniel Mitchell. (1992). 'Identifying Welfare State Regimes: The Links between Politics, Instruments and Outcomes.' *Governance* 5(1): 1–26.

Clement, Wallace. (1980). 'Searching for Equality: The Sociology of John Porter.' *Canadian Journal of Political and Social Theory* 4(2): 97–114.

– (1981). 'John Porter and Sociology in Canada.' *Canadian Review of Sociology and Anthropology* 18(5): 583–94.

Coughlin, Richard M. (1980). *Ideology, Public Opinion and Welfare Policy*. Berkeley: Institute of International Studies.

Crompton, Susan. (1991). 'Who Is Looking after the Kids?: Child Care Arrangements of Working Mothers.' *Perspectives on Labour and Income* 3(2): 68–76.

Economic Council of Canada. (1968). *Fifth Annual Review*. Ottawa: Economic Council of Canada.

Esping-Andersen, Gøsta. (1990). *The Three Worlds of Welfare Capitalism*. Princeton: Princeton University Press.

Flora, Peter, and Arnold J. Heidenheimer. (1981). 'The Historical Core and Changing Boundaries of the Welfare State.' Pp. 17–34 in Peter Flora and Arnold J. Heidenheimer (eds.), *The Development of Welfare States in Europe and North America*. New Brunswick, NJ: Transaction Books.

Fraser, Nancy. (1989). 'Women, Welfare, and the Politics of Need Interpretation.' Pp. 144–60 in Nancy Fraser (ed.), *Unruly Practices: Power, Discourse, and Gender in Contemporary Social Theory*. Minneapolis: University of Minnesota Press.

Gilbert, Sid, and Bruce Orok. (1994). 'School Leavers.' *Canadian Social Trends* Autumn: 2–7.

Goodin, Robert E., and John Dryzek. (1987). 'Risk-Sharing and Social Justice: The Motivational Foundations of the Post-War Welfare State.' Pp. 37–73 in Robert E. Goodin and Julian LeGrand (eds.), *Not Only the Poor*. London: Allen and Unwin.

Guest, Dennis. (1985). *The Emergence of Social Security in Canada* (2nd ed.). Vancouver: University of British Columbia Press.

Guppy, Neil, and Bruce Arai. (1993). 'Who Benefits from Higher Education? Differences by Sex, Social Class, and Ethnic Background.' Pp. 214–32 in James Curtis, Edward Grabb, and Neil Guppy (eds.), *Social Inequality in Canada: Patterns, Problems, Policies*. Scarborough: Prentice-Hall.

Hay, David I. (1994). 'Social Status and Health Status: Does Money Buy Health.' Pp. 9–51 in B. Singh Bolaria and Rosemary Bolaria (eds.), *Racial Minorities and Health*. Halifax: Fernwood.

Helmes-Hayes, Richard. (1990). '"Hobhouse Twice Removed": John Porter and the LSE years.' *Canadian Review of Sociology and Anthropology* 27(3): 357–88.

Hobhouse, Leonard T. (1911). *Social Evolution and Political Theory*. New York: Cambridge University Press.

– (1964 [1911]). *Liberalism*. London: Oxford University Press.

Huber, Evelyne. (1996). 'Options for Social Policy in Latin America: Neo-Liberal Versus Social Democratic Models.' Pp. 141–91 in Gøsta Esping-Andersen (ed.), *Welfare States in Transition: National Adaptations in Global Economics*. London: Sage.

International Labour Organization. (1992). *The Cost of Social Security, (1984–7)*. Geneva: ILO.

– (1993). *Workers with Family Responsibilities*. Geneva: ILO.

King, Desmond S., and Jeremy Waldron. (1988). 'Citizenship, Social Citizenship and the Defence of Welfare Provision.' *British Journal of Political Science* 18: 415–43.

Leibfried, Stephan. (1993). 'Towards a European Welfare State? On Integrating Poverty Regimes in the European Community.' Pp. 133–56 in Catherine Jones (ed.), *New Perspectives on the Welfare State in Europe*. London and New York: Routledge.

Lero, Donna S., H. Goelman, A.R. Pence, M. Brookman, and S. Nuttall. (1989). *Parental Work and Patterns of Child Care Needs*. Ottawa: Statistics Canada.

Liberal Party of Canada. (1993). *Creating Opportunities: The Liberal Party of Canada*. Ottawa: Liberal Party of Canada.

Manga, Pranlal. (1993). 'Socio-Economic Inequalities.' Pp. 263–74 in Thomas Stephens and Graham Fowler (eds.), *Canada's Health Promotion Survey 1990 Technical Report*. Ottawa: Minister of Supply and Services Canada.

228   Julia S. O'Connor

Manga, Pranlal, and Geoffrey R. Weller. (1980). 'The Failure of the Equity Objective in Health: A Comparative Analysis of Canada, Britain, and the United States.' *Comparative Social Research* 3: 229–76.

Marsh, Leonard. (1975 [1943]). *Report on Social Security for Canada.* Toronto: University of Toronto Press.

Marshall, T.H. (1964). 'Citizenship and Social Class.' Pp. 64–122 in T.H. Marshall, *Class, Citizenship and Social Development.* Westport: Greenwood Press.

Martin, Andrew. (1986). 'The Politics of Employment and Welfare: National Policies and International Interdependence.' Pp. 157–241 in Keith G. Banting (ed.), *The State and Economic Interests.* Toronto: University of Toronto Press.

Mesa-Lago, Carmelo. 1994. *Changing Social Structure in Latin America: Toward Alleviating the Cost of Economic Reform.* Boulder: Lynne Rienner.

Moscovitz, Alan. (1986). 'The Welfare State Since 1975.' *Journal of Canadian Studies* 21(2): 77–94.

Myles, John. 1996. 'When Markets Fail: Social Welfare in Canada and the United States.' Pp. 116–40 in Gøsta Esping-Andersen (ed.), *Welfare States in Transition: National Adaptations in Global Economies.* London: Sage.

Muszynski, Leon. (1985). 'The Politics of Labour Market Policy.' Pp. 251–304 in G. Bruce Doern (ed.), *The Politics of Economic Policy.* Toronto: University of Toronto Press.

National Council of Welfare. (1987). *Welfare in Canada: The Tangled Safety Net.* Ottawa: Ministry of Supply and Services.

– (1988). *Child Care: A Better Alternative.* Ottawa: Minister of Supply and Services.

– (1989). *Poverty Profile 1988.* Ottawa: Minister of Supply and Services.

– (1990). *Welfare Incomes 1989.* Ottawa: Minister of Supply and Services.

– (1993). *Incentives and Disincentives to Work.* Ottawa: National Council of Welfare.

– (1995a). *Poverty Profile 1993.* Ottawa: National Council of Welfare.

– (1995b). *The 1995 Budget and Block Funding.* Ottawa: National Council of Welfare.

– (1995c). *Welfare Incomes 1994.* Ottawa: National Council of Welfare.

Nelson, Barbara. (1984). 'Women's Poverty and Women's Citizenship.' Pp. 209–31 in Barbara Gelpi, Nancy Hartsock, Clare Novak, and Myra Strober (eds.), *Women and Poverty.* Chicago: University of Chicago Press.

Oakes, Jeannie. (1985). *Keeping Track.* New Haven: Yale University Press.

O'Connor, Julia S. (1987). 'Age Structure, Class, and Patterns of Public Pension Expenditure and Quality: A Cross-National Analysis for 1970–1980.' Paper presented at the 22nd Annual Meeting of the Canadian Anthropology and Sociology Association, McMaster University, 3 June.

– (1989). 'Welfare Expenditure and Policy Orientation in Canada in Comparative Perspective.' *Canadian Review of Sociology and Anthropology* 26(1): 127–50.

– (1993). 'Gender, Class, and Citizenship in the Comparative Analysis of Welfare State Regimes: Theoretical and Methodological Issues.' *British Journal of Sociology* 44(3): 501–18.

– (1996). 'From Women in the Welfare State to Gendering Welfare State Regimes.' *Current Sociology* 44(2): 1–130.

– (1998). 'Employment Equality Strategies and Their Representation in the Political Process in Canada: A Story of Possibilities, Contradictions, and Limitations.' Pp. 85–112 in Caroline Andrew and Manon Tremblay (eds.), *Women and Political Representation in Canada / Les Femmes et la représentation politique au Canada*. Ottawa: University of Ottawa Press.

O'Connor, Julia S., Ann S. Orloff, and Sheila Shaver (in press). *States, Markets, Families: Liberalism and Social Policy in Australia, Canada, Great Britain and the United States*. Cambridge: Cambridge University Press.

Olsen, Gregg M. (1994). 'Locating the Canadian Welfare State: Family Policy and Health Care in Canada, Sweden, and the United States.' *Canadian Journal of Sociology* 19(1): 1–20.

Organization for Economic Cooperation and Development. (1976). *Public Expenditure on Education*. Paris: OECD.

– (1985). *Social Expenditure 1960–1990: Problems of Growth and Control*. Paris: OECD.

– (1988). 'Women's Activity, Employment and Earnings: A Review of Recent Developments.' *Employment Outlook* July: 129–72.

– (1990). 'Child Care in OECD Countries.' *Employment Outlook* July: 123–51.

– (1992b). *Economic Outlook Historical Statistics*. Paris: OECD.

– (1993). *Education at a Glance: OECD Indicators*. Paris: OECD.

– (1994). *New Orientations for Social Policy*. Paris: OECD.

– (1995). *Economic Outlook: Historical Statistics*. Paris: OECD.

Orloff, Ann Schola. (1993). 'Gender and the Social Rights of Citizenship: The Comparative Analysis of Gender Relations and Welfare States.' *American Sociological Review* 58: 303–28.

Osberg, Lars. (1992). 'Sustainable Social Development.' Pp. 227–42 in Robert C. Allen and Gideon Rosenbluth (eds.), *False Promises: The Failure of Conservative Economics*. Vancouver: New Star Books.

Pateman, Carole. (1988). 'The Patriarchal Welfare State.' Pp. 231–60 in Amy Gutmann (ed.), *Democracy and the Welfare State*. Princeton: Princeton University Press.

Persson, Inga (ed.). (1990). *Generating Equality in the Welfare State: The Swedish Experience*. Oslo: Norwegian University Press.

Picot, Garnett, and John Myles. (1995). *Social Transfers, Changing Family Structure, and Low Income Children*. Ottawa: Statistics Canada. Report No. 82.

Pierson, Christopher M. (1991). *Beyond the Welfare State: The New Political Economy of Welfare*. University Park: Pennsylvania State University Press.

Porter, John. (1965). *The Vertical Mosaic: An Analysis of Social Class and Power in Canada*. Toronto: University of Toronto Press.

– 1970). 'Research Biography of a Macrosociological Study: *The Vertical Mosaic*.' Pp. 149–81 in J. Coleman, A. Etzioni, and J. Porter, *Macrosociology: Research and Theory*. Boston: Allyn and Bacon.

– (1987[1968]). 'The Future of Upward Mobility.' Pp. 65–86 in John Porter, *The Measure of Canadian Society* (2nd ed.) (Wallace Clement, ed.). Ottawa: Carleton University Press.

– (1987[1979]). 'Education, Equality, and the Just Society.' Pp. 241–80 in John Porter, *The Measure of Canadian Society* (2nd ed.) (Wallace Clement, ed.). Ottawa: Carleton University Press.

Porter, John, Marion Porter, and Bernard Blishen. (1982). *Stations and Callings: Making It through the School System*. Toronto: Methuen.

Poulantzas, Nicos. (1972). 'The Problem of the Capitalist State.' Pp. 238–53 in Robin Blackburn (ed.), *Ideology in Social Science: Readings in Critical Social Theory*. London: Fontana.

– (1973). *Political Power and Social Classes*. London: Verso.

Rawls, John. (1971). *A Theory of Justice*. Cambridge: Belknap Press of Harvard University Press.

Richer, Stephen. (1988). 'Equality to Benefit from Schooling: The Issue of Educational Opportunity.' Pp. 262–86 in Denis Forcese and S. Richer (eds.), *Social Issues: Sociological Views of Canada*. Toronto: Prentice Hall.

Ross, David P., Rick Shillington, and Clarence Lockhead. (1994). *The Canadian Fact Book on Poverty 1994*. Ottawa: Canadian Council on Social Development.

Ruggeri, Giuseppe C., Donald Van Wart, and Robert Howard. (1994). 'The Redistributive Impact of Taxation in Canada.' *Canadian Tax Journal* 42(2): 417–51.

Scharpf, Fritz W. (1984). 'Economic and Institutional Constraints of Full-Employment Strategies: Sweden, Austria, and West Germany 1973–82.' Pp. 257–89 in John Goldthorpe (ed.), *Order and Conflict in Contemporary Capitalism*. Oxford: Clarendon Press.

Schmidt, Manfred G. (1984). 'The Politics of Unemployment: Rates of Unemployment and Labour Market Policy.' *West European Politics* 7(3): 5–23.

Sclar, Elliot D. (1980). 'Community Economic Structure and Individual Well-Being: A Look behind the Statistics.' *International Journal of Health Services* 10(4): 563–79.

Statistics Canada. (1993). *Education in Canada, 1991–92.* Ottawa: Minister of Industry, Science and Technology.

Taylor, Malcolm G. (1978). *Health Insurance and Canadian Public Policy.* Montreal: McGill-Queen's University Press.

Therborn, Goran. (1986). *Why Some Peoples Are More Unemployed than Others.* London: Verso.

Thompson, Stella, et al. (1993). *Winning with Women in Trades, Technology, Science and Engineering.* Ottawa: National Boards of Science and Technology.

Tomasson, Richard F. (1984). 'Government Old Age Pensions under Affluence and Austerity: West Germany, Sweden, The Netherlands, and the U.S.' *Research in Social Problems and Public Policy* 3: 217–72.

Tuohy, Carolyn. (1993). 'Social Policy: Two Worlds.' Pp. 275–305 in Michael M. Atkinson (ed.), *Governing Canada: Institutions and Public Policy.* Toronto: Harcourt Brace Jovanovich.

Vermaeten, Arndt, Irwin Gillespie, and Frank Vermaeten. (1995). 'Who Paid the Taxes in Canada, 1951–1988?' *Canadian Public Policy – Analyse de Politiques* 21: 317–43.

Vermaeten, Frank, Irwin Gillespie, and Arndt Vermaeten. (1994). 'Tax Incidence in Canada.' *Canadian Tax Journal* 42(2): 348–81.

Vaillancourt, F. (1985). 'Income Distribution and Economic Security in Canada: An Overview.' Pp. 1–75 in F. Vaillancourt (ed.), *Income Distribution and Economic Security in Canada.* Toronto: University of Toronto Press.

Walters, Vivienne, Rhonda Lenton, and Marie Mckeary. (1995). *Women's Health in the Context of Women's Lives.* Ottawa: Minister of Supply and Services Canada.

Wannell, Ted. (1990). 'Male-Female Earnings Gap among Recent University Graduates.' *Perspectives on Labour and Income* 2(2): 19–31.

Wilensky, Harold. (1975). *The Welfare State and Equality: Structural and Ideological Roots of Public Expenditure.* Berkeley: University of California Press.

Wilkinson, B.W. (1986). 'Elementary and Secondary Education Policy in Canada: A Survey.' *Canadian Public Policy* 12(4): 535–72.

Wilson, Elizabeth. (1977). *Women and the Welfare State.* London: Tavistock.

Yalnizyan, Armine. (1994). 'Securing Society: Creating Canadian Social Policy.' Pp. 17–71 in Armine Yalnizyan, T. Ran Ide, and Arthur Cordell (eds.), *Shifting Time.* Toronto: Between the Lines.

Yates, Charlotte. (1995). '"Job Ready, I Ready": Job Creation and Labour Market Reform in Canada.' Pp. 83–106 in Susan Phillips (ed.), *How Ottawa Spends 1995–96.* Ottawa: Carleton University Press.

Contributors

PAT ARMSTRONG, School of Canadian Studies, Carleton University

RAYMOND BRETON, Department of Sociology, University of Toronto

WALLACE CLEMENT, Institute of Political Economy, Carleton University

JAMES CURTIS, Department of Sociology, University of Waterloo

JAMES DOWNEY, President, University of Waterloo

RICK HELMES-HAYES, Department of Sociology, University of Waterloo

JULIA S. O'CONNOR, Department of Sociology, McMaster University and National Economic and Social Council of Ireland

MICHAEL ORNSTEIN, Institute for Social Research and Department of Sociology, York University

Name Index

Abele, Frances, 42, 55
Abella, Rosalie, 122
Acker, Joan, 187, 225
Adams, Ian, 204, 225
Agocs, Carol, 108–9, 116, 139
Ahrne, Göran, 48, 51, 55
Albo, Gregory, 147, 174, 176
Allen, Robert C., 229
Anderson, Kay J., 41–2, 55
Andrew, Caroline, 122, 140, 187, 225, 229
Arai, Bruce, 218–20, 226
Arat-Koç, Sedef, 142
Archibald, Kathleen, 116, 140
Armstrong, Hugh, 12, 29, 54–5, 117–21, 123–5, 128, 138, 140
Armstrong, Pat, 12, 17–19, 21, 25–6, 29, 54–5, 117–20, 121, 123–6, 128, 130, 135–8, 140–1, 151
Aron, Raymond, 37, 150
Atkinson, Anthony, 225
Atkinson, Michael M., 231

Backhouse, Constance, 143
Badets, Jane, 73, 86, 108–9
Banting, Keith G., 206, 213, 225, 227
Barbalet, Jack M., 185, 225

Barrett, Michèle, 142–3
Barrett, Stanley R., 109
Beach, Charles, 225
Beattie, Christopher, 75, 109
Behiels, Michael, 76, 109
Bell, Daniel, 107, 109
Bellah, Robert N., 98–9, 109
Benston, Margaret, 117, 140
Bernier, Luc, 77, 109
Berry, John W., 99, 109
Betcherman, Gordon, 225
Beveridge, William H., 205, 225
Bienefeld, Manfred, 48, 56
Billig, Michael, 108–9
Billson, Janet Mancini, 87, 109
Blackburn, Robin, 230
Blishen, Bernard, 7, 10, 29–30, 33, 122, 143, 218, 230
Bolaria, B. Singh, 218, 225, 227
Bolaria, Rosemary, 218, 225, 227
Boldt, Menno, 112
Bottomore, Tom, 146, 176–7
Bourne, Paula, 143
Bovey, Wilfrid, 76, 109
Boyd, Monica, 10, 30, 42, 55, 87–8, 108–10
Bradbury, Bettina, 119, 141

238   Name Index

Osberg, Lars, 221, 229
Overall, Christine, 133, 143

Page, Edward, 174, 177
Pal, Leslie A., 96–7, 113
Palmer, Howard, 88, 113
Panitch, Leo, 171, 177, 179
Pareto, Vilfredo, 38, 58, 146, 150
Park, Frank, 149, 179
Park, Libbie, 149, 179
Parkin, Frank, 39, 58
Parr, Joy, 119, 143
Pateman, Carole, 229
Pearson, Lester B., 167
Pelletier, Réjean, 77, 113
Pence, A.R., 227
Penz, Peter, 225
Persson, Inga, 204, 229
Phillips, Susan, 231
Picot, Garnett, 224, 229
Pierson, Christopher M., 184, 229
Pierson, Ruth Roach, 127, 132, 143
Pinard, Maurice, 80–1, 108, 113
Pineo, Peter, 10, 30, 32–3
Ponting, J. Rick, 63, 68, 70, 72, 97, 108, 111, 113–14
Popper, Karl, 4
Porter, Alan, 4
Porter, Arthur, 3
Porter, Eileen, 4
Porter, John, 3–43, 45–7, 49, 50–8, 60–2, 75–6, 86–7, 90–2, 104–5, 107, 109, 113–14, 116–18, 120–5, 128–9, 132, 139, 143, 145–6, 148–55, 157–60, 163–70, 172–6, 178–84, 187, 193, 195, 218, 222, 226–7, 229–30
Porter, Marion, 9, 33, 122, 143, 218, 230
Poulantzas, Nicos, 43, 59, 171, 223, 230

Presthus, Robert, 146, 149, 179
Pross, Paul, 97, 114
Pupo, Norene, 128, 134, 143

Rae, Bob, 165
Rainwater, Lee, 225
Rashid, Abdul, 125, 143
Rasporich, A.W., 110
Rawls, John, 49, 50, 57, 59, 183–4, 230
Redekop, John, 28
Rees, Tim, 142
Reitz, Jeffrey G., 87, 88, 99, 105, 107, 109, 112–14
Richardson, James, 28, 30
Richardson, Trudy, 136–7, 143
Richer, Stephan, 218, 230
Rosanvallon, Pierre, 95, 114
Rosenbluth, Gideon, 229
Ross, David P., 194, 206, 215, 230
Rowat, Don, 5
Runciman, W.G., 108, 114
Ruggeri, Giuseppe C., 213, 230
Russell, Susan, 122, 143

Satzewich, Vic, 42, 55, 59, 110
Savard, Pierre, 140
Savas, Daniel J., 97, 114
Scharpf, Fritz W., 202, 230
Schmidt, Manfred G., 202, 230
Sclar, Elliot D., 218, 230
Scott, John, 147, 179
Scott, William G., 29–30
Selbee, K., 10, 32
Shillington, E. Richard, 194, 230
Shils, Edward, 4
Shiose, Yuki, 108, 111, 114
Siggner, Andrew J., 65, 70, 114
Siltanen, Janet, 54
Sinclair, 132, 143
Smart, Don, 146, 178

Subject Index

Aboriginal(s) (Native peoples), 15–16, 35, 42, 52, 60–72, 103–7, 122, 125, 129, 131; Assembly of First Nations, 71; changing relations, 60–72; 'citizens plus' approach to, 63, 65; corporate vs individual integration of, 66–7; economic base of, 66–7; establishing a territorial base, 66–7; 'First Nations,' 65; 'fourth world,' 68; gap between leaders and communities, 71; Indian Register, 108; institutional control, 65–6; land claims, 63, 66–7; linguistic families, 70; Native Council of Canada, 68; Native Indian Brotherhood, 68; Native Indian Council, 64; organizations resisting change, 71–2; pan-Aboriginal identity, 65; population, 69–71; rebuilding community structures, 65–6; recognition as political actors, 67–8; 'Red Power,' 64; relations with foreign governments, 68; self-government by, 60–72, 95; size of bands, 70; social and economic conditions compared, 64–7; social identity, 65–6; transforming institutions, 68–9; White Paper on Indian Policy (1969), 64, 66; women, 67–8

abortion, 132
abuse, child, 53; partner/spousal, 53, 133–4, 138
academia, 116
Action travail des femmes, 129, 139
advanced/modern capitalism, 44, 149, 152, 161
affirmative action, 16, 18, 23
agency (individual), 20–1, 43, 46, 48, 51, 147
American Sociological Association, 7
Anglican bishops, 146
Anglophone–Francophone relations (see English–French relations)
apprenticeship, 121, 131
Ascription and Achievement (1985), 6, 9
Asian population, 16, 42
Assembly of First Nations, 71
assimilation, structural, 121–2
Australia(n), 42, 51, 54, 181, 187–203
authoritarianism, 150
authority, 45, 150

banks, 158–9, 160–2, 165
benefits, government, 188–96, 206–12; cutbacks in, 206–12; education, 193–6; health, 191–3; social protection, 188–91

tion, 25; separation of Quebec, 98; sovereignty association, 78–81, 83–4, 98; status anxiety, 82–3; strategic nationalism, 78; survival nationalism, 75
functionalism, 167

gender, 7, 9–10, 19, 24, 44–6, 49, 52, 148; and class, 43, 46, 120, 219–21; and education, 219–21; and income, 220; and the welfare state, 197–213, 219–21; and work, 198–201, 220; as a relational category, 21; attitudes, 46; bias, 129; differences, 45; discrimination, 129; identity, 48, 120; ideology, 118; inequality, 17, 19–20, 23, 25–6, 36, 118, 123; multiple jeopardy, 87; relations, 19–20, 22, 25, 46
Germany (West), 51, 161, 181, 187–203
global restructuring, 47
Globe and Mail, 154, 176
goods production, 36, 44–5, 48, 50

Hawthorn Report, 63
health: benefits, 188, 191–3; and socioeconomic status, 13, 217–18
health insurance, 150
health/medical care, 17, 126, 133, 137–8, 170
hegemony, 36, 39, 42, 51, 149–51, 175
history (discipline of), 174
hospitals, 172
households, 53, 118–20, 122–5, 130, 132, 134–5, 138; division of labour in, 53, 132; domestic economy of, 118–19, 132–3; heads of, 46; income, 125; inequality between, 126; lone-parent, 125; low-income, 43; modern, 46; power relations in, 46, 53, 133; traditional, 46; two-parent,

126, 132; unconventional, 46; working-class, 119
housework, 46, 52
housing, 53
human capital theory, 130
Hydro-Québec, 77

ideology, 38, 42, 44, 51, 53, 102–7, 146, 149, 151, 156, 161–4
immigrant(s), credentials required of, 15–16, 131; national origins of: Asian, 37, 49; Caribbean, 37, 49; Central American, 16; European, 49; Latin American, 16; South American, 16; women, 131, 139
immigrant group relations, 20, 22, 25, 60–2, 85–107; and socioeconomic equality, 94–5; anglo-conformity model, 88; and the state, 93–4, 106; assimilation, 41, 99–101; cultural maintenance, 106; de-ethnicizing institutions, 90–3; ethnic diversity, 41, 98–101; ethnic identity, 48, 60–1, 106, 120; ethnic mobilization, 107; ethnic stratification, 8–9, 13, 16–20, 23, 25–6, 41, 86–90, 96–7, 105–6, 166; ethnic structure of opportunity, 96–7; ethnicity and social inequality, 105–6; ethnicity as a base of exclusion, 92–3; ethnicity as a base of inclusion, 92–3; ethnicizing institutions, 90–3; Franco-conformity in Quebec, 91; internal organization of ethnic communities, 94; language issues, 89–91; management of conflict, 95–6; nativistic ideologies, 102–3; Official Languages Act, 93; reactions of 'majority Canadians,' 97–8; recognition and status, 95; relative deprivation, 101–3; status